A MEMOIR

DREAMING IN SPANISH

An Unexpected Love Story in Puerto Vallarta

SARA ALVARADO

LITTLE CREEK PRESS®
AND BOOK DESIGN
MINERAL POINT, WISCONSIN

Little Creek Press
5341 Sunny Ridge Road
Mineral Point, WI 53565

To contact Sara directly: SaraAlvarado.com

ORDERING INFORMATION
Quantity sales. Special discounts are available on quantity purchases by corporations, associations, and others. For details, contact info@littlecreekpress.com

Orders by US trade bookstores and wholesalers.
Please contact Little Creek Press or Ingram for details.

Printed in the United States of America

Cataloging-in-Publication Data
Names: Alvarado, Sara, author
Title: Dreaming in Spanish
Description: Mineral Point, WI Little Creek Press, 2023
Identifiers: LCCN: 2023904002 | ISBN: 978-1-955656-48-1
Classification: BIOGRAPHY & AUTOBIOGRAPHY / Personal Memoirs

Book design by Mimi Bark and Little Creek Press
Book cover flower art: Jessica Gutiérrez

PRAISE FOR *DREAMING IN SPANISH*

"*Dreaming in Spanish* is the bitter, sweet, and sour of the complexity of life. A true story that is written with love, honesty, and grace. The story of a woman who embarks on an adventure to heal her soul and save her life. As she faces big challenges, uncertainty, romance, and love, but more than anything, a learning experience. With ugly truths but in the end, always truths. Truth is the best tool to create awareness of the problems we face as a society."

—**MARISOL GONZALEZ,** Mexican writer, poet, Moth GrandSLAM storyteller, teacher, artist, book reviewer, filmmaker, and entrepreneur

"It's easy to love this vulnerable, tell-it-like-it-is healing journey. Alvarado's self-discovery, self-compassion, and resilience buoy us all. I didn't want to put this down."

—**HEIDI ROSE ROBBINS,** author of *Everyday Radiance: 365 Zodiac-Inspired Prompts for Self-Care and Self-Renewal*

"It's one thing to break free of the forces of sexual assault and substance abuse, and quite another to bravely pursue a new kind of future, one of struggle but also joy, beauty, and lasting love. In this thoughtful and generous memoir, Alvarado reminds us of the profound power of second chances, courage, and self-acceptance. What begins as a careful recollection of misspent youth transforms into a messy and complicated love story—the best kind."

—**SUSANNA DANIEL,** author of *Stiltsville* and *Sea Creatures*

"Soul-filling! This enchanting story of hope, humanness, adventure, and love brings us face-to-face with our own understanding of what it means to surrender and begin to trust again. Sara Alvarado shares a story from Madison to L.A. to Mexico that allowed my soul to feel the weaving of courage, heartbreak, hope, strength, softness, and surrender on the same day. This memoir grabbed my heart."

—**ALLISON CROW,** author of *Unarmored: Finding Home in the Wild Edges of Being Human*

"*Dreaming in Spanish* is one of those books that everyone on a healing journey should read. Through her story, Sara—with an authorial voice that is refreshing, witty, and radiates raw, authenticity—helps you remember the importance of having faith in where life takes you and to trust the reroutes even when life can feel maddeningly overwhelming. Sara articulates the complex emotions behind motherhood, love, sobriety, and spirituality—and, generally, navigating the twists and turns of being a human. By the end, you are left feeling less alone and with more conviction that the universe *truly* has your back. But don't get it twisted—this uplifting memoir is peppered with tequila shots, party drugs, and plenty of F-bombs. This is the spiritual book for the people that scoff at spiritual books, and I could not recommend it more."

—**MADI MURPHY,** co-founder of The Cosmic Revolution and Cosmic Rx

"A stunner of a book! Sara takes us on an epic journey in multiple parts, in multiple lands, on multiple layers. But at its heart—make no mistake—this is a love story. It's a story of young love, of loving on strangers, of loving place, of loving mothers, of loving spirit, of loving babies, of loving ourselves, and of learning to acknowledge mistakes made and opportunities to do better. While perhaps done imperfectly, Sara made her mistakes with exquisite and extraordinary love."

—**TANYA GEISLER,** leadership coach and speaker

"This book is for all women—women who were never given a script, for those who reject the script they were given, and for those who do not believe in one. It's a book of adventure, but it's also a book of self-love and, in the end, seizing on the freedom to become who you want to be. In her memoir, Sara Alvarado is honest and transparent while also being compassionate and, above all, comfortable with uncertainty and self-doubt, something we can all learn from."

—**KAREN MENENDEZ-COLLER,** CEO of Centro Hispano

"Sara Alvarado's *Dreaming in Spanish* is equal parts a healing journey and love story that gives us permission to find the magic."

—**AMBER SWENOR,** author of *Unleashed: A Been-There, Rocked-That Guide to Radical Authenticity in Life and Business*, founder of Soul Seed

"*Dreaming in Spanish* is at once relatable and inspirational. This epic love story is frank and vulnerable, and Sara's insight and her unique way of viewing the world make it a must-read!"

—**ASHLEY QUINTO POWELL,** speaker, coach, and author of *Executive Motherhood: The Art of Having It All Without Doing It All*

"Sara Alvarado's *Dreaming in Spanish* is a story of seeking and finding, asking hard questions like what love should look like and where home is. This story is everything you want in a memoir—frank, generous, wise, and open-hearted."

—**MICHELLE WILDGEN,** author of *Wine People, You're Not You, But Not For Long,* and *Bread and Butter*

"Often, moms squeeze into tight, neat, socially acceptable boxes out of fear of being seen as "unfit" or "unsafe." We sanitize our stories and deny our humanity, hoping to be seen as "good" mothers. Through *Dreaming in Spanish*, Sara Alvarado gives us complexity and fullness and an invitation to be whole"

—**SAGASHUS LEVINGSTON, PHD,** author of *Infamous Mothers* and *Covet: the "Disrespectful" Health and Wellness Journal*

"*Dreaming in Spanish* is an entertaining and beautifully vulnerable memoir that will just as soon make you laugh as make you cry. Alvarado's honest and confessional tone is a welcome antidote to the filtered and curated world of media that we all grapple with on a daily basis. You'll finish the book feeling like you just had a long conversation with your most adventurous friend."

—**SUSAN GLOSS,** USA Today Bestselling Author of *Vintage* and *The Curiosities*

"Sara Alvarado's memoir, *Dreaming in Spanish*, details her story from a Midwestern white girl who studies Spanish and tries to escape her demons with alcohol, men, and mischief by heading south of the border. Her brutal honesty, unforeseen tragedies, and ultimate redemption from her past serve as a reminder of how hard life really is, even with the privilege that skin color and economic status provide. Sara's memoir is important to showcase that there are times in our lives, sometimes in the depths of our journey, when we can learn the most about ourselves."

—**OSCAR MIRELES,** poet laureate of Madison, Wisconsin (2016-2020)

— For us —

PROLOGUE

I HAVE LIVED most of my life in a place where the four seasons are distinct, sometimes extreme, and always telling.

This story is from a season in my life that was incredibly distinct, pretty extreme, and quite telling. It is my story, told from my memory and recounted from numerous journals. Some names have been changed. Some have not.

Memory is tricky. In writing this memoir, there were times I called on my memory or read through my journals and could feel exactly where I was at that moment in time—the veil was so thin. While other times the distance between now and then was as extreme as a Wisconsin winter and a Puerto Vallarta summer—almost impossible to comprehend, yet quite possible to work through.

This book couldn't have been written without sharing traumas from my past that may be hard to read. My content warning includes substance abuse, sexual assault, rape, and unexamined privileges.

As a white woman in my mid-twenties, I was incredibly brave and introspective, while also lacking significant cultural and racial awareness. This story is from a time when the privileges I was born with—that I hadn't earned—were tucked under the rug, supporting me without direct acknowledgment or a deeper understanding of harm and impact. The corners of the rug were beginning to curl up slightly, while so much was yet to be revealed.

In being truthful to who I was during this time, I show the self-confidence my mom instilled in me, that as a woman, is likely unrecognizable to my ancestors. I also show the ignorance and entitlement that often comes with whiteness, which the next generations will likely be appalled by. I am embarrassed to show some of who I was back then, and it's scary to do so publicly.

There are some ugly truths and a limited perspective, but also deep wisdom and limitless love. Both/and. I'm grateful for the learning and support from friends, healers, coaches, and teachers I've worked with to complete this book. And I'm grateful for the love and healing I've experienced in writing and sharing this story.

PART ONE

Chapter 1

MADISON TO PUERTO VALLARTA

DECEMBER 1999

WITH AN OVERSTUFFED backpack and no itinerary, I left Madison, Wisconsin, before dawn on December 15, 1999, ready to start a new life in Puerto Vallarta, Mexico. I was a twenty-four-year-old train wreck with a polished paint job, hoping my love affair (gone bad) with sex, drugs, and alcohol wouldn't follow me.

By age fifteen, I had rocked the Madison nightlife with my fake ID. At eighteen, I had dominated the house parties and clubs at the University of Minnesota in Minneapolis, instigated all-nighters all over Europe and walks of shame in Central America. At twenty-three, I was ready to rage the Los Angeles party scene. Parties were my life, and I was the life of the party even when I tried to avoid it.

A Mexican beach was my next destination, and a new life was my goal. After fifteen hours of travel, I arrived at the Guadalajara airport with my Mexico guidebook, a walkman, some mixed tapes, and a couple of books crammed in my carry-on. I started the trip with two books, *Overcoming*

Addictions: The Spiritual Solution by Deepak Chopra and *Conversations with God* by Neale Donald Walsch. Determined to quit the party life and motivated for the next adventure, I finished Chopra's book on one of the flights and left it there for someone else to serendipitously find.

It had been two weeks since I sat on an uncomfortable couch across from a middle-aged white therapist who told me I needed to "get a handle on my addictions" in a tone that insinuated he didn't believe I could. With his notebook in his lap, the lights low and soft, he suggested I find an outpatient program and commit to six months of celibacy.

I didn't argue with this advice. Part of me thought he was right.

I couldn't imagine a life so different, so I tucked his prescription in my back pocket. It was one of those times when you think, *Oh no, that can't be right, but, yeah, it's probably totally right.* After that appointment, I drove straight to the bookstore. The book *Overcoming Addictions* seemed to jump off the shelf like it was meant for me. As alone as I was at that moment, I felt supported by the universe. Someone was watching out for me, leading me if I was willing to follow.

Eighteen months earlier, I had left Minneapolis for Los Angeles to get away from a toxic relationship and start a promising career in real estate. Dreams of a better life in Los Angeles ended quickly. I was only there nine months before I escaped, not unscathed, from a reckless lifestyle where the pour was heavy and money wasn't clean. I ended up back home in Madison, and it took another six months of the same party lifestyle, unfulfilled plans, and one horrific night when I was drugged and raped before I tried running again—this time to Mexico.

It was a bold move, traveling alone, with no one to visit, no hotels booked, and no job prospects, but I was the kind of young, pretty, white woman who could sashay into a bar, take her pick of almost any guy, and enjoy free drinks all night long.

THE AIRPORT WAS eerily quiet when I arrived, and the tourist stations were already closed. As the luggage tumbled down the baggage carousel, other passengers confidently claimed theirs, hurrying out to a car or a loved one. I struggled with my heavy bags, not sure why there weren't airport employees available to assist me. Everything felt hard.

I had grossly overestimated my language proficiency. Getting through customs had been a challenge, trampling my confidence. All I wanted to do was cry, but I worried that if I started, I wouldn't be able to stop. Instead, I scanned the terminal, hoping to find someone I could trust.

After using my broken Spanish to ask a few people for help, a woman guided me to a kiosk and taught me how to purchase and use a phone card. My guidebook listed options for cheap hotels close to the bus station, so I went to work battling fear, fatigue, and a complicated phone system in a different language. I secured a room and hailed a taxi.

I took a deep breath in the taxi and gave myself a pep talk. Hold it together, Sara. You're almost there. The drive took forever, making me nervous again. The driver talked fast, and I couldn't understand most of what he was saying, but he didn't seem to notice.

When I was finally in my rundown room, I closed the door, locked it, threw myself on the bed, and burst into tears. After five minutes of ugly, loud sobbing, I washed my face, crawled under the covers, and called my parents.

My mom answered. Her tender, loving voice brought back my tears. *Please don't let her hear the fear in my voice,* I pleaded. I didn't want her to worry. After some broken static, I heard my mother say, "I'm glad you arrived safe." But we could barely understand each other with the poor reception, and then I felt an electric shock through the phone, and the line went dead. I was in tears again. I didn't try calling back.

IN THE MORNING, I made it to the Guadalajara bus station with my determined heart feeling strong. *Don't look back. Keep going,* I told myself. In the plush, air-conditioned bus, I got lost in the dramatic scenery: steep cliffs, stunning mountains, and no signs of life. We passed through a small town where clothes hung on laundry lines behind wooden shacks, and half-naked kids happily played next to skinny, stray dogs. The familiar and fitting song "Landslide" by Fleetwood Mac came through my headphones, and I felt back on track. I was here for the adventure, to escape the past, and to improve my Spanish.

It was mid-afternoon when I arrived at the bus station in Puerto Vallarta. I wasn't hungry or tired and had plenty of daylight to find a place to stay that night. My optimism was contagious, and everyone seemed to be smiling with me. The small bus station was clean and welcoming, which fueled my feeling that today was a new beginning and that I was going to be okay.

Trusting my guidebook again, I picked a hotel in the low price range and found a taxi driver. As I checked the book to tell him where I wanted to go, he looked at me with kind eyes and asked if I had a reservation. What a sweetheart. He knew I didn't. In the nicest way possible, he told me that it was high season in Vallarta, and most hotels were booked solid. I didn't blink an eye, and with confidence, I said, "Well, let's go find one that has a room for me tonight." I jumped in his taxi, rolled the windows down so I could feel the salty air on my skin, and beamed with anticipation to see the ocean again. As we zoomed toward downtown, I took in the views.

There were mountains! How did I not know there would be mountains? Yet here they were, a luscious mountain range covered in palm trees with the city of Puerto Vallarta snuggled between them and the magnificent ocean. My anticipation turned to excitement at what life could be like here.

The first hotel we stopped at didn't have any vacant rooms. I opened my book, but before I could start searching, the cab driver offered to take me to another hotel a block away. I closed my book and smiled. "Vamos." This one had a room for me. The driver's kindness reminded me to focus on the positive. He had graciously spoken slowly for me and praised my Spanish language skills. He was the first of many locals who showed an almost uncomfortable awe of my Spanish-speaking ability and a genuine concern for my well-being.

But wait. Did I call it a hotel? Really, that is not the right word for where I ended up. It wasn't technically a hostel, but it certainly didn't have any features of the kind of hotel I was used to. After paying for one night, I cautiously found my room. Walking through the worn-down, dark, and damp plaza area to the second floor could have killed my optimistic buzz. And if I didn't feel so enthusiastic about arriving in beautiful Puerto Vallarta, I would have melted into sobs upon entering the hotel room like I had the night before. But I didn't. I threw my twenty-pound backpack on the bed, fished out my flip-flops and sundress, and grabbed my sunglasses. Within ten minutes, I had shed the weight of my heavy bags and the confinement of my travel clothes and was headed to the beach. I was pulled to the ocean, to a new sense of freedom.

The five-minute walk to the beach from my hotel clarified a lot. Puerto Vallarta was a tourist town west of Guadalajara in the state of Jalisco. White people wandered about in vacation mode, while brown people hurried around them in work mode. I stood on the corner assessing the scene. I wasn't a touristy traveler and had never been drawn to destination resort towns. I had a lot to learn. But first, the warmth of the sun and the depth of the ocean called me. I had landed. I was hopeful to call this city home.

The beach was full of families, couples, and friends. There wasn't a cloud in the sky. I looked beyond the crowded beach at the mountainous backdrop and the far horizon where the sky met the ocean. My bare feet nestled into the warm sand, and I breathed it all in. The sun was low in the sky. I didn't know how I would make this place my home, but it didn't matter. The ocean brought me back to my center, the all-knowing place in my heart.

The fear and uncertainty I held contrasted with the beauty and confidence of the ocean waves, always crashing, ebbing and receding. This powerful ocean reminded me of my direct connection to God, the universe, and that inner voice that made so much sense when everything around me was confusing, chaotic, and scary. I understood God to be a higher power, an energy force, something bigger than myself. God was the divine feminine and sacred masculine, creating oneness.

Growing up, I knew God the way he was portrayed in the churches and media—an old white man in the sky—but by the time I was in my early twenties, I had created a more intimate relationship with God, who had become a feminine, mystical, and playful figure. I began to trust my intuition, read spiritual books, and follow the whisper I heard in my heart, which connected to the energy of an ancient divine wisdom within. She was not a separate male, dominant authority figure who instilled fear; she was pure love, the rush of inner knowing.

The ocean swelled up before me and pounded the shore, helping me be present in the moment. I knew I had to stop drinking and partying so hard. I knew I had to heal the broken parts inside of me. I knew I didn't need to do it alone.

It had been one month since the rape and ten years of drinking, drugs, and using sex in damaging, unhealthy ways. Had I hit rock bottom? Would I find a different path, or was I destined to keep running only to find that the location didn't matter? This death sentence of a lifestyle was available everywhere I went. Some would say (specifically my mother) that I was an alcoholic. But it was more than that. I was addicted to the lifestyle. It wasn't just the booze; it was the boys and the cocaine bumps in the bathroom, the after-parties, one-night stands, and wild adventures that were fun until they weren't. And when they weren't anymore, they left me battered and defeated.

I was floundering for a new way. Desperate. Although it seemed like I kept running to escape the inescapable, I wanted to believe that I was running toward something better. Running away and running toward. It's a paradox—not possible, totally possible.

I might have only been in Mexico for 24 hours, but I already had my short and ambitious to-do list written in my notebook:

1. Find a place to live
2. Find a job
3. Stay celibate for six months (I had five months left)
4. Quit drinking and drugs
5. Dream in Spanish. Immerse myself in Mexican culture and the Spanish language.

I had come to achieve something for myself and felt capable and ambitious. I had dreams, and my to-do list was going to help me get to a better place. I had to believe it was possible.

Chapter 2

MINNEAPOLIS, MINNESOTA

1993–1998

WHEN I FIRST LANDED in Minneapolis as a college freshman, I floated on a cloud of relief. I had escaped my hometown of Madison, Wisconsin, and my toxic relationship with my father, and I was certain I'd never go back. It felt like I had been waiting my whole life to leave. I didn't care about the education, so I'd picked a school I could easily get into, in a big city where I could get lost.

In Minneapolis, I lived in two distinct worlds: the working world, where I was responsible, respected, and reliable, and the party world, where I rounded out my day jobs with my side hustles of selling weed and fake IDs, and where I was known as fun, Crazy Sara. I worked and I partied. During the last two years of my five-year college career, I dropped to part-time and chipped away at my Spanish major while focusing most of my attention on an almost full-time job as a leasing agent for a medium-sized property management company in Uptown, Minneapolis. I loved being a working girl. And I was determined to graduate even if it meant cheating and schmoozing professors to get a passing grade. Where I was average at school, I got the praise I wanted for my work accomplishments. My dad worked in real estate, and the fact that I was working as an almost full-time leasing agent, maintaining a less than one percent vacancy rate on 326 units, made him proud.

After my fourth year of college, I took a trimester off and went to Central America for a couple of months. Midway through, in Costa Rica, I fell passionately in love with hot, sexy Marc, and we spent weekend benders high on cocaine, clubbing in San Jose, and camping on the beach in Playa del Coco. We were only together for three weeks before I had to return, but it felt like we had known each other for years. Marc ended up following me back to Minneapolis and became my party boyfriend, who was cool with me kissing girls while guys hit on him at the gay bars on 1st Ave. But it turned out he wasn't who he said he was, according to his birth certificate, and it wasn't long before his provocative, fun side turned volatile and possessive. That's when Los Angeles landed in my lap.

The opportunity to move to L.A. came a couple of days after one of our arguments became particularly explosive, and I jumped out of his truck to get away from him while he was driving. I was increasingly fearful of what I had gotten myself into and knew moving away would be the best way out of what was becoming an abusive and toxic relationship.

After graduating in the spring of 1998, I hoped moving to L.A. would give me new freedom. I didn't want another boyfriend. I wanted to date all the boys, flirt with all the girls, and commit to none. I wanted to work the party scene like it was a job. And get a job that could turn into an exciting career. So I did.

Chapter 3

PUERTO VALLARTA, MEXICO

DECEMBER 1999

THE HOTEL, if that's what I could even call it, was four blocks from the beach on Basilio Badillo Avenue. That first night in Puerto Vallarta, I found food for dinner and went to bed early, feeling strong. As I lay in the dark, the sound of cockroaches scurrying across the floor clarified my first priority—I needed an apartment ASAP.

The next morning, as I walked to the beach to say hello to the ocean, the smell of bagels lured me into a small shop called the Big Kahuna. A friendly white woman was working behind the counter. Donna was in her thirties, from Canada, and was helping the owner, Cesar, during the high season. The more I learned about the high season, the more I worried about finding a job and a place to live. But friends seemed easy to come by. That first morning in Puerto Vallarta, I made my first friend over coffee and a bagel.

Donna took me to the dance clubs and introduced me to her friends, who were mostly gay, single vacationers. I felt at home instantly. Here I was again in the party scene. Having not researched much about Puerto Vallarta before arriving, except to confirm it was in the same time zone as Madison and the sun would set into the ocean at the end of each day, I found it interesting, if not a bit disappointing, that I had landed in a place where I could saddle up to the bar surrounded by loud white people, order shots of tequila, and spend the night dancing. While I enjoyed the lure of the fun, I felt a pit in my stomach.

I'm not here for this. I'm here for something else. I reviewed the list I had made for myself that I had now memorized. *I am trying to get away from this,* I thought. This isn't part of the plan.

Maybe all the partying was just during the holidays. Maybe the tourists would leave in January. Maybe then I'd untangle from this party scene and settle into a healthier routine somewhere less touristy. I wanted to trust my ability to turn my life around, so I wrote a little prayer in my journal and reminded myself to drink water between my vodka tonics and not to sleep with anyone.

My parents had reluctantly agreed, earlier that year, that my Grandma Harriet could transfer a gift of ten thousand dollars to me directly. Years prior, her gifts went to my college fund, but I had graduated and was now experiencing a new kind of extravagant privilege as a twenty-four-year-old with only myself to care for.

Before leaving for Mexico, I called my grandma to update her on my upcoming trip.

"Grandma, I figured out my plan," I told her. "I'm going to take the next year to explore Mexico. I'll find work along the way, and the money will help so much." I tried to reassure her that this plan was a great idea. "I want to dream in Spanish, so I need to immerse myself. I'll be okay. Don't worry." She gave me her blessing as well as the privilege of financial security, which I grappled with. Even though my dad's voice was in my head, reminding me that money was tight and there was never enough, I could also see I had more than others. This inner conflict lay mostly unexamined in my subconscious.

As I faced a low vacancy rate and high tourist prices, the money shrank. But I was determined not to fail. The doubters in my life motivated me, the ones who questioned how moving to Mexico would help me get my shit together. I had something to prove to them and to myself.

A POSITION WAS OPEN to teach English at the University of Guadalajara Proulex downtown. The school was on the second floor of a quaint brick building next to the bridge over the Rio Cuale. Two large wooden doors welcomed me up a steep staircase and into a charming plaza. Everyone was on break during the holidays except for the director, who was in the office when I entered. He was casually dressed in khakis and a polo shirt with the school logo. He explained how the school worked, the different levels, the time blocks, and that most students were adults wanting to learn English for their work in hospitality. As he looked over my resume, I sensed that he wasn't even reading it. He had already decided to hire me. But instead of offering me a job, he offered to discuss the opportunity over drinks later that night. Being self-conscious about my lack of experience and desperately wanting to work, I agreed, even though I was uneasy.

After I left his office, confusion flooded me. *This can't be normal to invite a potential new teacher for drinks,* I thought. But it also didn't seem normal to apply for a job teaching English after having just graduated with a Spanish degree. The lines about what was appropriate and what wasn't were blurry when it came to men.

Our date over mojitos was slimy but effective. Classes would start after the first of the year, giving me time to study, prepare, and hopefully find an apartment.

EVERY DAY, I looked for an apartment. I slowly started meeting locals and making friends in new crowds, in addition to my touristy, party friends. I thoroughly enjoyed the hours we spent lying on the beach and dancing at the clubs, but I also allowed myself to stray and close down corner bars with the locals. I befriended the bartenders and waitstaff. The local guys swooned over my Spanish and my gutsy, solo adventure. They gave me tips for finding a place to rent. Everything seemed either ridiculously expensive, meant for rich tourists, or super low-end, unappealing, and not particularly safe, with nothing in between.

A new friend had helped me find a nicer hotelito, Hotel Yazmin, which was great but not guaranteed. Over the next month, depending on their reservations, I got bumped out repeatedly. When I couldn't stay there, I returned to the cockroach hotel. I was desperate to settle. I had gotten out of the United States just before Y2K. The most fretful moment was coming soon. Would the computers crash? I remember people in the Midwest withdrawing their money from the banks and stocking up on water and food while I planned my escape thinking I'd avoid the chaos by spending New Year's on a beach in Mexico. Here, no one seemed worried.

Between apartment showings, I contemplated my life. I found respite at coffee shops, where I would order a cup of regular coffee, add a bunch of cream and sugar, and make it last for hours while I journaled obsessively and struck up conversations with strangers. I wondered how I would integrate into this world, what that would look like, if I could heal and become the person I wanted to be. Who was that, though? I didn't even know.

TEN DAYS AFTER ARRIVING, it was Christmas. My Christmas present to myself: the Pacific Ocean, the sun, the sand, and the Spanish language. Instead of being in Madison, eating a traditional Christmas Eve dinner with my family, attending an evening mass, and getting to bed early, I was on my own, far away. I was proud of my brave adventure but also worried about the comfort I had found in Donna's party scene. I didn't want tanta fiesta, but I didn't know how else to spend the holiday.

Donna and I ordered Thai takeout on Christmas Eve and shared it at the bagel shop. Her friends stopped in with a bottle of wine. After drinking margaritas on the beach all afternoon, it felt like the appropriate thing to do. We switched to tequila shots when we got to Paco Paco's, the internationally known gay dance club. I could have been in L.A. again; the scene was so familiar. Donna crashed at my hotel room and held my hair back as I puked, half-naked, into the toilet. Most of my clothes were strewn on the floor. She laughed as I begged to die. Then I laughed as she tripped over her own feet. And we struggled over the one measly pillow. Then we passed out with the lights on.

We woke up on Christmas day wrecked. My body was torn up, but we were determined to get back to the beach. This was holiday living.

Donna and I created "the spot" where all our friends and acquaintances would come and hang out. Then we walked to the far end of the beach and smoked the rest of a joint we had saved from the night before. Poncho, a new local friend, had become my weed guy. Donna returned to our spot where her friends were sprawled out, half naked and hungover, while I stayed at the ocean's edge for some alone time.

The high was the perfect way to relax into my own body and feel alive again. I had wanted to die at the end of the previous evening, mostly because of the sheer amount of alcohol in my bloodstream, but also the familiar fear of failure. Now I stood at the edge of the water, the sun's warmth on me. I became entranced by the beauty of the ocean, and my body tingled with anticipation. I pretended I was being filmed for a movie, and I slowly undid the messy bun on top of my head and dramatically shook out my long hair. Then I gracefully stepped into the lapping waves. But I quickly stepped back. I didn't want to enter the ocean delicately; I wanted to leap in with abandon. I turned around and walked up the shore, and then, when it felt like I was far enough away, I turned toward the ocean and ran leaping, laughing until I dove into a wave and it crashed above me. I swam and swam, diving deep, holding my breath, and listening to the underwater world. When I got tired, I floated on my back, closed my eyes, and allowed the sun to calm me, nurture me, kiss me all over.

I was having so much fun with myself that when I got back to my towel, I lay down quietly so as not to encourage conversation and let my body sink into the sand. I pretended to nap. When the chatter around me stopped, I propped myself up on my elbows and gazed out at the ocean. *Had I made the right decision? Was this where I was supposed to be?*

As my eyes grazed across the bay, a whale jumped out of the water, and I watched in awe as her tail disappeared into the deep blue sea. I looked around to see if anyone else had seen it. No one had. It was just for me. The delight of her gift spread through me. Moments later, the whale appeared again, and I marveled. I was quick to thank God.

Thank you, God. Oh, thank you, thank you! I don't know what I'm doing or what I'm supposed to be doing, but I'm here, and I feel you loving me and supporting me. I promise to keep trusting you. Thank you.

I tucked my spiritual moment, my Christmas present to myself, into my heart and finished the day at a wild dinner party. As much as I enjoyed the evening, I was detached, observing the scene, mingling with people I didn't know, and longing for more meaningful connections. Donna must have recognized my unease. She pulled me aside and asked if I was okay. I told her I was fine. Her intuition sensed differently, and she lovingly touched my arm. Her concerned smile struck me, and tears welled up in my eyes instantly. "I need to be alone," I said. "I think I'm going to head out."

Walking alone on the beach late at night didn't frighten me at all. I was overcome by the beauty of the dark ocean, with her crashing waves on the shore and the sounds of holiday cheer. Music fought for my attention nearby and far away as it poured through open windows and doorways and elevated the joy in the air. I didn't have to choke back my tears anymore. Alone, I cried. There wasn't a clear path to a different life yet. If anything, this town was more of the same than more possibility for a positive change. Still, I could feel the determination rising inside of me, and as long as I stayed focused, I believed I had a chance of finding my way.

Chapter 4

LOS ANGELES, CALIFORNIA

SEPTEMBER 1998–MAY 1999

AFTER COLLEGE, I moved to a guest house in Beverly Hills that was owned by my dad's friend, Gary, a big-shot mortgage broker. My two years as a leasing agent in Minneapolis gave me enough work experience to know I could do well in real estate. The company I had been working for offered me a fantastic job with great potential in an attempt to keep me, but the opportunities in L.A. felt bigger and more exciting. Plus, I needed to get away from volatile Marc. I was young and enticed by the potential of balancing a successful career by day with wild parties on the beach at sunset and after hours on the strip, clubbing until dawn.

My guest house was a dream of a setup for five hundred dollars a month. The 8,500 square foot Beverly Hills estate was gated, like all the rest, but I didn't enter through the front like Gary, his family, and the staff; I had a back entrance. My back alley offered me a parking spot and access to the backyard, where I could enter my guest house and the outdoor kitchenette, which was behind a garage-like door. It was so cool! The guest house looked directly at the back side of their house from across the luscious backyard and was around four hundred square feet.

With Sedona orange tile floors, large windows, and massive built-in closets across one whole wall, it had character and was delightfully cozy. What I loved the most was the California king-sized bed where I could hang out all day if I wanted. There was still room for a little couch, coffee table, a TV, and a separate bathroom. The bonus was that I was friends with Gary and his wife, Deb, who always invited me over to eat takeout. Deb and I would hang out on the days I didn't work. I'd dish about the party scene, and she'd school me on Kate Spade bags. I knew my setup at the guest house was dreamy. I needed nothing more.

This arrangement could have been a solid rock to leap from. But, the holes in that living situation eventually ended up sinking me.

Before moving to L.A., I had decided to take an acting class while I was still in Minneapolis. That's where I met Mitch, who was also moving to L.A. around the same time. One night, months into my L.A. life, I was out with Mitch and some friends at a club. Someone had hooked us up with cocaine, and we were drenched in sweat on the dance floor, feeling on top of the world. Later, on my way out of the bathroom, I stopped at the mirror and took a long, hard look at my reflection. Normally I would reapply my lipstick and strike a pose before sashaying back to the scene. But instead, I leaned in close to the mirror.

I was wicked high. What I saw terrified me.

The reflection showed my flushed face, bloodshot eyes, and a desperate longing for something better, something different. I gripped the sink and studied my dilated eyes. It wasn't necessarily my appearance that shook me. What terrified me was that I could see where my life was going. Like I was watching someone else's life. I saw myself frantically seeking the next party, another drink, another guy to buy me another drink, or a nod from the bartender letting me know he was interested, which meant unlimited free drinks.

Usually, I didn't let myself look in the mirror long enough to risk an abrupt moment of harsh reality. I gasped for a breath as a wave of fear came up through me, but the air felt stuck in my chest, like I couldn't get it out. My heart started beating faster. I didn't know if it was a panic attack or the coke. I pinched the skin on my arm to bring me back to the present moment. I felt myself disconnecting from my body. Not wanting to end up on the bathroom floor, I ran cold water over the inside of my wrist and forced myself back out into the club. I told my friends that I was going to hook up with one of the guys we had met that night. That felt like the safest escape at the time. It was easier to leave with a stranger than be with friends or by myself, where the recent reflection in the mirror might remind me of my lack of control.

The next morning, when I woke up in the random guy's bed with little memory of the night before, I was relieved I was alive, even though I felt like death. The fact that I didn't know how I got there filled me with shame. I checked and confirmed that my car was out front. *I could have killed someone. I could have been killed. What the fuck was I doing?* The guy told me to sneak out the back door so his grandma wouldn't see me. *His grandma?* The trajectory of this lifestyle loomed dangerously.

L.A. opened the door to more risk than I was prepared to handle. I thought I was tough. I thought I had the chops to get my shit together and have it all, but the lifestyle was more like a slow fire that was getting too hot.

I had landed a really good job as a property manager in Riverside, but after a month or so, I quit. My ability to keep a full-time job had disintegrated. After six months, I preferred working for a temp agency because I liked the flexibility of scheduling myself depending on my benders. Then one night, I was talking to a woman at the bar about wanting to make more money, and she encouraged me to check out the escort business.

"You'd be so good. You're a natural conversationalist; from what I can tell, you can work a room well. It's easy money. The men are harmless," she said.

I made some calls, then signed up with an agency. They promised me there were no expectations to offer sexual interactions of any kind. Escort only. My first job was an easy one. I pounded back double vodka tonics before the guy arrived, and I treated the evening like a first date. But instead of assessing whether I would actually like the guy, I used my acting skills and pretended I liked him from the first moment we met. At the end of the night, clearly disappointed that I would not jack him off, he tried to berate me before shoving a handful of cash in my hand. I had confidently, almost fearlessly, stood my ground, but as soon as I got the money, I took off and couldn't stop shaking. *What was I doing?*

The following day, hungover and defeated, I called my mom. "Mom, it's bad. All of what I'm up to is bad. I don't know what to do."

My mother's familiar breath came through the line. "Come home, Sara. Come home, and you can figure out what's next, but you need to get out of there."

She didn't know. I hadn't been straight with her, and she didn't ask. But her intuition was strong, and she knew I was not well. She also knew that if I didn't tell her, it was because I couldn't.

I ended the conversation abruptly. I didn't want to go back to Madison. It was the last place I wanted to be. I was determined to stay, find a decent job, and never escort again.

A couple of months went by. I was still partying a lot, but I had found an office job, and things were manageable—until my dad's friend, Gary, who had always treated me like his little sister, assaulted me. It happened one afternoon when his wife, kid, and staff were out. I stopped by to get my mail and found him in the foyer getting ready to leave. He cornered me and started kissing me. I tried pushing him away, telling him to cut it out. He forced my skirt down and slammed his fingers into me.

I yelled at him to stop.

He told me I liked it.

I yelled, "No." I yelled, "Stop."

I yelled, "Stop," again, louder.

He finally did.

This was the third sexual assault I had survived. This was a man I'd trusted like family. This was my friend's husband. This was my parent's friend. I was shaken and in shock, and I moved quickly. Trauma responses vary from fight, flight, freeze, and fawn, but I was alone and scared, and my response was flight. Within two days, I'd packed all my belongings into my car, closed my bank account, and left without saying goodbye. On my way out of town, Ricky Martin backed up traffic, playing a live pop-up show at a block party in West Hollywood. I loved his song "Livin' La Vida Loca." I noted the irony and enjoyed my last L.A. traffic jam, singing loudly with the windows open and my car full of everything I owned. On the run, again.

Chapter 5

PUERTO VALLARTA, MEXICO

DECEMBER 1999

I DIDN'T EXPECT everything to become clear when I landed in Mexico, so I was pleasantly surprised when certain things did. For one, I was not at all interested in men—not a romantic relationship, a one-night stand, or even a flirty exchange. Although I noted my celibacy end date in my journal, and six months seemed like forever, saying no was easier than I imagined; I was so sick of men and their bullshit.

I was more hung up on the challenge of not drinking. I had already determined that I was an alcoholic. But I was a fun-time alcoholic, not some irresponsible, angry drunk. My friends loved Crazy Sara, and I didn't want to let them down. They counted on me to turn a regular night out into a full-blown party.

Christmas Eve clubbing had been intense, and though I'd planned to moderate by drinking water between cocktails, I lost track early and woke up with regrets.

I kept practicing drinking in moderation and was proud of the successful evenings, but then there was the night that I ended up on the beach with Roberto from Roxy's dance club. After having sworn off guys and being physically repelled by them in every way, I was full of shame and rage the next morning. I could barely remember how I had gotten so drunk, but remembered clearly almost breaking my celibacy promise and my fear as I yelled at him to stop.

Same story, different country.

Drinking and sex were too connected. I allowed myself to start the year 2000 with unbearably low expectations for myself. The world hadn't ended, and the computers didn't crash, but I feared my life would be the same until I crashed and burned.

I prayed about it. Party girl was also a prayer girl. I was deep into *Conversations with God* by Neale Donald Walsch and engaging with spiritual practices daily. Where I used to feel a connection to God every couple of weeks or when I remembered, now I was tapping into it daily. I was acknowledging God in my life, practicing gratitude, and witnessing beauty through a spiritual lens, sometimes intentionally and sometimes by accident. Like when I'd get signs that would surprise, delight, and ultimately remind me that God is always around, but I am not always alert to the messages. The signs could be as small as me craving a popsicle and then turning a corner and finding myself in front of a popsicle shop, or feeling worried about money and discovering forgotten cash in a pocket, or thinking about a friend I hadn't been in contact with for months and opening my email to find a message from her.

My spirituality was waking up inside me and bubbling to the surface. I felt God in the ocean. I felt God as the sun warmed my face. I felt the pull from somewhere deep inside. I saw God in people's faces on the bus. I heard God in the laughter from the kids on the corner. A butterfly would land on my knee, and I would smile at God or angels or a loving energy. It wasn't just the beauty that was all around me; it was intertwined in my thoughts, feelings, and experiences as I played with the idea that everything happens for a reason, and God is in everything.

The day after the close call with Roberto, I watched the sunset from the beach and talked to God. I needed God to step it up for me. I said, "I see you all around me, and I believe that you are within me and that I don't have to search for you outside of myself because we are one, but also, I feel like I'm doing this all by myself, and I hate it. I can't do it alone anymore. If you want something better for me, you need to help me."

I didn't receive a reply. I wasn't listening for one anyway. This realization that I was so alone made me angry, and I wasn't going to play nice about it. I wanted help.

Chapter 6

MADISON, WISCONSIN

NOVEMBER 1999

IT HAPPENED ON a Sunday in November of 1999, a month before I took myself to Mexico. I had agreed to meet up with a guy I had known in high school, Mauricio, though I hadn't seen him in years. I remembered him as sweet and funny. He invited me to a going away party for a friend at one of my favorite bars in Madison. We drove separately and met at the bar. I didn't know anyone there, but that was fine with me. I'd finished two vodka tonics by the time Mauricio arrived, though I was barely buzzed. He bought me a third.

I remember feeling fairly clear-headed as I sipped on the third drink. But that changed quickly. We were standing by the pool table when suddenly I couldn't feel my legs. And then things got blurry. I told Mauricio I needed to go outside for some fresh air. I didn't feel like I was going to puke; I just didn't have much sensation in my body and could barely walk. I held on to his arm as we went outside. He walked me toward the parking lot. I shivered from the November chill. He offered to sit with me in his Jeep, listening to music, until I felt better.

The next thing I remembered, I woke up in the back of his Jeep, teeth chattering and barely clothed. He was asleep in the passenger seat as I scrambled to find my pants. I was so cold and so scared. I don't remember how I got from that moment to my house, but somehow I drove home and ended up in my bed, with my clothes piled in the corner.

The next morning, sunlight poured into my bedroom window, and my head throbbed as I searched my mind for some memory of the previous night. I called my girlfriend to talk through what seemed like a black hole. My throat was dry and tight. "Kelly, I can't remember anything, but I have a really bad feeling," I said. She asked me questions to help me remember, then my mom walked into my room and sat on the edge of my bed. I got off the phone.

She softly petted my hair and asked, "Sara, are you okay?"

"Of course I'm okay. Just hung over. Why?"

"I had a horrible dream last night, and when I woke up, you weren't home. I was worried. I couldn't sleep until you got home safely."

"What was your dream about?" I asked.

"I dreamt that you were drugged, hurt, and needed help. You were stuck in the back of someone's van, and you couldn't escape. It was so vivid."

My heartbeat picked up speed, but I kept a calm face.

"Are you sure you are okay?" She looked carefully into my eyes.

"I'm fine," I told her and shooed her out of my room. Gingerly, I got out of bed, aware of the aches and pains. I wanted a hot shower. I wanted to remember what had happened. I checked my clothes and found blood all over my pants and underwear. A wave of nausea made me lurch to the toilet, but nothing came up. I was worried I would pass out, like my legs would buckle beneath me, so I sat on the cold floor to gather my strength.

I was more scared of remembering than I was of not being able to remember. As I showered, a couple of flashes came back to me, and I leaned against the tiled wall to steady myself. The contrast of the cold tiles and the hot water on my skin brought me into my body. I remembered lying on my back with him on top of me. I remembered trying to struggle free but not being able to move my arms. I remembered realizing I couldn't move my arms. It was like they were being held down. I remembered trying to scream no, but what came out was just a raspy cry. I remembered the silence. I remembered waking up so cold. So, so cold.

My mom's intuition, her dream, helped trigger my memory enough to know what I needed to know. And that was significant. I had enough flashbacks to put together what had happened. It wasn't hard telling my mom what I remembered, but I couldn't access my own emotions. I told her I wanted to see a therapist.

My mom squeezed my hand. "Yes, honey. Let me get you Garrett's phone number."

Garrett was the therapist my parents had taken me to during my senior year in high school. It had been many years since I had last seen him, and I didn't feel any connection to him, but I didn't argue. I just needed something to hold on to. I stood at the desk in the kitchen with my mom next to me and mechanically dialed the number. It was a Monday. My dad was at work, and my sister was at school.

"When would you like to see him?" asked the receptionist.

"Like, as soon as possible," I replied.

And as expected, she offered me some dates and times that were weeks away.

"No, I don't think I'll be in Madison then. Could you please put me on the cancellation list because my schedule is very flexible." Apparently, my flexible schedule seemed more noteworthy than my broken state of being.

Why was there blood? What had he done? Should I go to the doctor? Should I call the police? All I wanted to do was curl up in bed and sleep.

Later that afternoon, my mom tapped quietly on the door and peeked in. "Sara, you have a phone call." She handed me the cordless phone from the kitchen. It was the receptionist telling me there had been a cancellation for that evening. I confirmed the appointment and hung up.

"That's unbelievable, Mom. There was a cancellation, and she offered me a session for tonight. There are some angels working hard for me."

She smiled gently and whispered, "You are very loved, Sara."

That evening, I sat on a comfortable couch across from Garrett's swiveling office chair. Garrett was a white, middle-aged man with a sterile office. The pillows were stiff, and the colors were neutral. The office lacked warmth. Garrett lacked warmth. He was professional and a bit dry. Since I couldn't find my own emotions, I looked to him for a reaction and was confused and disappointed by his unresponsiveness. Maybe it had been a long day. Maybe he had wished his cancellation would have resulted in going home early instead of filling it with my wrecked self.

Without shedding a tear, I told him about the past five years since I'd last seen him: the drinking, getting high, one-night stands, the sexual assaults, the fun, the depression and anger, the parties, and the real reason I'd come, that I was drugged and raped the night before.

For some reason, I didn't cry. I wanted to cry, but I couldn't. I was too numb. I didn't feel anything, and I worried he wouldn't believe me. How could someone speak all of this out loud without any tears? After I spilled out all the stories in hopes of shocking him at least a little, he offered me his professional recommendation.

"Find an outpatient recovery program. And no sex for six months. Work on healing." Then we started to discuss my options for reporting the rape, but our time was up. Session over.

I spent the next couple of days mulling his suggestion. I reached out to the Rape Crisis Hotline to explore the process of reporting the rape. It would take a lot out of me, and I wasn't sure I had the strength to deal with the police. I wondered if I had deserved the assault. Was it inevitable, given my risky lifestyle? Maybe I signed up for this.

The first sexual assault I survived was at the age of fifteen, but it wasn't until the second one in college that I reached out for help. I believed that I needed to be resilient. I believed that being a victim was weak. I wanted to be a strong survivor.

I grew up hearing that everything happens for a reason, but I couldn't figure out how this applied to being raped. I told myself I needed a reason to justify what had happened, as if the rape needed to show me I needed to change my life. But I already knew I needed to change my life. Did the universe think a rape would catapult me to change? This is the story I made up in my head: God was pushing me into the next chapter of my life, and I should be grateful that it wasn't worse. At least I was drugged and didn't remember most of it.

But now I was a crumpled mess on the floor, wondering how to get up. I was so angry with men that it was easy to imagine no sex for six months. What I couldn't imagine was not drinking, smoking weed, and the occasional cocaine bender.

Chapter 7

PUERTO VALLARTA, MEXICO

DECEMBER 1999

I SPENT THE FIRST part of New Year's Eve with Donna and some new tourist friends. Even though I hadn't figured out how to live differently, I wanted to be on that path when the clock struck midnight, so I snuck away around eleven-thirty and wandered to the Malecon, the boardwalk. A couple of blocks away, everything shifted, and I found myself in a crowd of Mexican families, mostly dressed in white, celebrating. The loud music, the yelling, laughing, cheering, and smiling faces warmed me, contrasting how lonely and frigid I felt inside.

The next day I called my mom to tell her I was okay. I missed her so much. Surprised by the despair in her voice, I listened as she briefly mentioned a terrible argument she had had with my father. She was vague, and I worried about her. I worried for my sister, too. I remembered being present for their fights, but I had to focus on my well-being, so by the end of the conversation, when she promised me everything was okay, I decided to believe her.

"Sara, I have angels watching out for me. I don't need you to worry. It just puts negative energy in the universe. If you start to worry, stop, and instead send me positive, loving light."

TALKING ABOUT ANGELS and God was part of my life with my mom and friends, but it wasn't the norm in my Midwestern upbringing. In Mexico, it didn't take long to realize I was living in a culture where everyone I met seemed comfortable talking about God and angels.

There, God was not just a church or Sunday thing. God was not a topic reserved only for the grievous and glorious moments in life. God was not something people tiptoed around.

For example, the phrase "Si Dios quiere," *God willing*, was common.

"Nos vemos mañana. Si Dios quiere." *See you tomorrow. God willing.*

When Mexicans drove or walked past a church, they made the sign of the cross to honor God. No one bristled when the word Dios came up in conversation.

Playing with this new way of being in a relationship with God, I started to talk more openly about God with people I met, and not just Mexican people, but English-speaking people too. That's how Maria and I became friends.

Maria was from the United States. Her name was Mary, but she introduced herself to me as Maria one afternoon in the courtyard at the school because that's what she preferred. Her bright blue eyes and happy sing-song laugh made her very approachable. We instantly jumped into a conversation about synchronicity, spirituality, and the magic of living in Mexico. I had met a kindred soul.

She kindly offered help as I stressed about learning the curriculum for my classes and gave me sisterly guidance about how to navigate life as an American in Puerto Vallarta on a budget. Six months earlier, Maria had hit a low spot in Seattle with an ex-boyfriend and moved to Puerto Vallarta, where she could heal close to the ocean. Best of all, Maria spoke Spanish fluently and respected the Mexican culture—she wasn't there for the margaritas and the sunsets, like many tourists—and she loved dancing but didn't party hard. I had found a new friend more aligned with who I wanted to be. I started seeing less of Donna and more of Maria.

APARTMENTS STARTED OPENING up in mid-January. I had been living in hotels for a month. Two apartments were available for monthly rent (versus the typical weekly rates that the tourists snatched up). Both cost three hundred dollars a month furnished, but that was all they had in common. One was en el centro, a fantastic downtown location, spacious and close to everything. It was a one-bedroom unit with a clean bathroom and only blocks away from the ocean, the school, and a grocery store. The other apartment was farther from everything I was familiar with. It was a ten-minute bus trip away and then a steep walk up a brutal hill. But the view—oh my God. Standing on the front cement patio, I could see the full breadth of the bay from the southern tip of Cabo Corrientes to the northern tip of Punta Mita. The ocean lay in front of me with its powerful and peaceful presence. I had never had an ocean view. It was overwhelming to think I could wake up every day to this. Inside, the tiny studio apartment was one room with a bed, a tiny kitchenette, no door on the bathroom, high ceilings, a large window protected with bars, and a magical view of the Pacific Ocean.

Great location or great view? I could be happy in either place. But I needed to make a decision. Typically a decisive person, this choice had me in butterflies.

Chapter 8

MADISON, WISCONSIN

NOVEMBER 1999

IN EARLY NOVEMBER 1999, weeks before the rape, I had been exploring the idea of flying to India, meeting up with a friend, and traveling for the winter. Having grown up in Madison and then five years in frigid Minneapolis, I had lived through too many winters. Late in October, my friend and I started emailing about the possibility of traveling in India together, but I was having a hard time getting him to commit. By early December, I was reeling from the rape and more determined than ever to get out of Madison.

One afternoon, after talking to the Rape Crisis Center about my healing process, I made the decision not to report the rape. I threw away the bagged clothing I had been saving and impulsively bought a plane ticket to Mumbai. My bedside table was stacked with books about India, travel guides, and a notebook with information I had been gathering from people who had traveled there. After booking the flight, I sent an email to my friend, and I spread out the map on my bed and studied it with excitement. That evening he replied that he'd accepted a job in Australia; he had meant to email me earlier. He still wanted to meet me in India before his new job started and suggested that we travel together for a couple of weeks before he returned to Australia by the end of January. After that, I'd be on my own.

I wandered into the kitchen and leaned against the counter where my mom was making dinner.

"Everyone is telling me not to travel alone in India. I'm sure I'll meet people when I get there, and it'll probably be okay, but I don't know," I told her.

"Where would you go if you didn't go to India?" my mom asked.

"I don't know. I really want to go to India. I've been dreaming about this for so long."

She stayed quiet.

"I guess I could go to Mexico. I could practice my Spanish."

"Which one feels right to you?" she asked.

"I don't know. I'm so confused."

"Ask your body."

"What?"

"Ask your body for the right answer. Your body knows."

"Okay, Mom." I sounded like her snarky teenage daughter again and not the older, kinder version of myself that I had become, but she didn't react. She had stopped cooking to give me her full attention.

I softened my tone. "How do I do that?" She dried her hands with the kitchen towel and took one of my hands in hers.

"You put your hand here." She placed my hand on my solar plexus, the upper belly, under my breasts. "This is your third chakra, your knowing place. Close your eyes, say the thing like it's happening, and listen to how your body responds."

"What do you mean, 'say the thing'?" I asked.

"Say, 'I'm going to India,' and then feel what you feel. Then say, 'I'm going to Mexico,' and feel how your body responds."

I closed my eyes. "I'm going to India." I waited. I tried to feel my body.

My eyes were still closed as I shook my hands out, took a deep breath to clear the energy, and then put my right hand back in the same place and said, "I'm going to Mexico."

This time, I didn't need to wait. My body started to rock, and I sensed a rush of warmth. I smiled and opened my eyes.

"I'm going to Mexico! Oh my God, Mom! I'm going to Mexico. That was amazing!"

We laughed as we pulled out a map of Mexico. "I want to see the sun dip into the Pacific Ocean at sunset."

With new confidence, I hurried back to my room and canceled my ticket to India.

That's how I learned the trick of listening to my body when my brain couldn't decide. The act of protecting my heart from harm meant I learned to shut down and numb and compartmentalize in ways that no longer benefited me.

Chapter 9

PUERTO VALLARTA, MEXICO

JANUARY 2000

FOR SOME REASON, it didn't occur to me to check with my body about the apartment decision. I took the bus to visit the oceanview apartment for a second time, praying for a sign. The place was far away, not very accessible, and so small. As I slowly made my way up the steep hill, I navigated between the cobblestone streets and the skinny sidewalks and peeked in the windows and doorways of the homes I walked by.

At the top of the street, I looked up at the three-story terracotta concrete apartment building. Completely out of breath, I sat on the patio ledge, wishing I had worn tennis shoes instead of flimsy flip-flops. Sweating and panting, I gazed out at the ocean, wondering what to do, and a warm feeling came over me. I became giddy with excitement. This was it. My body had offered me the answer without asking.

I've always loved nesting. It doesn't matter where I am or how long I will stay; I always set up my space just for me. I spent a couple of days shopping for the basics and charging it all on my credit card. The apartment had a bed and some curtains that covered the large window, and that was about it. I purchased sheets, a pillow, some kitchen essentials, a plastic table, and four plastic chairs. My colorful sarongs now served as a tablecloth and a curtain for the bathroom door. I snatched up discounted Christmas lights from the sale rack for evening charm. Later I added a rocking chair.

It was a five-minute walk down the hill to the beach and a ten-minute hike back up. I could scan the ocean from one side of the bay to the other from my front patio. At night, the town's lights twinkled between the mountains and the shoreline. The ocean moved mysteriously under the light of the moon, and when there was no moon, the sheer blackness of the sea was just as powerful. The move was significant. Maybe I could listen to my intuition more deeply. Maybe my path would bend toward healing.

I didn't miss Donna, life at the bagel shop, or the nightclubs. I craved stability. I didn't want to party with random tourists. My heart was set on meeting Spanish-speaking friends, becoming a great English teacher, creating a healthier life, and healing from a painful past.

Still, most of the teacher friends I had acquired liked to party. I could go days without ending up dancing on a table or wondering what had happened the night before, but I hadn't figured out how to drink less recklessly when I did drink. If I couldn't handle drinking in moderation, I would have two options: check myself into a recovery center or quit altogether.

Chapter 10

SAN DIEGO, CALIFORNIA

MAY 1999

WITHIN THREE DAYS of leaving L.A., I picked San Diego as a landing spot. My friend, Kyle, had offered me numerous invitations. He was from Texas, but we had met while on a study abroad program in Seville, Spain, in 1997. Kyle was tall, dark, and handsome—cliché, I know. Kyle was also in a committed relationship, as was I. He made it clear that he was determined to be faithful to his girlfriend and would respect my relationship with my boyfriend. I took his lead. He showed me that not all guys wanted me for sex, and he was evidence that there were trustworthy men in the world. In Seville, we spent a lot of time together, smoking hash, studying at cafes, and going on adventures. Kyle had eventually moved to San Diego.

From the moment I arrived at his second-floor flat, Kyle and his roommates welcomed me and cared for me like a sister. They listened and believed me when I told them what Gary did. They didn't defend him, ask me what I was wearing, or question if I had been flirting back.

They also liked extreme adventures and raging parties.

"Who wants to go skydiving?" Brian asked as he stood in the doorway of the living room, watching us smoke a joint, the coffee table full of beer bottles.

My hand shot up like I was in grade school. And that's how I ended up jumping out of a plane at ten thousand feet, soaring above the ocean, mountains, and the Mexican border, jacked up on adrenaline. These were my people.

My first Saturday night in San Diego was brutal. After hours of drinking, smoking weed, and clubbing, I ended up on the floor in a bathroom stall, grasping the toilet. The next morning I couldn't scrub off the smell of booze stuck on my skin. Was shame a sharper scent than the stale alcohol? My new guy friends and I sat around the table moaning and sucking down salty Bloody Marys. I wasn't the only one full of regret, but I still felt so alone.

Later that night, we agreed to take it easy but fell short. All of us fell short. As fucked up as we were, it was a beautiful night, so we said yes to a midnight hike at Torrey Pines Beach. We walked through the stunning hills overlooking the Pacific Ocean while marijuana and alcohol coursed through our beautiful bodies and messed with our brilliant brains. I was higher than I was drunk. I was the only woman in the group, but I felt safe and respected.

Between the moon, some twinkling stars, and the random clouds tinted with a mystical reflection of the city lights, everything around me seemed brighter than I would have expected in the middle of the night. Ocean waves pounded on the shore below. Glimpses of sand dunes made me feel like I was in a faraway desert. It was breathtaking. A couple of guys ahead of me were engaged in deep conversation, but I didn't want to talk to anyone. My heart yearned to be present amid this beauty. My head was spinning.

What the fuck are you doing, Sara? How did you let yourself get so fucked up again tonight? You promised to take it easy after last night. You really can't live like this anymore.

And then I heard another voice, still in my head but clear as day. *It's okay. Everything is going to be okay. There is another way. Trust me.*

I stopped to look up at the moon. One of the guys had slowed down and was close enough that I could touch him. I grabbed his arm and held him tight next to me. I wanted to believe that voice so badly. I wanted to trust it.

"Do you believe in God?" I asked him.

"Yeah," he replied.

"Do you believe in angels?"

"I don't know. I guess I can see how angels might exist, but I don't know for sure."

"I do," I said. "I know there are angels all around me. I just know it."

We walked in silence, my head no longer spinning. Everything was going to be okay. I would make it out of this. I would make it through this. I trusted there was another way.

That was the night I would recall when I needed to remember I wasn't alone and didn't have to live the party-girl life anymore. When I'd find myself hugging another toilet, sick with horrible sinus problems after a coke bender, or peeing in a stranger's bathroom the morning after, I would think back to that night and pray it was true.

Chapter 11

PUERTO VALLARTA, MEXICO

JANUARY 2000

IT HAD BEEN EASY to feel confident about my decision to move into my oceanview studio apartment once I allowed myself to share the decision with my higher power. It could have been that my body knew, or an angel was helping me make the decision, or God was giving me a sign. I was open to all of those possibilities and that maybe all of those were the same thing. I grew up Jewish and Catholic and had an understanding that God was the same but different in different religions and could show up in different ways for different people. That was how I believed in God.

Now, believing in God wasn't enough for me. I wanted more. In reading more books, I was learning there was a way I could be in a relationship with God on a regular basis, and I could co-create with God more, too. I wanted that and knew I had to practice it to get it. Like doing anything well, it takes practice to create a habit.

Practicing meant that everything was more extraordinary when I remembered how to allow God into the ordinary moments of my life. That moment on the ledge of the patio was an example of how to co-create. I trusted the energy I felt. It brought me to the place I was meant to be. The next extraordinary (or miraculous) moment occurred during an afternoon with Maria. We had planned for her to visit my new place and then spend the afternoon at the beach. After our Saturday morning class, we got on a bus and headed north from downtown. When we got off, I pointed to the top of the hill and showed her our final destination. "That's it!" I exclaimed.

I apologized for the hike as we neared the top of the hill, sweating and puffing along. When we finally made it to my apartment, I unlocked the door and proudly showed her around. "Mi casa es tu casa!" It was all the more special knowing how hard it had been for me to find a place. We were still catching our breath after the one-minute grand tour, so we took two of my new plastic chairs to the balcony with glasses of cold water and looked out at the ocean.

"This is amazing, Sara. You found such a great spot."

"I know. I still can't believe how incredible the view is. I can hear the waves crashing at night. I feel so lucky."

We sat quietly a bit longer. We didn't know each other well, but we already felt comfortable enough to be in silence.

"Okay, enough gazing. Let's get on the beach," I finally said.

WE CHANGED OUT of our work clothes, packed our beach bags, and headed back down to the beach. We passed the gas station and some taco stands, and we crossed two busy streets where the buses sped by loudly, making conversation harder. The beach at the bottom of Calle Honduras was not a super touristy spot, although there were tourists everywhere this time of the year. The mixture of tourists and locals was about fifty-fifty. It wasn't too crowded, and we easily found a spot under the hot sun with no one around us. We flipped from our stomachs to our backs for hours to ensure we were evenly tanned. We would randomly take turns running into the ocean to cool off.

It's fascinating how easy it is to share your darkest secrets when you don't have to look at the person you are talking to. I suppose that is why confessions take place where the priest can't see you and why parents get juicy intel when carpooling kids. That's exactly what happened on the beach that afternoon. My struggles with the party scene and my addictions tumbled out very matter-of-factly, with little trace of my emotional distress and desperation.

WANTING HER TO know more, I continued. "My dad drank a lot when I was little and then quit cold turkey when I was around twelve. There is a history of alcoholism on his side of the family. I know I have it, but I don't know what to do about it. It's not like it's ruining my life. But there are days I feel ruined. And other times, it doesn't feel like a big deal at all, and I have so much fun dancing and drinking with my friends."

"I know all about alcoholism, Sara." She said in a supportive, kind voice. "I am an Al-Anon regular. It's like AA but for those who are impacted by alcoholics in their life. Do you know there are AA meetings in English here?"

"There are?" I could feel the energy around me shift. It was like a breeze swept through and changed something inside of me. I knew immediately that's where I belonged.

Maybe I wouldn't have to do it by myself. Maybe there was hope. But, shit, this means I don't have an excuse anymore, either.

As I listened to Maria openly share her experience with the twelve-step program, my brain kept interrupting me. I didn't want to not drink ever again. I didn't know who I was without alcohol. What if I couldn't do it? Maria was telling me how nice the people were and how I should at least check it out. Maybe she was right. And then, I thought, How ironic would it be to attend AA meetings in English, in Mexico?

Chapter 12

MADISON, WISCONSIN

1986

GROWING UP, I was witness to my father's unhealthy use of alcohol. I was going to say I grew up with an alcoholic father, but I'm not sure that is accurate. I grew up with alcoholism in my family. Maybe that works better. It's complicated, right? I want to be careful to tell my story, not his. My memories are my own, and sometimes they aren't always clear. I'm not sure what my mom's story would be as it relates to my dad's drinking, or my sister's for that matter. My dad quit drinking when my sister was one or two years old. She doesn't remember him coming home drunk. She doesn't remember the loud fights that happened when he had been drinking. But I do.

I remember one night especially well. My dad didn't come home for dinner like he was supposed to. Infuriated, my mom left a bloodthirsty note on his empty plate, the table still set for the dinner he missed. We all went to bed. My dad must have called to let her know he was sorry for being late and perhaps offered a plausible excuse. My mom took the call in her bedroom, and unfortunately for all of us, she forgot to retrieve the note she had left him earlier.

Later, I woke up to screaming and yelling as plates were thrown against the wall and smashed to pieces on the floor. In reaction to the fear that blazed through me, I went into action. I was only eleven, but I felt a strong sense of responsibility to my tiny baby sister, so I called my best friend Brooke, who lived four blocks away, and whispered that I was coming over. I carefully took my sister out of her crib, bundled her up, and made my way down the hardwood stairs, not worrying about the creaking noise. The shouting was too loud for that to matter. I sat on the second step, still out of sight, waiting for the right time to escape out the front door.

As I sat waiting, snuggling my sister on my lap, I imagined how distraught my mom would be when they found us gone. I didn't want my mom to worry or be upset, which made me doubt my decision to escape. But before I could sneak out the front door, my mom discovered us huddled on the dark stairs, frozen in fear. I hadn't found the courage to leave. It's not that I thought he would hurt us physically if he saw us trying to escape, but he was loud and angry, and I was terrified. I vividly remember the relief when my mom found us. Tears streaked her face as she gently got us back into our beds.

IT WAS SOON after that, or maybe it was another year later, when he quit drinking. I don't remember him deciding to quit. I just remember that after a certain point, he was sober and proud of himself for getting sober on his own because AA meetings were full of nasty cigarette smoke, and he'd rather go play basketball than sit in a smoky room talking. It wasn't discussed much, but my dad didn't beat around the bush when it came up. He let us know that he didn't handle alcohol well, that alcoholism ran in our genes, and that we should be careful. These were the messages that created my belief system. I believed that alcoholism was bad, a horrible disease that I could get because I was my dad's daughter. But at age fifteen, when life seemed better with vodka, I didn't care about any of that. I just wanted to escape.

Chapter 13

PUERTO VALLARTA, MEXICO

JANUARY 2000

MY DAD'S ADMISSION of his struggle with alcohol and our family history of alcoholism likely made it easier for me to talk with Maria openly. Feeling relieved I'd found a friend who wouldn't give me a hard time for saying no to a drink made the next couple of hours even more relaxing.

As we were packing up our things to head home, some guys who had been checking us out from a nearby bench came over to chat with us. Felipe was the friendly, talkative one, and even though he wanted to practice speaking English with us, he quickly switched to Spanish when he realized we both spoke fluently (relatively speaking). Felipe and I quickly realized we were neighbors by pointing to where we both lived at the top of the hill. He was young, not even twenty years old, and lived with his family while attending school so he could work in hospitality.

I was anxious to become friends with anyone who was a local, so when he invited me to meet him and some of his friends at the neighborhood bar, I said yes with a little too much enthusiasm.

"Jueves, dos por uno, en La Estocada." He explained where the bar La Estocada was located. I told him I'd see him later that week at six o'clock, and we went on our way. It didn't phase me to make plans with a strange neighbor guy to meet up for the two-for-one beer special within an hour of deciding to go to an Alcoholics Anonymous meeting and within two months of being raped. This was my confusing life, after all.

I fell asleep that night, confident that I would be okay. It was not perfect, but I felt angels around me, helping me, supporting me, loving me. I didn't feel as alone, and the conversation with Maria felt like it was divinely crafted. My new apartment, job, and friends were bringing new surprises. Reviewing the list in my head again, I realized how much I had accomplished:

1. Find a place to live ✓
2. Find a job ✓
3. Stay celibate for six months: four months to go ... so far, so good
4. Quit drinking/drugs: not quite, but I could feel it happening
5. Dream in Spanish and immerse myself in the Mexican culture and Spanish language: I was getting closer every day

THERE WAS A MOVIE THEATER on the corner of Insurgentes and Aquiles Serdan, just past the Rio Cuale River, only a block from where I was teaching English. This was where the AA meetings were held, and I was anxious to check it out. The corner was busy and loud. Sometimes, a line wrapped around the block when a new movie was released. I had walked by many times without noticing the raggedy, faded sign on the second-floor balcony that read "English AA Meetings." I paused by the front entrance but talked myself out of it and kept walking. *At least I know where it is,* I thought. Even with the sign, though, it felt far away. I couldn't imagine what it would look like or feel like or if I would be welcome. I needed someone to help me get through that front door. Until then, it would be something I probably should do but wasn't quite ready to do. First, I needed to find a gym. I had to prioritize my healthy new habits. But there weren't any gyms that I liked. They were either affordable but run-down or too expensive and fancy—the common paradox of a staggering wealth gap.

Running the hills in my neighborhood was exercise enough, so that's what I did. I ran the obstacles of the narrow, uneven stone streets with my walkman, my tennis shoes, and extreme focus. The beauty took my breath away, more so than the exertion of my legs pounding the road. Hot pink bougainvilleas cascaded down neglected concrete walls. The blue sky was piercing against the deeper blue ocean. The hills were dotted with white, orange, and yellow houses, green palm trees, and mountains in the background. Everywhere I turned, something captivated my attention and gave me a reason to stop and stare in awe.

And then there were the sounds. Sometimes I would turn my walkman off just so I could take in the children yelling, the dogs barking, and the friends laughing. Doors and windows were open; there was no barrier between a living room and strangers on the street. Laundry dried on the patio railings, and kids played with toy cars on the sidewalks. I ran by, slowed down, avoided people, sped up, jogged, walked, looked away when it felt too personal, and stopped to gaze at the ocean when it moved me. My runs in the neighborhood filled me up in ways I'd been craving. *Please keep me healthy,* I prayed. *I don't want to be sick in bed and hungover. I want this life.*

ON MY WAY TO CLASS Thursday morning, my calves burned from the unfamiliar hills. I stopped at the corner to wipe my armpits discreetly, not wanting to arrive at school looking as disheveled as I felt. I drank too much the night before and struggled through my morning classes. Once home, I nursed my hangover with ramen noodles and took a long nap. The sound of kids screeching with joy woke me. Feeling better, I lounged in bed reading, packed my beach bag with a blanket, my book, journal, and a bottle of water, and headed to the ocean to watch the sunset. This was my new life. I journaled, prayed, and felt waves of gratitude move through me. The sky was a brilliant blue, streaked with purples and pinks, and the air was balmy. Looking around at the palm trees and the happy children playing in the water, I promised myself I wouldn't get drunk that night.

After the sun dipped into the ocean, with my colorful sarong around my waist, I made my way to La Estocada to meet my neighbor, Felipe, and his friends for happy hour. The front of the restaurant was open to the busy street. I marveled at how nice it was to live where there was so much fresh air. The restaurant didn't seem welcoming at first, though. The front room was furnished as a dining area with several four-top tables and was empty. The walls were adorned with beautiful, vibrant murals of bullfighting scenes.

Squinting a bit, I could see a back room with a pool table. It was dark, but I thought I could make out some people. Felipe was not one of them. I found a table close to the bar, ordered a Corona, and told the bartender I was waiting for friends. He brought me two beers.

"No, gracias, quiero uno, nada mas," I said as I pushed the other beer toward him.

"Pero, es Jueves—dos por uno," he replied, smiling. *But it's Thursday—two for one.*

"Esta bien, pago por uno, y no quiero dos," I insisted. *I'll pay for one, but I don't want two.*

It made it hard to manage my alcoholism when it seemed like everyone wanted me to drink.

The bartender had a great smile. He introduced himself as Juan Carlos. After an hour, it was clear that my neighbor wasn't showing up. But I made a new friend. Juan Carlos and I talked for hours. I was pretty sure he was gay, which made me feel less guarded. I opened up more than normal. I stereotyped him based on his gentle spirit and a motion he made with his hand. Also, I didn't feel the typical aggressive interest coming from him; he made me feel comfortable. His deep brown eyes were kind. He was attentive and interesting. We talked about what I was doing in Puerto Vallarta, where I lived, where he lived, and how long he had worked at the restaurant. We talked about the classes I taught and my students, and I asked him what it was like living in a tourist town. A lot of the conversation was light and friendly, but as the night went on, there was sincerity and genuine interest in one another.

"Regreso pronto," I promised him as I left that evening. I knew I'd be back soon. If this is what the neighborhood hangout was like, I was happy. Cheap beer, good people.

Saturday evening, Maria and I met at Roxy's to go dancing. I didn't drink at first, but then a cute guy offered me one, and I didn't say no.

My plan didn't work again. But this time, instead of ending up drunk at the beach with the random cute guy, I went to La Estocada. I didn't hesitate to walk in at two in the morning. I strutted in like I owned the place, alone and confident with the alcohol flowing. Juan Carlos was working the tables and welcomed me.

"Are your friends here now?" he teased.

"No, I came to see you."

"Come sit over here with my friends." He motioned to a table, and before I could say anything, he pulled out an empty chair for me. Between serving customers, he sat with us. I was used to going out alone, making friends with strangers at bars, and drinking all night long. As people started leaving, Juan Carlos grew more attentive, and at last we were alone, engaged in deep conversation. I told him about the guy that had been catcalling me earlier and how pissed I was. I was hating on men and was not scared to tell him all about it. He listened intently, his soft eyes offering me space to let my guard down. I don't know if I was unusually open because of the alcohol or because he felt like an old friend, but I told him the truth instead of making up stories about why I was here in Puerto Vallarta.

"I'm trying to get better," I said, gazing down at my beer. I told him I wanted to quit partying so hard. I told him I was getting signs de Dios to attend an AA meeting but was scared. And he listened with compassion, so I told him about the rape and the past sexual assaults that felt like multiple stabs at a similar wound. I told him how angry I was but also how numb I was and that I wanted to heal and be healthy. I twirled my hair, nervous he would write me off as unhinged and damaged. But his eyes were steady, so I trusted him, still unable to trust myself.

It was probably close to four in the morning when Juan Carlos offered to accompany me home. The other waiter covered for him, and we walked up the hill together. I was exhausted from the truth-telling and the long night of drinking. We stood at my front door and looked out at the ocean and the city. The houses and hotels lit up the hills with tiny lights dancing at the ocean's edge. It was a piece of artwork—alive and breathing. It didn't sleep, this town. But the pause right before dawn was like a whole new world.

I finally turned to unlock the door to my safe haven studio. Juan Carlos squeezed my arm and asked me to come back and visit soon. Then in Spanish, he said, "And, Sara, good luck at the AA meeting. I'm proud of you."

Maria had told me that there was an AA meeting every day at five. My current excuse not to attend was I found spiritual solace in the sunset, which happened around six. But that stupid therapist's voice was in my head: "I recommend an outpatient program, Sara. You really need some help. I don't think you can do this on your own." Oh, how I wished he had committed me to an inpatient program. I wished he had called someone right then. This business of self-discovery and discipline was too hard to do alone. Couldn't people see I was dying inside?

I'm going to do it, I told myself. *I'm ready. On Monday, at five, I'll go. I won't tell anyone. I'll just go. Maybe I won't even tell them my name. Maybe I'll sneak in late and leave early. Isn't there a pamphlet or something? Why are AA meetings so mysterious?*

Meeting Juan Carlos the weekend before my first AA meeting gave me a helpful boost. This time, instead of pretending I was someone I wasn't, I bared my heart and soul to him. He was one of the only people who knew I felt defeated about my attempts to quit drinking and that I was scared. So on Monday afternoon, on my way to the AA meeting, I stopped by his restaurant before getting on the bus. I didn't go inside; I didn't need to. He was standing by the front entrance like a welcoming host. I didn't stay long. But it was long enough for him to give me the biggest, warmest hug. It was a lingering hug, strong and tight. I fit perfectly in his embrace and remember wanting to melt there. He was taller than me, but only a little bit, and my head rested on his shoulder. He smelled like cologne, and I loved it. My fear felt loved and held and comforted in that hug. The familiarity of his soul gave me pause. The pause allowed me to stay in his embrace longer than normal. That hug was everything I needed to get me through that first step, the first AA meeting. I thanked him and told him I'd come back to give him an update.

Chapter 14

MADISON, WISCONSIN

SUMMER 1999

IT HADN'T BEEN LONG since I first started to identify myself as an alcoholic. When I arrived back at my parents' house in Madison after my short stint in Los Angeles, it was my mom who talked with me. She took it upon herself to tell me exactly what she thought in the most loving, compassionate way.

In the car one afternoon, she asked me what it was like when I went out at night. She specifically asked me if, after a couple of drinks, my body told me it was time to stop. She got technical with me about how the brain works and used herself as an example. She told me that after she had a glass of wine or two, she physically could not have another one. Her brain sent her body a signal to stop. I had a hard time comprehending that. She told me how some people's brains don't give them the same signal.

"How is it for you when you are out with your friends, Sara?" she asked.

"I never get signals. Ever. I have challenged myself to have easy nights and drink more water, but somehow I completely forget my plan and find myself nursing a wicked hangover the next day."

She slowly shook her head with understanding. As we talked in this non-threatening and informational way, she told me quite bluntly that she thought I was an alcoholic. I didn't flinch. She also told me it sounded like I was a binge drinker like my father had been before he quit. I didn't like being compared to my dad, but I sensed the truth in what she was saying. Maybe it was the way she set up the conversation. Perhaps it was how she made it sound like it wasn't my fault; it was just how my brain was made. Or maybe it was just the right time for me to hear exactly what I needed to hear. I don't know, but it resonated with me, and I didn't get defensive.

After that conversation, I started to see myself as an alcoholic. It could have gone a couple of different ways. I could have denied this label entirely because I didn't need a drink every day.

I could go a week without getting drunk.

I was high functioning.

No one else had suggested my drinking was problematic.

But I had been exposed to enough education about alcoholism to know that drinking daily wasn't the only way to be an alcoholic.

I was a "party like a rock star" binge drinker, and most of my friends seemed to like that about me. But my mother gave me a new way of seeing myself.

I watched myself at the bar, working the bartender like I was on a mission. I wasn't just there for the drinks like some alcoholics were; I was there for the experience. If it wasn't fun, we needed a new party. If there wasn't a party, I would find one, and if I couldn't find one, I would make one. I took my label of being a "crazy fun party girl" very seriously. And now I had a new label: alcoholic.

The first time I used my new label wasn't at an AA meeting. No, not yet. I was at a bar in downtown Madison about a week after the conversation with my mom. My friends were ready to call it a night, I had been flirting with the bartender, and I had met some new random friends.

I was not ready to leave.

My two friends had to work the next day (imagine me rolling my eyes), and they were trying to talk me into going home. I bluntly replied to their proposition, "Sorry, ladies. I can't leave yet. Go on without me. I'm an alcoholic," I said, laughing. "I have to close down the bar with my new friends."

They didn't argue. They went home without me. We were no longer teenagers that stuck to the buddy system. We were young adults, and I had convinced them that I was okay on my own—a grown-ass woman. After that night, I referred to myself as an alcoholic casually, seeming comfortable owning my new label.

Owning my alcoholism was one thing, but understanding it was another. At that point in my life, I thought alcoholism was a horrible disease that would kill me if left untreated. But I also believed there was no treatment except never to drink again. If I couldn't stop, I would need to be able to manage it to avoid drastic consequences.

My understanding of alcoholism and my relationship with alcohol has changed a lot since then, but let's stick to where I was at the age of twenty-four, terrified that I might have to stop one of the things I really loved.

Chapter 15

PUERTO VALLARTA, MEXICO

FEBRUARY 2000

THE LOBBY AT THE movie theater, where the AA meetings were housed, was full of people coming and going. An old woman crouched in the corner of the landing halfway up, begging for money. I felt lonely for her. And I felt lonely for myself. Fear crept up, and my hands got sweaty. The hallway on the second floor was full of posters promoting AA with slogans: One Day at a Time. Keep it Simple, Stupid. Let Go and Let God. There was also a board with notes attached to it, all in English. Someone needed a ride to a nearby village that weekend. Someone had a dog for sale. There were apartments for rent and an invite to a fundraiser for Feed the Children. People lingered in the entryway. The meeting hadn't started yet. I was early and not happy about it. One long, deep inhale, and I opened the door.

I was twenty-four years old—a fresh, bright, blue-eyed, tan young woman with long, thick dark hair, fit curves, bright sundresses, painted toenails, and a skip in my walk. I did not belong here.

But there was joy here. Older people laughed together in chairs. The lighthearted atmosphere was beyond confusing for me. These people had this disease that meant they could never drink alcohol again. It should have been a terribly depressing, sad room. How could these people seem so normal and happy living sober lives?

The meeting started. I had assumed everyone would be as anxious and conflicted as I was or maybe even depressed and defeated. I had pictured a gathering of lonely and desperate alcoholics in despair. Perhaps that is why I had avoided coming, because I wasn't in complete despair, though I'd had moments. Yet here I was, two days sober, gathering with Friends of Bob who were introducing themselves as being sixteen years sober, thirty-two years sober, twenty-eight years sober. Lifetimes, really. My mind grappled with this information. *Not one drop in sixteen years? Were they really happy?* I was skeptical as I listened to them share, wondering if one day they might tell me about their secret lives outside of AA, where they had a Bloody Mary once in a while because it's not that big of a deal, right?

That first day, I received many outstretched hands welcoming me to this dark yet joyful and loving room full of long-time sober snowbirds. They belonged here. They had money and stability. They had a history together. Being sober was their life, their identity. I didn't belong.

Being sober was more foreign to me than living in a Spanish-speaking country alone. I felt like an outsider and more alone in that room with English-speaking people who shared my culture and heritage than I did living in my new neighborhood. But the spiritual energy in that room was undeniable. I felt a divine sense of knowing. *This is where you are supposed to be, Sara,* I told myself. *Just sit it out. Just stay. Don't ask so many questions. Don't try and figure it all out. Just be here.*

So I stayed. Then, as soon as the meeting ended, I rushed out to avoid anyone who might try to make friends with me.

JUAN CARLOS was eager to hear about my first AA meeting, and I was equally eager to tell him. He had a way of making me feel completely comfortable, like I had known him my whole life and was safe even in all of my anxiety and fear. There was no sign of judgment from him.

I stopped at the restaurant the next day after work and was welcomed with another big bear hug and his wide charming smile. When I told him that I ended up trashed and hungover again the night of my first meeting, he laughed lightly, like he was acknowledging the path to healing and recovery was not easy. His understanding confirmed that he saw me not as a failure but as a work in progress.

At this point, I still knew him as the bartender/waiter. It didn't occur to me that he was also the owner of the restaurant. At only twenty-seven, he seemed so young, but he had lived a lifetime in the restaurant business already. After he graduated from middle school, his mom had offered him the choice of continuing with school or going to work. He could tell what she wanted, so he started working as a dishwasher at a popular and touristy franchise restaurant, Carlos O'Briens, which overlooked the ocean on the Malecon boardwalk. After working his way up to kitchen staff, busboy, then waiter, he moved to Cabo San Lucas, where he also worked as a head waiter and got experience managing all aspects of the restaurant and bar. He knew every part of the restaurant's operation and learned enough English to make friends with tourists, party with them, and earn great tips. This also allowed him to get a visitor visa and travel to the United States and Canada.

He worked in Cabo for three years before coming back to Puerto Vallarta with enough money saved to open his own restaurant. La Estocada had been open for two years when I met him. He was always there. His brother, Edgar, worked in the kitchen. His sister, Reyna, and her daughter, Claudia, who was in her late teens, worked the afternoon shifts, and he hired waitstaff to help out at night. He wore an apron around his waist, his clothes were always well ironed, his shirt meticulously tucked in, and his hair gelled back. He was very together.

I, on the other hand, came and went in all states of dress. Sometimes I'd trail sand in after an afternoon at the beach, showing up in my bikini and flip-flops, a sarong tied around my waist. Other times I'd stop in after class in my work clothes, then casually slip off my shoes and prop my bare feet up on an empty chair.

WITHIN A COUPLE of weeks, without much conversation about it, we were spending a lot of time together. Early in February, he showed up at my door unannounced on a Sunday afternoon. He stood there with a plastic bag and asked me if I had plans that evening.

"No. ¿Qué quieres hacer?" *What do you want to do?*

He held up the plastic bag. "I got these oysters at the ocean today. I thought we could make them for dinner."

I invited him in, and he placed the plastic bag, heavy with oysters, on the counter. The shells clinked on the hard surface. My stomach turned.

"Are they still alive? I don't know how to cook these. Are we supposed to cook them?" I had never eaten oysters in my life.

I don't remember what happened next, but I imagine I made it clear that I had no desire to do anything with a plastic bag full of slimy oysters freshly removed from their ocean home. I do remember getting ready later that night for our first official date.

Our friendship began in Spanish. My fluency was improving every day, and even though Juan Carlos spoke English fairly well, our conversations and interactions were in Spanish. Yet as fluent as I was, there were gaping holes at times. I'd asked him to slow down, or I'd stop him mid-sentence to let him know I didn't understand. He was skilled at using other words to define words I didn't know. This is incredibly helpful for people who aren't native speakers. It goes something like this:

"Vamos a la cascada." *Let's go to the cascada.*

"¿Que significa cascada?" *What's a cascada?*

And then he'd describe, in Spanish, that a cascada is when water comes off a mountain, like there's a river, and then the river falls into a lake. As he spoke, he made all sorts of motions with his hands until, finally, my eyes lit up, and I yelled, "Si, si, a waterfall!

Many people who are not accustomed to communicating with others who don't speak their native language don't understand this interaction well. So if I were to say that I don't understand something, "No entiendo esa palabra." Many people will repeat the word over and over, thinking that I couldn't hear them.

Juan Carlos got it. He was always patient and spoke slowly, deliberately, and clearly.

Weeks later, he told me he never intended for us to make the oysters at my apartment. He came to visit that day to show me the oysters he had just bought and to invite me for dinner at a restaurant owned by his friend, where they would prepare these gorgeous delicacies just for us. Our first date. A date I wasn't expecting at all.

That afternoon, I was confused for a number of reasons. "But I thought you were gay."

"¿De veras?" *Really?*

We had been flirting for weeks, but I hadn't been a hundred percent sure what to think of him, and now it was clear he was interested in me.

"No!" I laughed, trying to make it seem like I was joking, "But you said you were happy being single. And I told you I wasn't interested in having a boyfriend."

He remained serious. "Si, yo se, pero I like you, and I want to take you out to dinner."

Two hours later, he arrived driving a taxi. He owned the taxi, and his brother drove it during the week. Sunday was his brother's day off. This delighted me. I loved watching people try to flag us down as we drove through town with the music turned up loudly.

I remember everything about the restaurant. It was on the second floor with an ocean view. We had the whole patio area to ourselves. It was dark and romantic, and all the staff knew Juan Carlos and practically tripped over themselves to make the night special. I felt like royalty. Juan Carlos asked what I wanted to drink. I paused. It felt like the kind of night for a glass of wine. I hadn't committed to never drinking again, and I couldn't imagine a romantic evening like this without wine.

"Vino tinto, por favor."

He ordered us a bottle of red wine. The waiter left, and another man appeared with a bouquet of red roses and baby's breath in a vase and set it in the middle of our table.

I was surprised at the extravagance of this centerpiece, and as I looked around, I realized this was a special delivery. They never gave us a menu, and they never took our order. This night was made just for me.

Juan Carlos' eyes sparkled. He had orchestrated this evening with great care. It was at that moment that I looked at him differently. We had become close friends, and now I wondered about him in an investigative, curious way. I wanted to know less about what he did and how he did it and more about who he was and his beliefs.

That night we talked about God and religion, education and intuition, and culture and our families.

When the plate of oysters arrived, the earlier misunderstanding was now cleared, but I pushed back. "You are assuming I like oysters. Why can't I order what I want to order? So there's no menu? You ordered everything for me?" I was not the kind of woman who liked whatever her boyfriend liked or who would do whatever he wanted to do, and expensive wines didn't always impress me. "If you want me," I told him, "you will want me for who I am and not who you think I am. You need to know more. I am more than I seem. We all are." I wasn't complaining and wasn't put off by his well-planned evening. I simply wanted to question his intentions and let him know that wining and dining me was not the way to my heart. Knowing and loving me exactly as I am was more important than fancy meals and flowers.

He took my banter in stride, watching me carefully with an amused twinkle in his eye. Juan Carlos wasn't a fast talker or fond of small talk. He didn't get defensive when I challenged him. Instead, he used very few words to convey his genuine interest in me and his growing respect for me. He wasn't like the men I was used to dating. The men who checked off a box on my "to date" list were firefighters, stock brokers, surfers, professors, artists. In the past, I'd aimed to date men who would either teach me something I wanted to learn, introduce me to people I found intriguing, or fulfill a fantasy I'd made up. Juan Carlos didn't check any of these boxes. He could have, but it happened too fast. He came out of nowhere and offered me a comfortable place to be, right there in his heart. From there, he held out his soft, gentle hand, and we looked at the world together for no reason other than to experience what was right in front of us. We didn't need each other; we simply liked being together.

Juan Carlos brought out a tenderness in me. Where I once was on guard and suspicious, I became vulnerable and tender. I allowed him to care for me in ways I was only beginning to care for myself.

Even on that first official date, I felt I already knew him. I already knew us.

He drove me home and parked at the top of the hill. I got out and walked around to his side of the taxi. He stood against the car and held both my hands. My whole body tingled with electricity and heat. I was short of breath. In an unusual state, I was intimidated by him and this electric connection, the intensity taking me by surprise. I leaned close and inhaled him. My heart pounded. He stood still, not moving. He was waiting for me, and I couldn't resist him. I inched my face up toward his, trusting he wanted this as much as I did. It was the softest, most gentle kiss. What began as precious and delicate turned quickly into lust and desire. We were both breathless. I remember, more than anything, how much I loved inhaling his breath. I wanted to breathe him in. My exhale was his inhale. It was a magical kiss. The kind of kiss that sends you into a daydream for days.

Chapter 16

EVANSTON, ILLINOIS, AND MADISON, WISCONSIN

1970s–1983

MY MOM IS ONE of those magical humans, an earth angel. She was my spiritual goddess guide. She was wise, grounded, and intuitively knew me like she had a sixth sense.

It was my mom who helped me realize I was an alcoholic, and it was my mom who helped me realize I had been drugged and raped. It was my mom who taught me how to listen to my body and tap into my inner voice. It was my mom who believed I could be whoever I wanted to be, and it was my mom who reminded me I was exactly enough the way I was. It was my mom who not only whispered to me but showed me that love was all that mattered.

My mom taught me the value of practicing gratitude regularly by being a grateful and joyful human. She was intentional in choosing gratitude and joy in her life, and as I grew up under her wing, I was similar. As a teenager, I went dark for a couple of years, but in college and beyond, my mom and I frequently talked about how fun it was to be happy, love life, and see the positive in everything. We oohed and ahhed over a simple glass of water, how the Almond Joy bar was perfectly made for us to share, and how beautifully the sunlight played through the hanging crystals. She looked at me like I was the most treasured human on earth, always telling me I was beautiful and smart, and she was in awe of me. She praised me way more than she ever criticized me. I don't remember her thinking I wasn't good enough, ever. Imagine that, in a world where we are taught to doubt our capacity and our potential and to see ourselves as less than others, my mother insisted I was amazing and wonderful.

She didn't believe in the four Cs: complaining, criticizing, comparing, or competing.

Someone always had it worse; no need to complain. There is good in everyone; no need to criticize. We are all wonderful in our own ways; no need to compare. A win-win is always possible; no need to compete.

Many of my friends struggled with dysfunctional, toxic relationships with their mothers. I suppose I confuse some people when I talk about my relationship with my mom, as my friends who have marvelous father-daughter relationships confound me when they talk about their dads.

My mother, Deborah, was raised in a Jewish family in Evanston, Illinois, the middle daughter with one older and one younger brother. She grew up surrounded by love, and like many, her childhood included some complicated experiences. When she was young, her dad's retina detached; from then on, he was blind in one eye and could barely see out of the other. My mom's mother, Harriet, became fully responsible for the household and finances, plus raising three young children. It was thought that if he got angry and yelled, it could worsen his eyesight, resulting in a home where no one yelled, and heated emotions were swept under the rug. My mother learned to go with the flow and put her needs aside.

My mother met my father right before her twenty-fifth birthday in the summer of 1973. She had been accepted into a dance therapy graduate program in New York City, which would begin in the fall, and my father, four years younger, was in an undergraduate program at the University of Wisconsin in Madison, living in the same house as my mom's brother, David.

It was a quick love affair. Within six weeks, while they were hitchhiking from Evanston to Madison, he asked her to marry him. While my mom was in New York City and my dad in Madison, they wrote love letters and planned their wedding. After my mom's first semester, she left the program and moved to Wisconsin to start a new life with my dad. They were married at an outside ceremony, by a rabbi and a priest, on a windy day in June 1974, in Spring Green, Wisconsin. The wedding was a joyous occasion despite an undercurrent of tension from a few family members from both sides who struggled with the contrasting religions and lack of tradition. But my parents were hippies, and all their friends were hippies, which meant love was what most people came to celebrate. Peace and love. Anything is possible.

I was born nine months and four days later, in Avoca, Wisconsin, on March 19, 1975. My arrival might have seemed appropriate based on the timeline, but my parents had just started a new life together in a small town where my dad had found an opportunity to work on a farm and live in a small house in the country. They had not considered becoming parents so soon. My mom was shocked when she found out she was pregnant. She proposed an abortion. They didn't have the chance to live together before they got married and were now trying to settle down in a township with a population of 463, in a little house with no running water and very few resources. My dad was working on a farm, and my mom had found work as a counselor at the local school. She had had an abortion a couple of years earlier with a college boyfriend, so she knew what she was proposing. Just because she and my dad were married didn't mean they were ready or financially stable enough to have a baby. My dad, only twenty-two years old, was absolutely against the idea. Not because of his Catholic upbringing but because he was married to the woman he loved and the idea of having a baby, while scary, was a natural part of the life he wanted. His confidence and conviction won her over, and so with trepidation and utter reverence, my mom fell in love with the idea of having a baby and becoming a mother.

I don't know what my mom expected from the marriage, but I don't think it was all she'd hoped. Her new husband had a strong personality, which contrasted her more accommodating ways. He was incredibly driven and persuasive. When he wanted something, he was tenacious in going after it. Even though he had a righteous tendency, he was also open-minded and respected a well-formed debate. He battled his own childhood issues that began when his mother almost died giving birth to him. His mom had extensive health issues during his childhood, spending months at a time in the hospital. While his father worked, my dad was alone or with other family members, missing the care of his mother.

My dad loved my mom passionately and told me he knew he wasn't ready to get married or start a family at such a young age, but he wasn't sure he'd ever meet someone else like her. He committed fully to whatever life would be like with her as his wife. That kind of passion showed up when he was frustrated and angry, too. He was a yeller, and my mom, although raised in a quiet, reserved home, became a yeller, too. I like to believe it was the angry feminist in her that chose to fight back instead of becoming a submissive wife.

OUR HOME LIFE revolved around my dad. He liked to work, and he knew how to party. I have vivid memories of him coming home drunk and loud, sometimes angry, sometimes rambunctious, making life unpredictable. My mom and I weathered these emotional storms. In a way, my mom and I grew up together. I was the Pisces to her Virgo and brought daydreams and a vivid imagination; she was more practical. She was my solid ground when nothing felt stable. She was more of a friend than a parent much of the time, but her profound wisdom and cautious ways offered me a responsible and loving mother who kept me centered and safe—or as safe as she could. She opened the door to creativity, dance, art, song, skipping, and joy in the little things.

Instead of lamenting the loss of her dancing career, she threw loud dance parties in the living room just for us. With the windows open, she belted out the lyrics to Beatles songs and insisted I dance wild and free with her. I gazed at her admiringly and told her how beautiful she was. I adored her. She adored me. We were dancers together. She didn't have to convince me. I was a dancer, too, not because I wanted to be like her but because I was born to dance. As I grew older, I constantly asked her to watch me as I took center stage in the living room and put on shows for her or anyone who came to visit. With my eyes closed, I moved through the room in my own world, not caring how I looked or who was watching. I was a dreamer and a dancer, and my mother was my biggest fan.

The fact that we had so much fun together made it easier for my mom to navigate the constant moving around. After the first year in small Avoca, my parents moved to Madison, and every year until I turned nine, we moved from apartment to apartment, from house to house. My dad started with contractor work and then got his real estate license. At first, they rented apartments, and later he would buy homes, fix them up, and sell or rent them. For my mom, moving ten times before I turned nine was far from ideal. Still, her ability to make every place our home, our special sacred landing place, was her specialty, and I don't remember feeling the displacement of such constant commotion. Perhaps I sensed her discomfort and made it my job to show her I was okay and could roll with it just fine. Change still doesn't rattle me.

Knowing how rattled she was with change, I can imagine her relief when, in 1983, my dad decided we were moving to the other side of town, to a wealthy community, where he promised her they would settle down and not move again. They lived in that home in the village of Shorewood Hills for the following fifteen years.

Chapter 17

MADISON, WISCONSIN

1980s–1990s

FOR OUR FAMILY of three, 1983 was a big year. Not only because we moved up in the world socioeconomically but because my dad had an affair that year that rocked our family. It didn't break my parents' marriage, but it shattered parts of us in ways we couldn't have anticipated. Like a cut that keeps getting scratched and reopened, over time, the impact of that quick affair showed up in different ways.

It's unknown to me if it was my years of begging my parents for a little brother or sister or the desire to move forward from the wreckage, but I finally got what I had been asking for when my sister was born a year later, in 1984, a couple of months after I had turned nine. I was my mom's best helper. Again, we were in it together. My dad, an eager participant when he was in the right mood, worked a lot and often came home drunk after going out with work friends. My mom, the grounded caretaker, also worked. On a typical Sunday afternoon, you could find her planning my Madonna-themed birthday party, changing my sister's diapers, scheduling a hair appointment to refresh her perm, and making sure there were enough cans of Spaghettios in the pantry—all while doing the laundry.

My mom continued to be one of my favorite people, even in middle school when my friends became more important, and I grew bolder. That was when I started questioning why she was married to my dad. Not because of the affair; I had tucked that into a far corner of my mind. Until I hit adolescence, I had simply been scared of my dad's temper and moods, but as I got older, my emotions became more complex, and a deep-seated anger started to bubble up. Amid my middle school angst, I decided he was an asshole and seethed with hatred toward him. That's the only word there is for it. My journals from those years are filled with raw hate and a dramatic desire to die.

Their marriage, as romantic as it might have seemed from the outside with their frequent displays of affection, was volatile. Yelling and name calling were the norm, and their fights were loud. My dad snapped easily. I went off and hid each time, and my mom ran in circles trying to accommodate his needs until finally standing up for herself. Then he would yell at her, then he would yell at me, and then he would bring home a puppy, and everyone would pretend to be happy. It couldn't have been easy for my mom to listen to me frequently question her decision to love the man she had chosen.

After one yelling match, I escaped the house, slammed the door on my way out, and sat in the car waiting for my mom to drive me to school. She came out with her coffee mug, which I held for her while she pulled out of the driveway.

"He's such an asshole," I blurted. "I don't understand what you see in him." My rage came out in my voice.

My mom didn't respond. Her silence might have been a sign of her tenderness, but I was too self-absorbed to notice. I kept complaining. "He's a jerk, Mom. Why are you still married to him?"

"He's got a lot going on, Sara. Work is intense right now. You could be a little nicer. It's not easy for him."

"That doesn't mean he has to be such a jerk." I looked out the window, feeling disconnected from my mom and defeated. I wanted to fight, and she wanted to make peace.

It was true that my dad did have a lot on his plate between a demanding career and graduate school. He did the best he could without many loving role models or a supportive childhood. My mom saw the hurt and the potential in him. She was steadfast in her loyalty. While empathy didn't come easily for my dad, forgiveness came very easily for my mom.

This left me with a strong desire to get out. I dreamed of the day I would leave for college.

As a teenager, I grew more courageous. I began to talk back and rebel—shoplifting, drinking, dating for the wrong reasons, breaking curfew, sneaking out at night, pushing my limits with teachers, basketball coaches, and whatever other rules (and laws) I decided were stupid or beneath me. I'm guessing that my mom knew I was struggling and hoped we'd make it through the teenage years without much lasting damage. She also had a toddler and a full-time job at the state capitol to manage.

My mom's parenting style is best described as a passive, permissive style. It probably seemed to balance well with the more authoritarian style my dad preferred. It was his way or the highway unless I could offer a reasonable argument, and at that age, I didn't possess the maturity to do so. Most of the time, it felt like he was just using his power to make my life hell.

That was a typical teenager's perspective, but what was not typical was how the door I kept slamming shut on my dad stayed open for my mom. She was easy to be around, not intrusive, and not overbearing. Her intuitive way of being helped her make smart decisions with my friends and me. She knew when to speak up and when to stay quiet. She became the mom that would pick my girlfriends and me up after an afternoon of partying at the park, our water bottles emptied of vodka and Mountain Dew, pretending she didn't know we were shit-faced.

After I failed a biology test in tenth grade, she took me shopping to cheer me up. "It sucks to fail a test," she said. That same year, my dad grounded me for coming home drunk, and my mom took me to get ice cream because she felt bad for me. "It sucks not to be able to see your friends," she said.

My mom also had a way of counseling my friends through heartbreak and self-esteem tribulations. She was there to help my friend, Cyndi, when she got kicked out of her house, and once she counseled my friend, Daria, to change the negative self-talk in her head. One afternoon, we were sitting around the dining room table, and Daria was frustrated with her math homework.

"I am so bad at math. I don't understand why we have to learn this," she complained for the third or fourth time. My mom was listening from the other room, and finally, she walked in and put her hand on Daria's shoulder.

"You are very smart, Daria. I know you are smart, and smart people can learn math. But until you believe it, you will continue to think you are bad at math."

Daria considered this for a bit, and then my mom asked her if she was willing to do something different just to try it out. Daria agreed.

"I want you to go to the bathroom and look in the mirror and say over and over again, 'I am good at math. I am smart, and I am good at math.'"

I laughed nervously. I knew Daria liked my mom, but I was worried that this would be too far-fetched. I didn't want Daria to think we were kooky. To my relief, Daria took on the challenge and went to the bathroom. She came back out and said she didn't feel that much smarter.

My mom said, "No, sweetie, it will take more practice. You will need to stop yourself every time you notice the thought that you are bad at math. You need to change the messaging in your brain. That message that you aren't good at math is coming true because you keep saying it. Change the message, any message that isn't working for you, and you'll see. It works."

Years later, Daria would repeat this story to me.

My friends adored my mother, and I enjoyed sharing her. She was a safe place to land for all of us. In contrast, my dad had a reputation for causing people to steer clear. And we did. They were two extremes; there was little middle ground in my childhood.

Chapter 18

PUERTO VALLARTA, MEXICO

FEBRUARY 2000

EARLY IN FEBRUARY 2000, I found myself settling into a quieter life in my new home with its ocean view. Further from the party scene, I had more time to read books and journal on the beach. I reflected a lot on my anger and my lack of respect for men and myself. The ability to observe how my past was creating barriers to healthy living gave me a reason to address the pain instead of hiding from it.

In reflecting on my past, I couldn't avoid the nagging question about my mom and why she stayed in what I deemed an unhealthy marriage. The more I tried to figure out her motives, the more confused I got. *Maybe she's not perfect. Maybe I should take her off the pedestal. We are all imperfect humans on our own imperfect paths.* Being able to confront my own ugliness, knowing my mom knew my ugliness and still loved me more than anything, helped me experience brief moments of that same grace for her.

Most of us are wounded in some way, and hurt people hurt people. I didn't want to hurt anymore, and I didn't want to hurt anyone else. I wanted to break the cycle, but at age twenty-four, I didn't know much about breaking cycles or healing journeys. I knew I wanted something different, and I was determined to make a change. I wasn't afraid of change. Maybe that was the rebellious spirit in me.

My whole life, I'd been the odd one out. But it was comfortable for me. I didn't like fitting in even as I longed to fit in. Paradoxically, there was a rebel in me who loved shaking things up, wasn't afraid to get in trouble, and constantly sought ways to challenge the status quo. And this was in direct contradiction to the part of me who wanted to be seen as a good student, a perfect girlfriend, and an easygoing human being. I was confused by my contradicting desires, but when I followed my heart, things made more sense, even if they didn't to the outside viewer.

Later in life, when I would tell people about my journey to get sober and how I found English-speaking AA meetings in Mexico, the common response was, "So you moved to Mexico to get sober? That doesn't make a lot of sense!" The stereotype of booze cruises, Corona on the beach, and the best tequila in the world didn't fit the story I was sharing. It wasn't a conventional recovery story.

When I moved to Mexico, I had imagined immersing myself in the culture. If I had done more research, I would have realized that Puerto Vallarta is a tourist town, attracting mostly North Americans and Canadians who visit the beaches and eat and drink to their hearts' delight at half the price. Looking like the typical tourist in a tourist town meant I was seen as the consumer, the economic prosperity of the city, and not someone who valued the people, their culture, history, and language. It was one of the reasons Mexicans constantly praised my Spanish and asked me where I was from. I didn't fit their stereotype. Walking in the touristy downtown, I observed the annoying way English-speaking tourists would engage with the natives with entitlement, arrogance, and disrespect.

"I speak Spanish. Más cerveza, por favor." It was embarrassing.

I knew the people in Puerto Vallarta appreciated and depended on tourism, which was likely one of the driving factors for the kindness constantly offered to rude Americans. Still, I didn't want any part of that. I wanted to be a local, not a tourist. I wanted to belong. I didn't want to consume the experience; I wanted to become a part of it. Hanging out at Juan Carlos' restaurant was one of the ways I stood apart from the stereotypical white people. As evenings playing cards, eating chicken quesadillas, and flirting with Juan Carlos became my routine, the regulars started treating me like a regular. I'd casually kiss the traditional hello on the cheek with Juan Carlos, his sister, Reyna, and her oldest daughter, Claudia. When his brother, Edgar, shyly made eye contact from the kitchen, I would nod and smile. And I would try and play with Paulina, Reyna's five-year-old daughter, who I usually found under the pool table.

Even though I was still drinking every once in a while, I tried being sober more than anything. When I visited the restaurant, Juan Carlos offered me a limonada, and if I asked for a beer, he'd serve me one without hesitation. He respected my journey. He trusted I knew what I needed. We even got drunk together a couple of times. On one of my drunken nights with him, I asked if I could call him Carlos instead of Juan Carlos.

"It's shorter, sweeter," I said.

"Esta bien, amor," he said.

One night, a couple of days before Valentine's Day, as Carlos and I sat on the ledge of my front patio, holding hands and looking out at the night sky over the dark ocean, I knew I had to share my conflicted thoughts with him. I was afraid of being in a relationship. I was in Mexico to dream in Spanish and get my shit together. Men were a distraction, and I was weary of the wounds they had caused me. I blurted out, "I didn't want a boyfriend. Maybe we should just be friends."

Carlos replied slowly, "I didn't want a girlfriend either, Sara. My restaurant gets all my attention, and I don't have the time or energy for a serious relationship. But we can't be friends. I like you too much. This is different." We sat in silence, and then he said. "Let's see what happens."

I knew it was different, but I was still unsure about the timing.

"I want to return to the States at some point and get my PhD and become a professor. I don't want to live in Mexico forever." I threw it out there as a warning. I'm a wanderer—a free spirit.

"Mira, Sara, if this works out, great. But if it doesn't, that's okay too. I'll be fine with or without you." He stood firm in this statement. He was clear and intentional about wanting to be with me but not needing to be with me.

I inhaled deeply and didn't reply right away. It was potent. It was what tipped me over the edge into the deep end. I wanted to share my life with someone who was whole, with or without me. I had been with too many men who declared their undying love for me, like they couldn't live without me, before even knowing me. Carlos was clear; I will be fine with or without you. I choose you right now if you choose me.

And the celibacy goal? He already knew about my six-month no-sex promise. Again, he surprised me by honoring that without concern. He wanted to be different. He didn't want to be like all the other guys. He said we could wait. I wasn't as sure, but I admired his confidence.

"So what's the intention of being together?" The words translated well into Spanish, and Carlos seemed to get what I meant.

"To experience life together, I suppose."

"Okay," I said. It was all so similar to what I was reading about in *Conversations with God*. We are all on this life journey together and are okay exactly as we are.

I was used to boyfriends saying, "You make me whole," always making me cringe. Carlos wasn't like that. But I needed to go slowly, which was not how I typically moved.

We agreed we were more than friends and that we'd take it slow, knowing trust would take time and effort. "Whatever will happen, will happen."

Chapter 19

PUERTO VALLARTA, MEXICO

FEBRUARY 2000

MY ROUTINE OF GOING to work, the beach, La Estocada, and my studio started to feel steady. It grew easier to blend in, even though I still stuck out as a white girl in a world of brown faces. Yet, I walked in my neighborhood like I belonged there. I fit in with the teachers at school. I could be a tourist on the beach and also engage at the corner grocery store like a local. Often, people pegged me as a tourist and asked where I was from. I hated that question. "I live here," I told them.

"¿Si, pero de dónde vienes?" *Yes, but where do you come from?* All I heard was that I was different and didn't belong. Where is someone from? Where did someone grow up? Where do people live? There are so many iterations and different contexts to grapple with in these questions. I am from the same land you are from if there are no borders. We both breathe the same air. I was very particular about the words I used when having this conversation with people. Years later, this would serve me greatly in understanding the microaggressions Black and brown people regularly endure with questions about their background.

I felt this longing to belong in a foreign country, but I could not find any sense of belonging in the AA meeting room. I went to more meetings but kept my distance. What if they were all pretending? I couldn't trust them. But really, I couldn't trust myself. I was still drinking, and I thought they would hate me if they knew. It all seemed too hard, too unattainable. But I kept going because I didn't know what else to do. And I kept drinking because I didn't know how not to.

Carlos and I talked at length about spirituality and religion. He came from a very Catholic family with ten brothers and sisters. We talked about the point of marriage and partnership, played with different ideas together, and left space for the possibilities of what we could believe. He was open-minded and didn't care what people thought of him. That became clear as I learned more about him. He owned the restaurant and a taxi but lived with his mom and didn't have a car. He was saving money and investing in his dreams, and his willingness to make sacrifices was notable. Carlos knew I was talking with some AA members about getting a sponsor and working the program, and I admitted the sacrifices seemed like too much. I still hoped I could get my drinking under control so I wouldn't have to quit for the rest of my life.

Maria encouraged me to meet this guy, John, from AA, to help me find some answers about the program. John's weathered, older face and slow, calm demeanor gave me the feeling I could skip the small talk and throw all my concerns on the table. He wasn't taken aback. The first concern was this never-drinking-again thing and who I was if I wasn't a party girl or Crazy Sara. What about my bachelorette party, with shots, champagne, and maybe a little coke?

During our talk, John made clear to me that each journey is unique but what brings everyone in the room together is the basis of the program: one day at a time. He suggested that every time I want to daydream about my bachelorette party—which I confessed I looked forward to more than any wedding—to think only of today. And maybe even this one hour. Come back to the present.

"Don't try and figure it all out," he said. "Don't overthink it. If you want to get better, and it seems like you do, take it one day at a time and keep showing up."

He made sense. He didn't hit on me. I liked him. We smoked too many cigarettes and talked for hours. I told him about Carlos and how different it was with him but having a boyfriend was not part of the plan.

John slowly blew a smoke ring and said, "It seems like there is a lot in your life that's not part of the plan, Sara."

THE NEXT DAY was Valentine's Day, and people proudly carried bouquets to their moms or lovers. Stores were decorated, and street vendors offered roses for sale. The mood was all love. Teaching school that day was fun, with treats, heart-centered activities, and exercises.

Carlos was standing out front when I arrived at the restaurant after my last class. It felt like he was waiting for me, but that was his usual spot so he could greet people and make them feel welcome, appreciated, and important. It was that kind of friendly, fun atmosphere. He was beaming, and we hugged. I loved his hugs so much. He was excited to introduce me to his other sister, Martha. I walked into the bar area with Carlos right behind me.

The balloons and the decorations were amazing. Cut-out hearts in red and pink adorned the walls, and an arch of red, pink, and white balloons floated over the bar. A bulletin board where pool tournaments would showcase the brackets and score sheets was converted into specially made hearts listing the couples who frequented the restaurant:

- Chely y Jesus
- Armando y Maria
- Lety y Victor
- Maribel y Leo
- Mario y Guillerma
- Alejandra y Pancho
- Sara y Juan Carlos

I stopped in my tracks. I felt the realness of us. Like it had to be pronounced in a pretty red heart on Valentine's Day to be official. It was only February 14. I stood there feeling nervous and special at the same time. Carlos put his arm around my waist with an ease that felt like home, like the warm blanket my mom offered when I was scared. My nervousness slid away.

I went home that night, content and comfortable. It wasn't perfect, but it was good enough. My Spanish wasn't perfect, either, but it was good enough. My attempt at being sober wasn't perfect, but it was good enough. My desire to know God wasn't perfect, but it was good enough. And that was all I needed that night—to detach from perfectionism and sleep peacefully enough.

Chapter 20

PUERTO VALLARTA, MEXICO

FEBRUARY 2000

It was a deep penetrating irritation. I wanted to have contradicting lives and be contradicting people. There was the me I knew well, Crazy Sara, and there was the inner divine me who knew I needed to change—quickly.

The problem was that I liked the spontaneous, wild, and free Sara. She was mysterious and unpredictable. She went wherever she wanted to go, met new, random people, and fell in and out of love. But that woman also yearned to do what everyone else was doing and daydreamed about marriage, children, and stability.

The whole thing was a contradiction. How could I give up such a fun life, being such a fun person, only to step into a healthier, boring life and become a person I was completely unfamiliar with?

I walked around contemplating this and incessantly discussed it with my new AA friends. I wanted to have it all.

One night, I said fuck it to being sober and met Donna and some friends at a hip new spot. Sitting next to Barbara at the end of the bar, I realized she had come alone—something I would do. Barbara was a good thirty years older and had the stories to prove it. After I told her a little bit about myself, she shared her wild stories of travel, adventures, and lovers. She talked about the different countries she had lived in, the wisdom she had gained, and the experiences that could fill books. Her dangly earrings got caught in her wavy hair as she laughed with her whole body. Her flowy purple dress was adorned with long crystal necklaces, and her fingers were dressed up in big clunky rings. She glittered, not with diamonds or gemstones, but with earthy, vibrant colors, silver jewelry, and mischievous sparkling eyes. I loved her.

She was who I wanted to be when I grew up.

We partied until they closed up the bar. Too many shots and vodka tonics later, all the sparkle had dulled around me, and the flowy purple magic was replaced with the white ceramic toilet bowl. Again.

That smell of toilet water.

Only someone like me knew that smell. It's a faint smell of old water. It doesn't smell like urine, actually; it's a familiar, cold ceramic smell. The toilet itself is pretty clean. I didn't associate that smell with having the flu because most of the time I was covered in a dried sweat from dancing all night, my hair tied behind my head, and my shoes next to me. I'd reach around to find my purse, pulling it close while resting my head on that toilet seat.

I know the feeling of wanting to die but knowing I won't, and not sure which is worse.

The next morning, I could barely get out of bed, but I was determined to keep my teaching job, so I hid my wicked hangover behind my sunglasses and made my way to class. The sun hurt.

A couple of steps ahead of me, on the other side of the street, I noticed a young Mexican mom in a cute athletic outfit pushing a stroller with a water bottle in the cupholder. She looked great in her stylish sunglasses and bright tennis shoes. I glanced at my reflection in the window. I, too, looked great in my sunglasses and cute teaching outfit, but I felt like hell. It hurt to be me that morning.

She was walking fast, like me, but she walked to exercise her body. I was walking fast because I was late to work, again.

The mom pushing the stroller must have been exhausted, too, but for different reasons. My stomach ached, watching her. She was ahead of me on the sunny side of the street. I was walking in the shade, watching her in a way that would settle in my cells and shift my life. In reality, it wasn't she who changed me; it was my idea of who she was. It was me seeing myself in her.

She was who I wanted to be when I grew up.

I looked at my reflection in the shop window again. I was in front of one of those expensive jewelry stores that looked out of place next to the cheap tourist t-shirt shops. My sunglasses and lipstick gave me a rockstar vibe, but I could feel what the reflection hid. That person in the window wanted more for herself.

It was that desire that gnawed at me. Was it possible? This was all I'd known. This was the person I'd learned to love. And I was still learning to love her. But I hated her too. I hated her when she passed out on the floor in the bathroom, hanging on to the toilet seat.

I picked up my pace, not wanting to be late for work. I felt a wave of irritation and wondered why the sun was so fucking bright and why people were smiling and wishing me a buenos días when it wasn't even seven in the morning. I scowled at the smiling people and decided that the world was trying to annoy me on purpose, maybe for having too much fun the night before. Blaming the world was easier.

PART TWO

Chapter 21

CARLOS AND I had been back and forth about being in a committed relationship and had both agreed that we couldn't not be in a relationship, we couldn't be just friends, we couldn't deny what we felt. So even though neither of us wanted it nor felt we had time or energy for it, we chose it.

We intentionally and consciously acknowledged that our best-laid plans were great, but God might have other plans. I wish I could say we weren't scared. We were. But what was fascinating was that the fear didn't present itself when we were together. It melted away, even when we wished it would roar loud enough to end it all so we could go back to our original plans.

After running errands one afternoon, Carlos came over for a siesta to prep for the restaurant that night. I had finished teaching my morning classes and was enjoying a long midday break before my evening classes. He brought some food, and we were going to nap and relax before going our separate ways later.

I don't remember what the argument was about, but it started with something he had done or not done the night before when we were playing cards at the restaurant, and it started in Spanish. I was pissed because he was getting defensive instead of talking it through with me, and at some point, when I got heated and angrier, I switched to English, and then I called him an asshole.

He left abruptly, saying something like, "I'm not doing this."

I fought with him to stay while wanting to tell him to fuck off at the same time. It wasn't much of a fight, though. He had emotionally shut down and was gone within minutes. I was pissed. How could he just leave like that without talking it through? I curled up on my bed and cried. After I exhausted the tears, I journaled, realizing I really liked him and didn't want us to be this way, but I didn't know how to fix it. I resolved to pay him a visit after my class that night to clear things up.

The restaurant was empty when I arrived. We sat at a four-top table, the wooden chairs stiff, like the energy between us. The conversation was in Spanish again. I asked him what had happened and why he got so angry.

"I don't like name-calling."

"You were being an asshole. It wasn't that big of a deal."

"Name-calling isn't okay with me, and if that is how you are in relationships, I don't want to be in a relationship like that."

He didn't say he didn't want to be in a relationship with me. He said he didn't want to be in a relationship like that, but I didn't catch that right away. I felt the ground beneath me shift. I saw this magical love crumbling into pieces, and I didn't know how to stop it. My breath quickened. I had determined earlier in the day that I didn't want to lose him. At all. But now it felt like I was. He was drawing a line in the sand that I couldn't comprehend.

"But name-calling happens. It isn't that big of a deal. My parents call each other names all the time. It's part of fighting."

"It doesn't have to be. We get to decide what kind of relationship we want, and I don't want a relationship where name-calling is okay."

I stayed quiet for a bit. We get to decide? Who is this guy?

"Wait, so what you're saying is that we get to decide the rules? Name-calling isn't normal. It is a made-up rule that we can accept or reject?"

"Yeah. Pretty much." His patience with me was kind, once again, and his conviction in what he wanted and believed was strong and admirable. I was astonished by his maturity. I felt like a little girl learning a grown-up thing, but he wasn't treating me like a little girl. He was treating me like a capable, intelligent human being. "I want to be with you, Sara. But I don't want to be in a relationship where we call each other names and swear at each other when we are angry. Do you think you can agree to that?"

I stayed quiet. That was a good question. Could I? Had I ever been in a relationship, even with my parents, where these were the rules?

"I am scared I can't. It is what I grew up with and how I've been with all my other boyfriends, but now that you are telling me it doesn't have to be that way, I want to try. I do. I want to make up new rules with you. I want us to decide how we want to be together." We were still speaking in Spanish. The tension between us had eased, and Carlos reached across the table for my hand. It was like a jolt of electricity. We both felt it. Our eyes locked with a deep understanding.

"Te quiero," he said.

"Yo también te quiero." *I love you, too.*

The start of our relationship wasn't like a boat easing off of a dock and slowly gaining speed. It was like a stick-shift car driven by an amateur, starting confidently, slamming on the brakes, choking the engine, trying again with more ease, then going too fast, and then slamming on the brakes again.

Sunday nights were the only night Carlos had off, so those were our date nights. On February 22, 2000, we went dancing after a romantic dinner. I had a couple of beers but didn't get drunk. I didn't even enjoy my drinks and was uncomfortable at the nightclub. The music was loud, the songs were cheesy, and it was too loud to talk. So we watched all the drunk tourists, and finally, I asked if we could leave. What had changed? I was starting to want to be sober more. I also wanted to be with Carlos, and the loud bars made our time together feel impersonal and empty.

That was the last time I drank, though I didn't know it at the time.

One day at a time. Before I knew it, I had been sober for seven days. Then fourteen. And so on.

ONE MORNING, right after my early class, one of the students approached my desk. It was Alfonso, an older, sweet-natured man. Alfonso asked me if I had a class at nine. I didn't. Then he asked if I wanted to join him for breakfast. My first instinct was to say no. What if he hit on me? He was my student and an old man. But then I became more curious than suspicious and asked him if there was something particular he wanted to discuss.

"No, Maestra Sara, nothing in particular. I am curious about your life."

I smiled and said, "¡Vamos pues!" *Let's go!*

Alfonso was deeply spiritual, and God came up in our conversation before we even arrived at the restaurant. We went right there, easily. I told him I had been trying not to drink, and he told me he was proud of me, which felt great. I told him all about the AA meetings, and I remember feeling comforted by his concern for my well-being. Like he knew I was hurting inside and had something to offer me.

Over the next month, Alfonso and I occasionally hung out. We didn't stay in touch after the class ended, but while we were friends, he taught me the value of slowing down and trusting my intuition and how to meditate in a way that felt accessible and has stuck with me forever. While we sat on my front porch one morning after class, way above the city, he directed me to find a nonmoving object in the distance or nearby to look at.

"Don't look hard at it. Look at it softly, so you can also see all around the object."

I was looking at a spot on a rooftop. Then as I relaxed, I started to notice the clouds moving, even though I hadn't taken my eyes off the spot on the roof. A bird flew within my sight. There was a parasail and boats. I started to see, without directly looking at the movement.

"Now listen. What do you hear? There are layers of sounds, and as you listen carefully, you'll be able to notice each on its own, individually," Alfonso said. He was practicing alongside me.

I heard the buses. I heard the dogs—not just one dog, but three barking dogs. I wondered if they were talking to each other. I heard neighbors chatting nearby and children yelling further down the hill. The sounds were layered and distanced.

"Have you listened to every sound there is to hear?" he asked. I thought for a moment and listened again, noticing all the sounds I had identified.

"Yes," I replied.

"Now feel your senses. Feel the air on your skin, the hair on your head, your legs against the chair, your heart beating." And so I did. I felt the sweat on the back of my neck. I felt a fly land on my thigh. I felt my bra pinching under my arm. We sat there, so still, so focused, and so relaxed at the same time. Together, but apart.

This is the tool I use when I want to come back to the present moment, get grounded, and open my heart to messages beyond the human world. I use this time to connect with the divine, ask for support, and give gratitude to the universe and my higher spirit.

I was healthier than I had ever been. Healthy in mind, body, and spirit. The connection created in the moments of meditation helped me feel certain of the path I was on. I wished it would last. But still, I caught myself wondering and worrying about the future.

EVERYONE WARNED ME not to think about the future. Keep it one day at a time. But I'm a planner, so I calculated that by June 22, I'd be four months sober. It would be easy by then, right? I was scheduled to return to the States on June 15 to prepare for a family reunion in Italy. Then I would either stay in Italy and travel around Europe or return to Mexico. Either way, whatever happened, I was calculating life in four months, with approximately 120 days of sobriety. I wanted to finish the twelve steps by then too. Which meant I needed a sponsor quickly.

I tried to stay present as I focused my energy on these AA meetings, the teaching, the people, and my new life. If I planned too much, too far ahead, I'd start to freak out and get anxious. Then I'd take a deep breath, remember to live one day at a time, and focus on the moment in front of me.

The breeze, the sound of the birds.

Stay focused.

It was like I was grasping the ledge, and the only thing that kept me from falling was stopping to listen to what was happening in the moment. The act of listening, smelling, seeing, and experiencing the present moment is equivalent to the feeling of being underwater for as long as you possibly can. That first breath when you come up for air is all-consuming. There is no space to think, worry, or ruminate when all you want is air.

As long as I stayed in the present moment, it didn't have to be so hard. I could start allowing it to be easier.

I HADN'T EVEN known Carlos for a month yet, but he was already taking up a lot of space in my head and my heart. I found myself daydreaming about him and us. He was so different from anyone I had ever met. I felt good with him. I wanted to open my heart and keep it open. Until now, I was used to closing it to protect myself. My mom had given me a taped seminar full of fascinating insights that helped me see where I had been closing myself off. It was by Caroline Myss on energy anatomy, and it was also similar to the messages in the James Redfield book, *The Secret of Shambhala*, which I read on lazy weekend mornings. Sometimes, I could feel my mind expanding. But other times, I could barely breathe. My fear of the future shortened my breath and tightened my chest. The seminar encouraged me to become an observer of my own emotions, to help me learn more about myself and uncover the deeper work. Maybe if I could notice the fear, it would help me overcome it or meet it with love. I yearned to be free, to feel my feelings and not automatically shut down, numb out, or hide.

Carlos already knew the demons in my closet—the rape, sexual assaults, the challenging relationship with my father, and my struggles with drinking. One afternoon we started arguing about something small; I don't remember exactly what. I remember thinking he was a chauvinistic pig, like all the other guys I had met. I wrote in my journal that night and then reflected. How do I change that? How can I remember to remind myself that I am safe, I am loved, I am respected? How can I believe what my heart is showing me—that Carlos is safe, that I can trust him, and that I respect him? I wrote about not wanting to be scared. I didn't want to live that way anymore. What do I fear, anyway? I fear being loved for the wrong reasons. I fear failure. I fear being taken advantage of.

The next time we were together, I told Carlos I was scared of the love we had discovered. I told him I was scared that I was going to fuck it up. I told him I was confused as to why I feared something so beautiful. We talked at length. Naming my fears out loud moved that darkness into the light, where it shrank. We were learning to be vulnerable with and support each other.

What was I really scared of? Lack of control, maybe. We laughed about how whether I was single or not, I didn't have control and never would. I told him about the saying in English, "If you want to make God laugh, tell her your plans." I told him that I wished more than anything to see our relationship as a divine, precious gift and to honor and care for it.

BEING OPEN WAS way harder than it seemed. I continued to journal about being open to the highest good for me, for him, and for all of the universe. It reminded me of my mother and how she taught me to intention. She used the word as a verb—to intention something.

While I was growing up, my mother intentioned parking spots, arriving safely as our plane took off, or a positive diagnosis from a doctor. It went like this: "Dear Universe, it is my intention that we get the best possible parking spot (or other intention), if it is for our highest good, for the highest good of those around us, and for the highest good of all." Then she would make a *swoosh* sound, like she was sending it out into the universe, and say, "Thank you!"

If she came upon a fantastic parking spot, we got excited. And if she missed one, she would say, "It must not have been for our highest good." Or, "Maybe someone else needed it more than we did."

This untangled the belief that I should know what was best for me all the time because bigger things were happening not just for me but for everyone around me. What I thought was for my highest good might not be. My mom often reminded me that the universe was conspiring for me, not against me.

In talking with Carlos that night, we uncovered a conversation I didn't know I was missing and would continue for the rest of my life. How can I stay open to love? How can I live from a place of love, not fear? I pledged to be more aware of when fear was bubbling up in me. The reality was that men had angered me and created fear in my life for as long as I could remember. But it wasn't just with men. I feared rejection, too. And when I stayed open to love, I found myself less defensive or fearful of what others thought of me. I trusted that I would be okay if love was at the center.

And anger felt safe. It offered a barrier. It protected my tender heart. I could see how it was no longer serving me. When I got quiet and really tuned into my inner wisdom, I felt safe at my deepest core. Yes, I had been hurt and betrayed, but I had no reason to believe Carlos would hurt me. It became clear that I had been equating men and danger too closely. I was in a relationship with a kind, gentle soul I could trust.

AT AA, I shared about the recent argument with Carlos and my surprise at how this relationship was impacting me. It felt good to tell the truth without worrying about being told what I was doing wrong. As I shared, I kept circling back to how angry I was about the rape and how although I wanted to enjoy this new relationship, there was a dark cloud over me. I was confused as to how I could trust Carlos so openly and also be so fearful at the same time. Then one night, after journaling and crying and journaling some more, I decided to forgive the guy who raped me. I wanted to say it out loud and share it with the world. So, I went back to AA the next day to share it with strangers. I couldn't wait for my turn to talk. I shared my enthusiastic decision to forgive the rapist. Immediately I felt confident that things were going to be better. A bit later in the meeting, someone read from the chapter "Easy Does It," which explained about the compulsive addict. The addict who never leaves the bottle of beer half empty, who does everything with gusto. I saw myself in this reading. I tried to imagine not finishing a drink. Then I remembered my mom telling me she sometimes didn't finish her wine. I saw myself as a person who doesn't do anything half-assed. I didn't like it. I could see where, at times, it was forced. Was my desire to forgive the rapist a coping mechanism so I could tell myself I was all better?

Was it a way to claim I was all better without being all better?

At the time, I perceived only two options for recovering from a trauma: victimhood and survivorship. I was a victim of a violent act. Being a victim left me feeling broken, vulnerable, shameful, and tender. If only I had nurtured myself the way I would have cared for a friend.

Instead, I saw being a victim as weak. When I felt the tenderness and fear creep in, I got angry. I didn't allow myself to feel the sadness beyond the anger. I was scared that in feeling sad for myself and the girl in the back of that Jeep, I would crumble. I worried that if I permitted myself to be a victim and allowed myself space to heal, I would be weak. I had been fed the message that the goal was to survive, and you can't be a survivor if you are a victim. This binary thinking led me to fight the moments of tenderness and sorrow and instead shout forgiveness to the man who raped me. I would be a survivor, not a victim. Hear me roar!

The only one who saw me fall apart was Carlos. At night, when we cuddled in bed and things got sexy—my celibacy was still intact—I cried. He held me and reminded me that he wasn't going to hurt me, that I was safe. In the dark, I could be broken, but come daylight, out in the world, no one could see my pain. Carlos offered me a place to heal. When I tried to pretend I was fine, he would squeeze my hand, knowing it wasn't fine and indicating that it was okay not to be okay.

Chapter 22

IT IS A CURIOUS THING how Carlos contradicts himself. I would describe him as a rule-following stickler. It annoys me, but in a humorous, endearing way. If the speed limit is sixty-five miles per hour, it's hard for him to go seventy. The speed limit is the speed limit in his world. In my world, it is a suggestion that I rarely agree with, but Carlos likes rules. We both know that as much as this is true, he also sees his life as his own to live, doesn't need to follow all cultural or religious traditions, and challenges the status quo. For example, he respects his mother's Catholic religion but doesn't feel obligated to follow it. I was grateful to discover this about him, knowing we would be breaking some traditional rules by simply being together.

Carlos' family was traditional in many ways. His father, Cipriano, inherited land from an uncle with no children. Cipriano had helped him work the land, so when it became his, he continued to work it to provide for his family. He picked mangoes from the trees, brought pigs home to feast on, and used a machete to clear and care for the land he'd been given. He was a nurturer, a farmer, and a healer. People visited him when they were hurt or sick. He was known for healing broken bones, sprained ankles, dislocated shoulders, and other ailments.

Cipriano was born in 1911 and married a woman from Puerto Vallarta. She had two children but died when he was forty-seven years old. He needed a new wife and set his sights on a young girl, Marcelina, only eighteen years old—a twenty-nine-year age difference. One day she was washing clothes at the river, likely daydreaming about the young man she had been in love with who had recently been killed. Her heart broken, she was focused on the task at hand when Cipriano came for her. At the side of the river, he rode up on his horse and told her he was taking her to marry him. She objected, but she didn't have much choice. As she told me this story, while we were sitting around a large table in front of her daughter's house one evening, I could see her memory take her back to that very day in 1960, and her eyes welled up with tears.

He was as old as her father.

Cipriano took her on his horse that day to a small home on some of the land he owned. She tried running away twice. The first time she ran back home to her parents, but her mother was angry at her for leaving the family and didn't believe that he had stolen her. Her mother didn't let her come home. The second time she went to stay with her godmother, but Cipriano came for her. Marcelina finally surrendered. They were married, and eighteen months later, she had their first child, a daughter named Maria. Over the next twenty years, Marcelina and Cipriano had eleven children together. Every two years, they had another child. He brought her chocolates when she gave birth to a boy and didn't talk to her for a couple of days after she gave birth to a girl. There were four boys and seven girls. Cipriano seated the children in the pew at church so the boys were on the end to show them off.

In 1980, Carlos was eight and his oldest sister, Maria, was eighteen. The youngest child wasn't born yet, and there was still no phone in the house. Marcelina didn't think they needed one. Maria had just gotten her first job and wanted to communicate with work or be able to call home if she was going to be late, so she saved the one hundred fifty dollars it cost at the time to get a phone installed.

Cipriano worked the farmland, a thirty-minute horse ride away. Sometimes he'd take one of the donkeys with him to help bring back produce. Marcelina sent the kids out to sell whatever produce Cipriano had brought home or cookies she made. She counted the money precisely when they returned, always taking half and reminding her children to save their money.

They ate well, and Marcelina always made sure the children did their homework, behaved at church and school, and presented themselves properly out in the world. But was she happy? I'm not sure it occurred to her that happiness was an option. She was raised to be a good wife, which meant having as many children as God would bless her with, keeping the house well-maintained, and focusing on raising the children while also devoting herself to Catholicism. She was a homemaker, and she took her job seriously. She still does.

When Cipriano was seventy-one, they had their last child, Judith. Seven years later, at seventy-eight, he passed away after being in the hospital for three months. Carlos was sixteen years old.

In 1989, when Cipriano died, Carlos was working. Carlos' brother-in-law found him at the restaurant to tell him their father had passed away. Carlos worked hard. His father worked hard. And when his father died, working hard became even more important for Carlos and his older siblings. Marcelina, now a widow, still had young children to care for. While I grew up leaning on my mom for support, Carlos grew up helping support his.

Chapter 23

MY RELATIONSHIP WITH CARLOS was evolving fast, and as much as I was enjoying it, I was still scared and angry about the rape. Sometimes, my anger erupted if a guy whistled or cat-called me as I walked to work; I would snap back with Spanish swear words. But other times, when I was feeling peaceful after sitting by the ocean, reading a chapter from a spiritual book, or spending an hour journaling, I relished the attention. I was aware that I oozed with sexual, feminine energy. I was aware I could stop traffic if I wanted to. I would step off the curb to cross the street even if I didn't have the green light, knowing the sway of my hips, the skip in my step, my big smile, and maybe even my short skirt, could captivate attention in all the ways that objectified and oppressed women while paradoxically offering us a bit of power, too.

Understanding power in a culture designed with systems of oppression had not been explicitly taught to me. I was aware of the dynamics of "power over" and "power under," but I hadn't explored "power with" or "empowerment" when it came to my personal power. I was even more confused about my own empowerment after being raped, left utterly powerless, unable to even move my arms or scream for help.

In one way, it seemed like I ran away after the rape. I didn't report it to the police, even though I bagged evidence. I made anonymous calls to the Rape Crisis Center to understand the pros and cons of my next steps. And then I left the country as fast as I could. I wanted to believe

I was boldly running toward a better, healthier life but feared I was running away to escape the claws of addiction or the shitty men waiting to attack. I desperately wanted to trust myself, my decisions, my heart, and my path. I desperately wanted to trust in a divine energy and the messages that seemed so clear to me. In the clearest of moments, I did. Then the muddy moments swallowed me, and I wondered, *What if it's true? Wherever you go, there you are.* Was this what my life was going to be like? Maybe I wasn't destined to find my way.

I needed my mom. I needed her and wanted her to help me, hold me, and give me space to talk. I needed to cry on my mom's shoulder and feel safe. So I emailed her and asked if she wanted to come and visit me. I didn't tell her I desperately needed her; I was vague. She was busy, and I knew it would be hard for her to come, but mostly I was scared she wouldn't. And if I asked for what I really needed and she said no, how would I be okay? It was hard to explain the importance of her coming to see me since I was already scheduled to be in Chicago early in March for my grandmother's eightieth birthday party. I would see her then. How could I explain that it wasn't just that I missed her, but I needed her to be with me in this new space? To help me see that it was real.

My mother read between the lines of my vague email and asked me if I needed her to come or if I wanted her to come. Her email read:

It is likely that you too, like me, get confused about wants versus needs. It is probably easy for people to dismiss your needs because you seem so "whatever" and take care of your own needs so wonderfully. You are so independent and so competent and tuned in, and so thoughtful and so kind. It is important for you to be very clear about what you need and ask very directly for it. It is your absolute right, and given all of the above observations about you and your style, it is important that you practice using that voice, knowing the difference between "it would be nice" and "I need you."

I wrote back: Yes, Mom. I need you. I really need you. Please come.

Thank you, sweet Sara. You did a beautiful job asking for what you need. I'm very excited to meet Carlos. You are blessed with meeting wonderful people, and he sounds like a soulmate. Of course, Virgos, and Pisces have a very powerful psychic connection.

I don't remember telling her that Carlos' birthday was three days before hers, but she would have made it a point to find out with her love of astrology. In her email, she continued on to inform me that she had contacted Frank at Exotic Journeys, her travel agent connection, about plane tickets.

She scheduled her trip right away and sent me the itinerary. Frank had booked her on a direct flight to Puerto Vallarta and arranged it so she was on the same flight as me from Guadalajara to Chicago so that we could return together for her mother's birthday party. I was beyond excited. I used pink and purple markers to draw stars and hearts on all the days on the calendar that she would be there. I couldn't wait.

MOST MORNINGS, after teaching my eight o'clock class, I returned to my studio to prepare for the next day and correct homework. Teaching English was completely new to me, and I was scheduled to teach at a different level every new session, which lasted four weeks. There were ten levels. Each session was a two-hour class, five days a week, for four weeks, for a total of forty hours. Thankfully, the director started me out on the lower levels, and my new teacher friends graciously shared their tips, tricks, and exercises so I didn't have to start from scratch. And since I had no experience teaching English, I often turned to them. My small teacher crew consisted of four very different people: Chris from New York, Maria from Seattle, Jenn from Canada, and Leticia from Mexico City. Leticia was always working. And if she wasn't, she was always willing to cover a class. Chris balanced out his teaching hours by playing volleyball on the beach. Jenn and I were closest in age; she was twenty-two, on a work-abroad experience from Canada. I loved her instantly. But unfortunately, she lived on the other side of town. Maria was older, in her forties, and loved the social scene. Because I easily made friends, it wasn't unusual for me to create a teacher crew quickly, but it was a new experience not to have alcohol at every gathering. They knew and supported my desire to quit, but they didn't question me if I chose to order a beer with them, either.

My fluency in Spanish was very valuable, as I could switch from English to Spanish to explain how English worked and didn't work. I didn't believe in the method that one hundred percent immersion was helpful due to my personal experience during my collegiate study-abroad program in Seville, Spain, when one day our Spanish teacher explained the difference between ser and estar to our class in English. It was like bells were ringing, and fireworks went off. It all made perfect sense the way he explained it, and I looked back on the years of me not understanding how and when to use ser or estar and felt angry that no one had thought to explain it in my native language the way he had.

The more I learned about English through teaching it, the more I fell in love with the Spanish language. Or maybe it wasn't the language as much as the door it opened to a culture. Without the language, I would have had limited access to a deeper knowledge of humans who were just like the English-speaking humans I knew but also different. Linguistically, it also became easier to understand the rules of both Spanish and English. I was able to see how many of the rules in the English language didn't make sense. In turn, it became easier for me to understand how a student might translate "Tengo 25 años" into "I have 25 years old." I also really liked teaching. My confidence started low, which was one of the reasons I took time each day to prepare thoroughly. Showing up prepared felt amazing. I became confident in handling the lessons, the questions, and navigating the teaching time. Of course, a few days I showed up hungover and ready to wing it, justifying that the pay didn't warrant all the extra hours. But the extra hours made me a better teacher, and I felt better when I performed well. The students made it easy. Many were respectful and kind, motivated to learn for higher-paying jobs and bigger tips, while others were clearly in class because someone at home was making them. Either way, I was determined to make the class fun and engaging.

Chapter 24

NOT REALIZING YET that I'd already had my last drink, I was still playing around with the idea of being sober. Some days I was leery of the AA community and the rigid twelve-step program, while on other days, I wanted what they had badly—freedom from my dangerous lifestyle.

I was in Mexico to immerse myself in the language and culture, and the English-speaking AA community represented something I had decided to leave. And from what I could tell, it also meant fleeting friends. Getting to know people and investing in a relationship that would end, since many of the people in the room were only in the area for a short period of time, didn't sound so great. This was all before smartphones and Facebook. Whatever the underlying reasons were, it was easy to slip in and out of meetings without making real connections. I learned later that a handful of English-speaking AA members showed up all year round. I could have created meaningful connections, but that's not how my story went.

SIXTY DAYS into my adventure, I accomplished my goal: I dreamed in Spanish. Pieces of the dream became clear to me after I woke, and I remembered the conversation I had in my dream. I sat up, grabbed my journal, and wrote about it, unable to stop smiling. I couldn't wait to tell my mom about it and show her my life in PV.

IN FEBRUARY, the month of my mother's visit, the weather in Puerto Vallarta was in the eighties and sunny every day. I had been in my studio apartment for a little over a month, but it already felt like home. Carlos helped me find someone to paint the wall behind my bed bright orange. White Christmas lights decorated the front window, and I used a colorful sarape as a tablecloth over the plastic table. Lots of candles were placed on every table, countertop, and random ledges, and I burned incense regularly.

I had imagined my mom's weekend visit would include a brief introduction to Carlos, but as the days got closer and Carlos and I fell more in love, I couldn't wait for her to meet him and spend time with him. I was equally excited for Carlos to get to know my adoring and adored mama.

She oohed and aahed as I knew she would as we rode in the taxi from the airport to my studio. I showed her where I lived and the beach where I spent time. I brought her to one of my classes. She sat in the back, and then we went to breakfast with Alfonso. She came with me to an AA meeting and observed with love, compassion, and her full, non-judgmental presence. In her three-day visit, she fell in love with Carlos, as I knew she would, and as he got to know her, I am pretty sure he loved me even more.

When we had first started dating, he had asked me if I was different in the States. I didn't know what he meant, so he went on to explain that a lot of times, women come to Puerto Vallarta on vacation and fall in love, then when the boyfriend would go back to the States with his new girlfriend, he would see a more pretentious and uptight side of her. I had promised him I was the same here and there, but I had replied quickly, and maybe I wasn't. With my mom visiting, he spent time with us and could see that I was indeed a similar Sara when I spoke English and interacted with her as I was in Spanish with him. I didn't realize how important it was for them to have met when they did. And I didn't realize how important it was for my mom to know my life more intimately.

She slept in my little bed with me and woke up to the sound of the dogs barking, the roosters crowing, and the waves crashing. She held on for dear life as the bus rattled dangerously fast and was assaulted by the sewer smell and the pounding and drilling as we walked by construction sites. She took me out to expensive dinners and paid for our cab ride home so we wouldn't have to walk up the huge hill. She sat on the front patio with me, admired the sunset, and held my hand as we talked about the pain and suffering of life as well as the joy and miracles in it. Her witnessing my Puerto Vallarta life helped me embody its realness. It wasn't a dream I was having; it was real, and she could attest to it. There was proof now. When she went back, there would be someone from that world that knew my new world existed. She would know the faces of the little kids on the corner who I liked to play with, who knew my name. She would know the tightness in my calves from walking up the steep hill to get home. She would know Carlos' loving gaze, his warm smile, and of course, the delicious chicken quesadillas and guacamole, the perfect comfort food.

All the senses were turned up, especially the spiritual ones. My mom and I sat on the rocks and talked about God, angels, the universe, and love while watching the waves and spotting the whales.

"You found a magical place to heal, Sara. I'm so happy for you."

Her heart knew my heart and held it softly, allowing her healing energy to show me it was going to be okay. It really was. I felt it.

I loved her so much and wanted her close to me, but I didn't ever want to live in Madison again. I was where I needed to be, and that meant we would be far apart for now. I was in awe of how confident she was in our love and connection to each other, that no matter how far apart we were, we were intuitively and deeply connected, and we could always hold that truth with us.

Chapter 25

THE LONG WEEKEND in Chicago was a gift from my grandma. She was turning eighty, and I was turning twenty-five later in the month. My mom's mom, Grandma Harriet, and I, Pisces twins, were close, so when she had offered to pay for my ticket to come back, I quickly asked my friends to sub for my classes and packed for the cold March weather. It had been a little less than three months since I had arrived in Mexico, and I knew my family wouldn't believe I was on the path to recovery. Since I wasn't sure about my recovery, except that I wanted it badly, I didn't share much with them. What if I failed? What if I was meant to be that woman at the bar, traveling around the world, partying like a rock star forever? If I tried to escape that life and failed, then I would disappoint them all. So, the less they knew, the better. That way, I could make it look like my life was my choice, and even if I didn't feel like I had a choice, I could pretend I did. I was good at pretending.

My cousin, Toni, was in town from Santa Cruz for the big party. We had become close when I was living in Los Angeles. I was excited to see her again after so much had changed. I hadn't realized how much I wanted to confide in her, so we called her when my mom and I needed to be picked up from the airport. In the car, I spilled it all. I gushed about Carlos, how much I loved him, and how different he was from anyone I had ever dated. She asked me how he was in bed. I told her about my commitment to celibacy for six months and how I wasn't sure I would make it, but it felt right. She asked me about my recovery, and I said I wasn't sure about the AA meetings, but I hadn't had a drink in seventeen days. I had reduced my drinking dramatically since mid-January, but what I still couldn't do was drink in moderation when I drank. I could go a week without drinking, but I usually failed if I tried to limit myself to three drinks when going out with friends. I suspected that I was the kind of alcoholic who needed to stop entirely. She asked about my apartment, she asked about my job, she wanted to know everything, and I wanted to tell her everything. I told her about the books I was reading, the meditations I was practicing, and how conversations about God happened naturally in Mexico.

My mom and Toni listened in a supportive and loving way. Neither of them told me what to do, what not to do, or how to live my life. They were there for me in whatever way I needed them. I didn't have to have answers, and I didn't need to know what was next. They just wanted me to be happy, and that faith in me and my journey gave me a strength I didn't know I needed.

This was a stark contrast to my conversations with my dad that weekend. With him, I chose my words carefully. Based on years of experience, I held back anything that I knew wouldn't fit with what was right or wrong in his mind. I focused on how I was making money, gaining teaching skills, and learning Spanish. I didn't talk about my personal, spiritual, or love life. What he got was carefully curated.

I made it through the weekend without drinking and could still chop it up on the dance floor. My mom and I danced and danced until we were sweating.

I was so proud of myself and excited to return to Puerto Vallarta and continue this path of recovery. But mostly, I was excited to return to Carlos. Talking about him to my family and friends gave me a different perspective. They confirmed that my glow was as brilliant on the outside as it felt on the inside. They helped me become even more certain that I wasn't dreaming this new world. This was real. I was really living the way I wanted to live. Being back in the United States for a long weekend confirmed that I could be me in a new way.

Chapter 26

I RETURNED TO PUERTO VALLARTA with renewed energy and confidence. I also returned ready to plan my upcoming birthday celebration. On March 19, 2000, I would be twenty-five years old. It felt like a big one, but it also felt like another test. Can I celebrate a birthday without getting drunk and clubbing until dawn? How was I going to make it fun?

Playing around with what fun looked like as a sober person was not easy; my first thought always included booze. But it turned out that the hard part was thinking about it, and the easy part was actually living it. On a night out at La Estocada with my teacher friends, we all decided to make a trip to Guadalajara, not just because it was my birthday but because Jenn and Chris hadn't been there yet, and Leticia wouldn't stop raving about how much fun it was.

Carlos and I made plans to meet up with the gang for a couple of nights in Guadalajara, then spend a night on our own for my birthday in Lake Chapala, a nearby town. He hadn't left the restaurant for more than one night in a row since it opened, and we hadn't spent this much time together ever. I was like a giddy child.

In Guadalajara, Carlos showed me the best flea markets, where the vibrant colors splashed from vendor to vendor. Kind faces encouraged us to stop and buy something, and the smell of fresh churros sprinkled with cinnamon danced in the air. We wandered the irregular multicolored cobblestone streets, holding hands like the young lovers we were as we explored the charming plazas. I was in awe of the enchanting stone buildings and European-like cafes. We stopped and sipped cappuccinos and people-watched and kissed like we didn't care who was watching. Later, we met up with my friends for a long dinner and then hit the clubs, where we danced and danced until we were dripping in sweat.

Traveling with Carlos was everything I'd hoped it would be.

Lake Chapala was nothing like I'd imagined.

It was a delightful and romantic town. Even more romantic was the inn where we stayed. Carlos had made all the arrangements and wasn't surprised by the beauty. It wasn't a fancy inn, but it was unique and dreamy. Our room was simple, with buttery yellow walls, a king-sized bed with white linens, a white rocking chair in the corner, and white furniture. I ran to the bed and collapsed dramatically on it. I took off my tennis shoes, stripped off all my clothes, and enthusiastically jumped on the bed.

"Let's be naked the whole time we are here!"

Carlos laughed, but he didn't argue.

As we lay in bed that afternoon, the white curtains billowed in front of the sliding glass doors that overlooked the exquisite grounds. I felt like we were in a movie. Carlos was way more modest than I was. I stood up, still naked, to open the curtains so we could see outside, and he rushed to cover me. Whipping both of the curtains as wide as I could, I breathed in the fresh air and felt elated. There, in the yard in front of our sliding glass doors, was an elegant, dazzling peacock.

"This is dreamy in all ways, Carlos. I'm in heaven." I snuck back under the covers with him, insisting no one was around to see us, and curled up in his arms, inhaling the scent of his naked, beautiful self.

For the first time, we made love, so much love, in all the awkward, passionate ways that a new couple makes love. We were starving by the time we showered and left our cabin for dinner. I don't remember dinner or the next day. I only remember that room, the white curtains, the peacock, and the insatiable desire and vulnerability.

I had broken my six-month celibacy promise, but I had no regrets. Carlos was one of the healthiest things in my life, and I had decided to stop trying to plan everything the way I thought it should be and start opening up to what the universe had in store for me, especially if it was going to be this delicious.

Chapter 27

DURING THE MONTH OF APRIL, Carlos and I spent as much time together as we could (which wasn't much), playing house, having sleepovers, and having sex anywhere and everywhere, including the ocean, followed by fresh oysters and naps on the beach. Carlos worked and worked and worked, and when he wasn't working, he was with me. Sundays were our day for adventures to faraway beaches or boat trips and dinners out, followed by a movie. Sundays felt like mini honeymoons. The weekdays felt like a grind, with moments of erotic lovemaking and intellectually stimulating conversations.

Between classes, I took care of lesson prep, practiced meditation, prayed, journaled, and read my spiritual books. I spent time emailing my family and friends and taking care of domestic duties during the day so that I could spend evenings at La Estocada. Often, I woke up at four in the morning when Carlos finished work, and we'd talk until he fell asleep and I left to teach my morning class. One Sunday, instead of date night, we went out for lunch at his favorite seafood restaurant. We sat on the back patio under an umbrella with plates of ceviche, cut-up limes, and spicy salsas. Early that morning, when he had crawled into my bed, snuggling up close, I was too tired to talk even though my mind was racing. I loved him next to me. I loved listening to him breathe. I loved knowing he was alive in the world, and this intense feeling made me question everything. Things were not as they had been before. I was out of my comfort zone.

This realization threw me. I felt an urgency to know his life plans and make sure he knew that mine were suddenly up in the air.

When I asked him why he hadn't wanted a girlfriend before meeting me and why he was waiting to settle down, he didn't pause. He knew exactly why he was waiting. He told me that both his older brothers got married very young. His oldest brother, Jorge, moved in with his girlfriend, Luz, when he was only sixteen. And then Rafa did the same when he was eighteen. Neither of them was married. He learned what he didn't want by watching them. He saw the responsibilities that come with having a family and children at a young age, and he wanted to build something with his life before focusing time and energy on his own family. "I don't think it's bad to get married young, but I knew at a young age that I didn't want that for my life. You know, to each their own," he said.

"So you created your own dreams," I said.

"I got good at making and saving money. That's how opening my own restaurant became a reality." He told me his plan at that time was to spend five years building his restaurant. By then, he'd be thirty years old, the restaurant would be financially successful, and he could settle down with a wife and have kids. It was a great plan. I was impressed by his certainty.

Whereas Carlos was going to wait to get married and have children for financial stability, my reason was that I wanted to travel the world first.

But now, I was doubting everything. I loved him. I didn't want to leave to go travel the world, even though I still desperately did.

We had been sitting at the outdoor table on the back patio, and all our plates had been cleared. I ordered another lemonade. Here he was, doing this life thing on his terms, and I'd walked in with all of my uncertainty and unhealed trauma.

I told him I had no idea what would happen to us, but I knew I wouldn't have an abortion if we accidentally got pregnant. I had gone off the pill after the rape, and even though we mostly used condoms, we didn't have a perfect record

"What do you mean, Sara?" he asked. Telling him I wouldn't want an abortion if we accidentally got pregnant wasn't romantic, but it was my truth.

"Before you, if I were to get pregnant, I would have no problem getting an abortion. But not with you. You're different."

"Tan directa," he said. *So direct.*

"I don't have life planned out like you do. But I know what I know when I know it. Mostly though, you confuse me. We confuse me."

He was calmly leaning back in the chair while I sat up, my knee bouncing rhythmically.

"It's a good thing we have time," he said.

Chapter 28

I MISSED MY MOM TERRIBLY. I emailed her from the cyber cafes in the tourist areas of town and called her from the corner pay phone. And I also wrote her letters.

Dear Mom,

Good morning sunshine! I'm having a good morning here! I opened the little window on my door and pulled the curtains back. Another clear and sunny day. I made some coffee, then my bed, and I washed my face. With the classical Mozart music playing, I sat on my bed with my coffee and my journal and paused. Looking at my bedside table, I miss you terribly. I have this strong desire to pick up an imaginary phone next to my bed and call you. I just want one of those 'sitting on the bed' conversations. Sipping coffee, watching the morning turn to noon and talking to you. I don't want to stand on a corner at a pay phone and worry about the minutes as they pile up and suck away at the phone bill. This moment bothers me. I don't like not being able to call.

I have been going out with Jenn a lot. Jenn is the Canadian teacher I work with. She's full of fabulous energy. Every Saturday night we go dancing. Last night she said, "I LOVE going out with you, even if you don't drink." I feel really good not drinking. I was at a bar the other night, and I just couldn't imagine enjoying myself intoxicated. I am surprised I haven't lost any weight, though. Sometime soon I will stop smoking too—just not yet. It is really only at bars that I smoke—and for now it is helpful and keeps me busy. My period is still late, and that's weird, but I'm not worried.

Someone's music is fighting with mine. The kids down on the corner (remember them?) are playing a tag game and shouting randomly. No barking dogs right now. There is a nice breeze, and I am feeling content. I have the day to myself, and then at four p.m., I'm going to Carlos' house for a family dinner. I have one more week of classes and then a two-week break for Semana Santa. That will be so nice. Then, when I go back to classes, I will only have six weeks left until I see your beautiful face again. Know you are loved and missed dearly by me. Xoxo Sara Lilac

ONE SATURDAY MORNING in April, I headed to my neighborhood beach with my thermos of coffee, a banana, and my backpack. I stopped by the neighbor's casita to say hi to the kids playing pretend store, and I promised to pretend to buy something from them on the way home. The street was peaceful at nine.

I made my way to a spot on the sand warmed by the sun. As I opened up my mat, I thanked God and my strength for my sobriety. I loved the sun on my face. I closed my eyes, and the warmth of peace and gratitude filled me and brought me into the present moment. With my eyes closed, I could focus on the sounds—the waves, the birds, the cars in the distance. After a few minutes, I assessed my surroundings. A few steps away, a woman was passed out on her front side, face down in the sand, beside remnants of a bonfire that must have kept her warm throughout the chilly night—that and the alcohol that pulsed through her.

AT TEN, she rolled over and faced the ocean. Awake, alive, and likely very foggy. I knew how she felt. I knew the aches in her body. I knew the weakness in her movements, each movement demanding all her energy and radiating a new pain. Not a searing pain, but a pain that could be felt all over and throughout her insides. It cut through to her outsides and instantly faded her aura, depleting her energy and sucking out the glow that usually shines from her. There was no sparkle to her, no exquisite radiance. Her skin was dull, and her movement slow. She wasn't thinking clearly at all. I felt all of it like I was her. There, by the grace of God, go I. The cheesy AA slogan was not just a slogan; it was a truth that had pierced me.

I had to look away. It was too painful. My heart separated from her as it filled with warm gratitude.

I said a prayer. *Please take care of this woman, God. And thank you for taking care of me.*

Chapter 29

MOTHER'S DAY RATTLED ME, not because I missed my mom, though I very much did. There was something else that brought out my insecurity and pettiness. Carlos was hosting his mom and sisters at his restaurant for a Mother's Day celebration. In Mexico, Mother's Day isn't the second Sunday of May; it's always May 10. This day is sacred in Mexico. The nation stops on Mother's Day. People don't come to class, and some people don't work. The schools have major celebrations, dances, and performances. Mariachi bands are booked solid. Flower shops sell out of arrangements, and people make extra money selling bouquets in the streets.

Yet he didn't invite me. Instead, I was at home, crying. Didn't I belong yet? Didn't I deserve to be there? I couldn't tell if I had a right to these dramatic feelings or if it was PMS. Or maybe I was righteously angry with Carlos and myself for wanting to be with him all the time and not being able to. I was upset with myself for loving him as deeply as I did. I was also upset that my period was late.

THE NEXT DAY, he heard all about it, and he apologized for not inviting me and explained the family drama that was happening. I forgave him, embarrassed for being a bit dramatic. "I'm hoping it is PMS," I said and mentioned my late period. Quietly, he was worried that I was pregnant. Loudly, I declared I wasn't.

There were many days when we didn't have time together, when we were interrupted at the restaurant by customers, or I saw him only briefly between his daily errands. I was not feeling confident in our relationship.

One Sunday night, we finally had time for the two of us. As we walked along the beach on our way to dinner, I said, "My throat hurts a little, Carlos. I think it's because there are things I need to tell you, but I haven't. My throat chakra might be closed off, and maybe my telling you all the things will help. Nothing big, just little silly things that become life."

So many things spilled out of me. I told him how I had been dreaming in Spanish, about the classes I was teaching, and the volunteer program I signed up for called Feeding the Children. We talked about the Virgen de Guadalupe, the Madre de los desaparecidos, Jesus, God, and praying. He spilled, too. He told me about his sister and some trouble with her boyfriend and her kids. He talked about a frequent customer who drank too much and his other sister's husband, who was sick. Later that night, after we returned to my studio and made beautiful, slow love, we talked more. We talked about family and money. And then he told me he could live anywhere with me, that everything he was doing with the restaurant he was doing for us and our future. He wasn't immersed in the restaurant to avoid me but to bring us more opportunities to be together. We made a deal, and I was clear that I needed more time to talk about all the things—the big things and the little things. We turned a corner. I don't know what to call it, but it was exactly what we needed.

After turning that corner, I sent my parents an email from the cyber cafe downtown that said: "I just want you to know that Carlos is the guy I'm going to marry someday. He is the one. But don't worry. We aren't going to do anything crazy."

A week later, I got my period. Oh, thank God. In the bathroom, I sat on the toilet, looked up, and smiled. It wasn't heavy, but I used a tampon anyway.

Carlos shared my relief. I was not only relieved, but I was also a whole new level of grateful. I was the "get on my knees by the side of my bed and give all the thanks there is to give to all the higher powers that might exist" grateful. I had a skip in my step again. It'd been almost three months since my last drink, and the thought crossed my mind even though I was not tempted to have a celebratory drink.

I BROUGHT MY desire for the celebratory drink to an AA meeting. I went more regularly and became friendly with some of the women. Nora liked to save a seat for me next to her. We only saw each other in the meeting room, so I didn't know her well, but she reminded me of a sweet aunt I never had, one who smelled of sandalwood, always had a tissue in her purse, and looked at me lovingly. Her return to Canada was coming soon. I would miss her at the meetings, which were changing now that most of the snowbirds had left and summer was coming. In late May, those who were still there were the brave ones.

It was wicked hot, sticky, and uncomfortable. The streets were quieter. The locals talked about the slow season looming, and the non-natives who stayed through the summer talked about how fascinating the city was when the tourists were gone. I hated the heat and never planned on staying through the worst of it. My plan was to get out during the summer and return in the fall. I had booked a flight back to Madison for early June. My goal of learning Italian fell to the side as I had been so preoccupied with my love affair with Carlos and my pregnancy scare. My new plan was to wing it when I got there, hoping my Spanish skills would give me an edge.

"I'm starting to be glad I don't drink," I said to Nora as we waited for the meeting to start.

She squeezed my hand. "I'm glad you are finding some happiness in sobriety, Sara." She smirked. "And that you aren't pregnant."

I shook my head quickly and firmly. Like I was shaking off an annoying fly. Even thinking about the pregnancy scare filled me with dread.

"Thanking God over and over again," I said.

The meeting started, and when it was my turn, I introduced myself as Sara, an alcoholic, and found comfort in the routine of reading the steps. A small warmth of inspiration gave me pause as I listened to one person's story, and just as quickly, a pang of irritation and judgment hit me as I listened to another complain about something mundane. I started bouncing my leg to keep myself from bitching out loud. "Augh, this guy again," I whispered to Nora. She patted my bouncing knee lovingly but didn't whisper back. I doubted I'd ever be as cool, calm, and accepting as she was.

THE NEXT MORNING, I changed my tampon and stared at the white cotton blob floating in the toilet. There was no blood. Nothing. Was that the shortest period ever? Was my body disoriented from not drinking? Were my angels messing with me? Were they trying to teach me a lesson?

I chose not to worry. Carlos worried for me.

The next day there was still no flow. Carlos asked me about my breasts, telling me he thought they were tender and slightly enlarged. "No they aren't," I snapped back.

That is what denial looks and sounds like. All the signs pointed in a direction I couldn't fathom.

Chapter 30

BEING PREGNANT WAS NOT an option. I even wrote a list in my journal of the reasons why I shouldn't be pregnant:

- I'm traveling, living, and working in Mexico with nothing more than a backpack and a quest for adventure.
- I've known Carlos for four months, if that. Except for my mother, my family doesn't know this Carlos guy. I don't know all of his family. We barely know each other.
- I'm newly sober and have no idea who the heck I am or what I'm doing with my life. Just eight months ago, I was snorting coke in Las Vegas with friends on a bender weekend.
- My job hardly provides enough to support me, and I don't have health insurance. The recent purchase of a stereo system felt like a big purchase for me. (Okay, it was a large boom box.) Don't people need money to have offspring?
- I don't want to settle down, have a baby, or get married. I am not up for it, ready for it, and I don't desire it in any way. It's just not the time. I have a plan, and a baby isn't in that plan. My journal has a list of all my dreams for the next couple of years, and a baby is not anywhere on the list.

AND THEN THERE was Carlos, who would be a father. We'd never encountered a relationship like this: scary and not scary at all. It felt meant to be. Even though we were choosing it, sometimes we admitted that we didn't feel like we had a choice.

Like it was chosen for us.

We hadn't wanted this.

We thought we knew what we wanted.

We thought we wanted to do our own thing, on our own.

He wanted to grow his restaurant. I wanted to heal and see the world on my own. None of this worked with a pregnancy.

Carlos was sure I was pregnant, but as the indirect, soft, and loving soul he was, he didn't come out and say it. It had been two months since I had a full-on period. There had been spotting in recent weeks but nothing that would constitute a real menstruation cycle. And my breasts ... he knew because they'd changed. And it pissed me off that he was so much smarter about these things than I was. He grew up with seven sisters, and his mother had eleven children. He was an uncle to sixteen nieces and nephews and was practically raising two of his nieces and nephews currently. His knowledge about pregnancy, boobs, breastfeeding, labor, and all other pregnancy-related things was way beyond mine.

I finally agreed to take a test. We discussed the options: Option One, go to Rey grocery store and buy one of those stick tests. Option Two, go to a clinic.

I opted for the clinic. The clinic option gave me a feeling of security. Having someone break the news to me and then answer my questions would create a much better outcome than learning alone from a stick; I was certain of that. "So we'll go today?" I said when I finally accepted that it had to be done. Why not? Let's get it over with.

What I didn't understand then was that there is a vast difference between what we call a clinic in the U.S. and a clinic in Puerto Vallarta. Oh, how I wish I had known.

The door was wide open as we walked up the stairs. There was nothing to separate the street from any open business or home. If the door is open, you walk right in. The clinic was small, maybe ten blocks from my apartment, on the main street down from Carlos' restaurant.

I didn't know why we went there specifically. Carlos just led me there. I felt safe following his lead. But he didn't know what I was expecting, and it wasn't this.

Two women sat behind a counter, chatting enthusiastically. The place was empty otherwise. There were two chairs in what seemed to be a small waiting area. The woman stopped talking when we walked in and stared at me, the foreigner. I approached and told them I needed a pregnancy test and asked how much it would cost. They explained that I needed to pay two hundred pesos (ten U.S. dollars) upfront, they would take my blood, and then I was to return in a couple of hours. It didn't occur to me to question anything else about the process. Was there a doctor or a nurse?

"I'm nervous, Carlos," I confessed as we stood on the corner. We were scheduled to go back at five-thirty to get the results.

"Todo va a estar bien, amor." *It's going to be okay, love.* But there was concern in his eyes.

"I know. But if I find out I am pregnant, I'm not going to be happy. That is so sad. And I think of my mom and how she probably felt the same way when she found out she was pregnant with me. I want to be excited if I am pregnant, but I'm not sure I will be. That sucks." I kept talking in a frenzy. "I just want to know, and at the same time, I don't."

"It's better to know so we can figure things out. And no matter what, I'll be here. Te amo mucho."

"What about money? I want to buy a TV and a VCR, not a crib and a car seat." I heard what I was saying and quickly added, "I guess that is all material and meaningless. But what about you? What about us? I want to have more time to enjoy you. I want you all to myself and travel with you and go on adventures. I'm not ready for routine and financial pressure." Tears welled up in my eyes, and he hugged me. What else could we do but hold one another? And pray. Sitting at the park near the clinic, Carlos finally excused himself to answer his phone, which had been buzzing. I pulled out my journal, wrote to God, asking for strength, and prayed I had what I needed to handle this.

I tried not to pray that the test would come back negative. I knew that praying for the good of all, or God's will, was the way to go in the world of prayer. Don't be too specific. Then, I journaled a gratitude list:

- I'm so grateful for Carlos and our love.
- I'm grateful for my health and my heart and my smile.
- I'm grateful for my life and Mexico, the sun, and the ocean.

Finally, I went through a mental list of my most beloved family and friends and intentionally sent them love blasts. I imagined them all happy, healthy, and feeling my love. My fear subsided a bit.

The church was adjacent to the plaza area, and I watched as an older man exited and clutched the railing as he walked carefully down the stairs. He seemed so fragile. I felt so fragile. But I wasn't—I was strong. I looked up to the sky and promised I would trust the process and accept whatever was meant to happen.

We walked back up the steps of the clinic at exactly five-thirty. The sun was blazing hot like it was every day. No other patients were there, and only one woman sat at the front counter. Approaching the desk, she told us to wait. We sat on the chairs in the corner, so still and quiet. Ten minutes later, she reported that they were on the way. We waited some more.

Finally, a young man pulled up in a white car and jogged up the stairs with a bunch of papers. He handed them to the front desk lady, quickly turned around, and ran off again. I watched her as she searched through the pile of papers, looking for my name. By this time, I was standing at the counter with Carlos right behind me. Everything felt like slow motion.

I tried to lighten up the situation by saying, "Bueno, dime mi destino." Okay, tell me my destiny.

She ignored me. Then she folded a piece of paper, stuck it in an envelope, and handed it to me.

I hesitated before reaching for it. My mind was racing. What was happening here? This woman clearly wasn't a nurse or a doctor. At best, she was nineteen years old and didn't even have decent customer service skills, so surely she wasn't the one that was going to break the news to me regarding my future. Her blank stare caught me off guard. I looked at Carlos with desperation in my eyes. This was all going so wrong.

"What's this? Don't we get to talk to a doctor? What kind of clinic is this?" She was still holding the envelope. I couldn't bring myself to take it.

"Now we take the envelope to a doctor," Carlos explained calmly and gently put his hand on my lower back.

"You mean we wait until we are at a doctor's office to open this?" I snapped, jerking my body away from him. I was bewildered. This seemed ludicrous. I grabbed the envelope from her and turned toward the door. I needed an exit.

"No ... I'm opening it now. This is crazy."

So I stood in the doorway and ripped open the envelope.

Positivo.

There it was.

Chapter 31

TEARS STREAMED DOWN my face as I stared at the positive result. No. No. This can't be happening. How could I be pregnant? The tears turned to sobs as I held onto Carlos' arm in complete fear and shock.

He walked me across the street toward the plaza in front of the church, which loomed in front of us. My eyes moved directly to the hand railing that the man had gripped maybe an hour earlier when I had looked up to the sky and promised to trust and accept.

"Keep breathing," Carlos whispered. I was choking on my sobs.

I can do this. I can trust and accept. I need you, God, Angels, Universe, Source. Whatever you are, whoever you are, I need you.

But all I managed to say as I held onto Carlos' arm was, "Oh my God. Oh my God."

I started using some of my self-regulation tools. Breathe. Deep and slow, in and out. Just breathe. I concentrated on my breath, but then I'd get flustered and cry again. Finally, under a tree at the park, Carlos pulled me close and gently held my face in his hands.

"It's going to be okay. Todo va a estar bien. Te prometo." *I promise.* I stared into his eyes. I wanted to believe him. And then I did believe him. I knew it would be okay. There was a strong sense in my gut, and I knew this was exactly what was supposed to happen.

I took his hands and held them tightly, saying, "Yo se." *I know.*

The urgency of everything poured out. I needed to go to a doctor. How far along was I? We would need a home and a crib. And wait, what about my class tonight?

I called Maria and asked her to sub for me.

There was so much I needed to know. The practical part of being pregnant—the basic information. Where was the brochure? And then there was the emotional part of becoming a mother. I quickly decided I didn't know how to deal with the emotional part, so I opted to focus on the practical part.

Carlos and I walked to the coffee shop in silence, hands clasped tightly. I focused on each step across the concrete plaza. I looked at the ground as we stood on the corner. I knew that Carlos would watch out for the cars and tug on me when it was safe to cross. I knew I didn't have to worry about being taken care of. I wanted to be taken care of. I allowed him to lead me. I allowed myself to surrender. I released control.

A PAGE IN THE SUN was on the corner. Used books filled the floor-to-ceiling bookshelves, and sunlight streamed in the big windows and bounced off the sunny, yellow walls. The warm air moved ever so slightly by the hard-working ceiling fans. Only a scattering of customers sat among the empty tables, and the barista was bored behind the counter. We ordered drinks and sat down. Carlos was on his cell phone trying to schedule an appointment with his family doctor. I was in my head, which was buzzing. I was in the future, I was in the past, and I would stagger into the present every once in a while and focus on the ceiling fans.

Until then, I didn't know what my future consisted of. I had been to enough AA meetings to know the simple and grounding phrase "One day at a time," and I had been holding on to that for dear life. It had seemed like a smart decision to have such an open-ended, flexible plan for my future. Now, it was all irrelevant. I was having a baby, so I needed some well-thought-out plans quickly.

Carlos needed to get to work, and I needed to talk to my mom. We agreed that we'd take things one moment at a time and check back in later that night. Both of us were aware that this was a shock that needed to be tended to with compassion. How did we know that? I don't know. We just did. We loved and respected each other, and there was a mutual understanding that this wasn't what either of us had anticipated when we met four months earlier, but here we were.

AFTER CARLOS LEFT, I loaded up my phone card and found a pay phone at a dead-end street at the beginning of the Malecon boardwalk. It was still very loud, but it was the best I could do. I called my mom, but she had left for a girls' weekend in Door County. Next, I called my best friend from home, Brooke. She immediately reassured me that it would be okay. She was loving and supportive. She knew about Carlos; I had been emailing and writing her letters with juicy details. She'd known my period was late. And she knew she needed to hold me steady while the ground shook beneath me. Talking to Brooke was exactly what I needed. But I longed to speak to my mom. I needed companionship, someone who could help me talk through and process this in real life. I walked to the school, knowing class would be over soon.

I waited for Jenn at the base of the stairs.

"Jenn!" I called out the minute she came into view. She could see the desperation and sense of urgency in my eyes and hurried her step.

"Sara, what's going on? Why weren't you teaching tonight?" she asked as we walked toward the busy street.

"Let's go down to the river," I said. And then I blurted it out, "Jenn, I'm pregnant."

"What? Oh my God!" She stopped and looked at me as my eyes filled with tears, and she hugged me tightly.

"Are you okay?" she asked.

"I guess. I'm only freaking my shit out."

"Of course. Tell me everything."

I knew I could trust her to not be judgmental while processing aloud. "So this is what I know for sure. I know that I'm teaching through the end of this session, and then I planned on leaving for the summer, but I wasn't sure how long because I want to come back to be with Carlos. I have a plane ticket to Chicago and am leaving in a couple of weeks. Plus, I'm scheduled and booked for a family reunion trip with my grandma and all of her family—my mom's family and her two brothers' families—in Italy for the first two weeks of July. So before all of this happened—" I threw in a dramatic hand movement around my belly. "I was going to be gone for the summer, maybe stay in Italy longer but eventually come back to PV. And NOW I'm pregnant. Like really, legitimately preggo."

"But wait. Back up, Sara," Jenn said.

"Oh, right. So, Carlos had been hinting that I was probably pregnant for a couple of weeks, and I was in complete denial. Finally, today we went to a clinic, and they handed me a piece of paper in a sealed envelope that said "positivo," at which point I burst into tears because I knew I was going to have this baby and that my life will be forever changed." I took a deep breath. "So, yeah, no big deal."

I was trying to stay light. I always tried to stay light. It was a comfort zone for me.

"Do you think you'll get married?" she asked.

I looked at her curiously.

"I don't know. He is all set up and established here, and I'm just some wanderlust girl, and I don't even have insurance." I burst into tears. Again. It was a slap in my face, my irresponsibility. How could I bring a baby into this world with so much of nothing?

"It's going to be okay, Sara. You love each other, and Carlos is such a good guy."

"But we don't even live together. I barely know his family, and he doesn't know my family at all, except for meeting my mom over one weekend. How can this be happening?" I cried into my hands. Jenn had her arm around me. We were tucked away on a bench in an empty park and didn't have to worry about strangers staring.

"But Jenn, as much as this is all fucked up and not supposed to happen like this, I know we are supposed to be together, and I believe that everything happens for a reason. I just didn't think it would ever happen like this." I spun off into a spiritual riff about God and her plans and being in the right place at the right time for my life to unfold the way it is supposed to, even though it might not make any sense to me now.

"Sara, you might not have a lot of the things you think you are supposed to have to start a family, but what you and Carlos have is what's most important. You have love and respect for each other." She squeezed my hand, and I felt some of her strength transfer to me. I believed her. I knew she was right. I knew that I would be okay and that this was the right path, even though it wasn't the path I imagined I'd be on at the age of twenty-five.

"You're right. The details will work themselves out. It's going to be okay no matter what happens."

MY HEAD WAS still spinning as I looked out the bus window on my way to the restaurant, but I was able to keep it together by focusing on my breathing. Keep breathing. I needed my to-do list to be on paper and not in my head. I needed to stay focused and remain calm. When I arrived at the restaurant, I found a table, got into business mode and pulled out my notebook.

- Call Mom and Dad
- Find/visit a doctor
- Grade papers
- Work on lesson plans for the week
- Find someone to sublet my apartment for the summer
- Grocery shopping, buy candles
- Pay rent

I put the last item on the list even though I had already paid rent, just so I could cross it off and feel that hit of accomplishment. Carlos made me chicken quesadillas and spent as much time with me as he could before I left. I knew he would come up to sleep with me after work.

It was still dark when he slipped in the front door, even though the roosters reminded us it was early morning. We spent an hour talking until I needed to leave for class. I left him to sleep and was grateful for the time we had to talk through what was going through our minds. A baby? Is this happening? We discussed the immediate future of clarifying information and what needed to be prioritized over the next few days. We talked about what life might be like a year from now with a baby. That was harder to talk about and imagine, and we ended up cutting those conversations short when it got tough or I started to cry. We decided to take the one-day-at-a-time approach. At school, I felt some relief when Maria and my boss, Jose Luis, reacted to the news with kindness and compassion. I kept bracing myself for someone to be disappointed and was surprised when I received nothing but love and support. After class, Carlos met me out front.

"We're going to get an ultrasound," he said as he flagged a taxi.

"What? I thought we were going to the doctor."

"The doctor says we need to get the ultrasound first, and then we'll bring it to him afterward."

"Oh." It was all too confusing for me—too many moving parts. I hadn't even told my family yet, causing me significant distress. I leaned on Carlos' shoulder in the taxi and closed my eyes. The ride was bumpy, but I enjoyed the distraction and the man beside me, who felt like the only sure thing right now.

Chapter 32

THE ULTRASOUND CLINIC was similar to the testing clinic. It was a one-purpose place with no doctors or nurses answering my questions. Carlos had asked if we should find an English-speaking doctor, but I felt confident with my language skills even though I was freaked out about being pregnant. I wanted to be pregnant in Spanish.

As we entered the clinic, I took note of the dark, quiet waiting room and prayed for a good experience. Upon checking in, I was immediately ushered into a private room where two nurses were prepping for my appointment. They asked a lot of questions in Spanish, and I answered them all clearly. One of the nurses, whom I'll call Angelica, told me to get on the table for the ultrasound. I asked if Carlos could be in the room with me, so the other nurse left to get him.

Angelica, avoiding eye contact, instructed me to lie down. I asked her if she wanted me to take off my shoes, my dress, what? I was desperate for someone to give me clear instructions. Finally, I figured out she wanted me to lie down and lift my dress over my belly.

The back-and-forth conversation was in fluent Spanish, but it felt like pulling teeth. Carlos entered, and Angelica turned to him, warmly welcomed him, and asked, "What's the patient's name?"

I immediately felt the confidence flood out of me. I wanted to sit up and scream, "You've got to be kidding me; I'm right here. I speak your pinche language! I'm a person, not your patient!" But I was stunned and lay there wanting to cry, half-naked and silent. Why couldn't she have asked me what my name was? We had been speaking in Spanish the whole time. How could she call me a patient like I wasn't there, lying right next to her?

As she rubbed the gel on my stomach and used the ultrasound wand, we all watched the screen until we saw the heartbeat and the little brown blob that was our baby. It was real. So very real, and as much as I wanted to squeal with excitement, I was also horrified at the same time. How could I be carrying a tiny human being in my body? I looked up at Carlos, who was emotional and present. The squeeze of his hand reminded me that I wasn't alone. She told Carlos I was six weeks pregnant. The baby was due on January 25, 2001.

SO MUCH OF the joy and awe of that moment was clouded by the anger and invisibility I felt. The way she treated me stays with me. I don't want to let it go. It is an important reminder of how people are treated in this world. I tried to imagine how different it would have been if I hadn't spoken Spanish at all.

I was experiencing how stereotypes and biases are connected to language and the challenges that come with language barriers. Everyone yearns to be understood. As humans, we want to feel connected.

Words connect us. Experiences connect us. Smiles, laughter, and tears connect us. Love connects us.

I desperately wanted that nurse to connect with me, to show me a bit of warmth, a smile, eye contact. I wouldn't have felt as scared and alone.

But instead, that burning anger bubbled up. I promised to never forget. Now, when I meet people who don't speak English fluently, I understand the power of eye contact and a smile.

AS I LEFT the clinic, Carlos answered his ringing cell phone. It was my sister. I hadn't talked to my mom yet, and my sister was calling. I quickly questioned my game plan. Do I tell my young, soon-to-be sixteen-year-old sister that I was pregnant before my mom knew? I grabbed the phone, wanting to hear her voice. Her hello sounded so far away. My hello came out between sobs.

"What's wrong, Sara? Are you okay?"

"Yes, yes, I'm okay. I just left the clinic. I'm pregnant, Kat."

"You are? Oh my God!"

She gave me the phone number of where Mom was staying. I worried my sister was upset with me, disappointed. I couldn't read her voice. The ambiguity of it all, the distance between us, and the poor telephone reception made it all hard. I wanted something to be easy.

"I'll call you later. Please don't be upset with me. And if you talk to Mom before I do, please don't tell her. Just tell her to call me on Carlos' cell."

WE WERE NOW in another taxi, driving to the doctor's office with an envelope of ultrasound pictures, a date, January 25, 2001, and a baby's heartbeat. We pulled up in front of a townhouse on a quaint cobblestone street in a middle-class neighborhood unlike any I had seen yet. The homes were on tiny lots with the walls butting up to the neighbors and no space for a front yard, just a gate entrance to the home or parking space. Too many new things to process. And why were we at someone's house and not a clinic?

Carlos' family doctor had a home office with a large, dark wooden desk and two black leather chairs. It was more like an attorney's office. Dr. Javier warmly welcomed us. He was a stocky man with gray hair, which I hoped meant he was experienced and competent. But what I remember most was how kind, loving, and very gentle he was with us. His biggest concern was my stress level and how our family and friends would react to the news. He supported us in a fatherly tone. After an hour, we both felt relieved, more informed, and still overwhelmed. The bits and pieces were coming together. I was exhausted, but instead of going home to rest, I asked Carlos to drop me off by the church where I knew of a pay phone off a main street. I couldn't go back to my apartment until I talked to my mom.

THE PHONE RANG, but no one answered. I went into the church to pray and try to calm the fear that swelled in my belly. The roaring buses couldn't compete with the frantic thoughts that rang in my head. I slowly climbed the stairs, aware of how alone I really was. Mexico's midday heat pounded on me, and I discreetly wiped the sweat that dripped between my breasts, which were unusually tender and sore. The constant and strong smell of my sweat was still new to me, and the stickiness of it was distracting.

"Maestra Sara!" Lupita excitedly called out and rushed over. She adjusted her baby on her hip and hugged me tightly.

"I'm sorry I missed class this morning."

And then she noticed the tears that had welled in my eyes and abruptly asked, "¿Que te pasa?" *What's wrong?*

She stared at me with demanding and compassionate eyes. I blurted out, "I'm pregnant."

"Oh! Felicidades!" She exclaimed and then quickly grabbed my hands in hers, acknowledging the tears. "Escúchame. God only gives you what you can handle. I promise you; it's going to be okay."

I thanked her, and she told me I could call her anytime.

Her words rolled around in my head as I sat in the last pew in the hot church and prayed and prayed and prayed. *Please, God, give me strength.* I searched in my mind for the serenity prayer. *Please, God, grant me the serenity to accept the things I cannot change, the courage to change the things I can, and the wisdom to know the difference.*

Accept the things I cannot change. I am trying. I closed my eyes and felt the loving presence of a higher power surrounding me, and a gentle voice reminded me that I was going to be okay and that this plan, while not of my own dreaming, was actually what was meant to be for me. I was going to be the best mom ever.

And then I thought of my dreams of traveling and the fact that I didn't have health insurance, and I choked on my fear again. I gripped the back of the pew in front of me so that I wouldn't pass out. *Take care of me, God. I'm freaking out. What if I don't think I can do this?*

Another voice inside me replied, *You can do this, Sara. It's okay. I'm taking care of you.*

Promise?

Promise. Keep breathing and know I'm here. I'm always here.

Chapter 33

MY RELATIONSHIP WITH GOD, spirit, angels, and a higher power was grounded in oneness and not by religion. I had learned three distinct truths that I attribute to growing up under the influence of two different religions. Between my experiences with a Jewish mother, her strong Jewish lineage, and a father who was raised Catholic, I came to understand things in my own way:

We are all the same, and having a certain religion doesn't make pain or pleasure any different. There are joyous and devastating moments in life, and how we navigate them may differ, but our hearts are the same. Oneness.

Religion has a significant amount of ego oozing from a patriarchal, sexist, homophobic institution built on systemic oppression and closed-mindedness. I'm not interested in those ingredients.

Religion and an understanding, belief, and faith in God can bring great comfort to people and communities. Judaism works for some people in my family, as does Catholicism, and I honor that. No religion works for some too. I say, do your thing, do whatever works for you, as long as it doesn't harm others.

MY GRANDMOTHERS either hoped I would resonate with their religion or wanted to make sure they were doing their part to educate me. They were the ones who took me to temple and church and told me stories about their religions. When I was in middle school, my dad's mom, Grandma Bette, gave me a simple chain with a gold cross on it for Christmas. My mom's mom, Grandma Harriet, gifted me a silver chain with the Jewish star when I was visiting her one summer in my early teens. I wore them both, but never at the same time.

My mom loved being Jewish, but mostly she loved love and felt that love was its own kind of religion. The feminist in her rejected certain aspects of the Jewish religion, like how it historically relegated women to a lower status than men and that it wasn't until 1983 that a woman could be ordained as a rabbi. Yet my mother fully embraced many of the cultural aspects of Judaism and found power in her lineage. We celebrated and honored high holy days and other Jewish traditions. But she practiced spirituality more than Judaism. She had at one point self-described herself as a spiritual being having a human experience.

My father didn't seem to identify as Catholic, but he didn't necessarily reject it. I imagine it was a connection he had with his family and his childhood. I grew up with a strong understanding in our family that we could self-identify in whatever way we pleased, and we could change our minds, too.

As a twenty-five-year-old, I had a basic understanding of Catholicism and Judaism but a powerful desire for a deeper spiritual connection than what I thought religion could offer me. I wanted to cut through the rules of a religion and create my own relationship with my own God. I wanted what my mom had.

My mom had a calm and loving way of being in the world no matter what was happening. I know she experienced anxiety (she was human), but she found so much peace in her belief in a higher power, in love, and in the magic and synchronicity of the universe. She believed in angels and past lives. She believed in signs and spirit messages that could come from a conversation with a stranger, a message in a book, or lyrics in a song on the radio. She turned to animal medicine cards and angel oracle cards.

Oh, the angel cards! She kept them in a sweet little bowl by the front door, and occasionally she'd pull one and flip it over to read the message. Each card had one word on the back: surrender, patience, joy, commitment, harmony, adventure, love, communication, and plenty more. My friends pulled cards when they were over. And when I moved out, my mom gave me my own set of angel cards.

That's the kind of magic I wanted more of in my life. I don't know if past lives are real, but I don't need to know to have a feeling and comfort in that belief. I had met people who felt like old friends. Maybe I had known them in another lifetime. This way of choosing to live felt right for me. It's why I brought the book *Conversations with God* when I came to Mexico. My mom gave it to me on November 27, 1997, two years earlier, and it had journeyed with me on all my adventures, but I had never read it.

The inside of the book had a note from her:

I love this book because it speaks directly to what I know of Godness. It is with excitement and respect for your delectable questions that I pass your own copy onto you with love and thanks for the gift of you Sara, in my life. Your mother, your fan, your friend, & your student.

OH, MY PRECIOUS, poetic mother. I was ready to read it. And how beautiful the invitation was to start my own conversation with God. No, not start it, but acknowledge I had already been having one, and I wanted more.

The book was everything I thought to be true but had never had the time or place to explore. It certainly wasn't like the masses or services I had attended. It didn't offer answers to everything, and I still questioned horrific acts that happened every minute of the day all over the world. I didn't want to believe God intended or meant for those acts of violence and trauma to happen. Instead of turning away from the harder conversations and questions, I allowed space for the unknowing and the reality of injustices created by humans that needed to be addressed.

I felt the presence of God in the ocean, in children's laughter, and in the beauty and pain of life. I asked God for help. I thanked God excessively. I questioned God. I also practiced writing prayers to God in my notebooks.

The more I read, the more I was able to engage in conversations with God. As a feminist, I struggled with the word "God." It felt masculine to me, and that didn't resonate. "Goddess" didn't roll off my tongue, either, so I kept playing with different words to use for this being, this connection to spirit, this divine higher power. I mostly used "God" because it felt more accessible, but I still wasn't sure that was it for me. In writing this now, I still relate to not having a word, although I've come to use "universe" more than "God."

As comfortable as I felt making myself at home in that last row, the stiff wooden pew was starting to bother me. I was also getting tired of the heat. I tried meditating. I focused my sight on one place on the wall where gold paint flickered in the light and noticed all I could notice while keeping my vision held. *It's okay. It's all okay. I can handle anything. I'm strong. I'm Sara. I'll always be Sara.*

Later that night, after my evening classes, I went straight to the restaurant. My stomach was growling. Carlos came right over to hug me and see how I was doing. He probably thought I was a ticking time bomb. Who knew when I'd freak out and burst into tears again. But I could feel myself shifting into this place of acceptance. If this was going to be my life, I was going to love it.

"How was your afternoon?" We sat down at a table together.

"It was good. But I still haven't talked to my mom yet. I need to talk to her. I left your cell number for her to call me back." I said.

"I told my mom." Carlos grabbed my hand. He seemed fine, though, and not as nervous as I felt.

"What did she say? How did it go?"

"She is happy for us. It was fine." I could tell that was all I was going to get out of him, and I wondered what it would be like to have her as my mother-in-law and my baby's abuela.

"I'm starving. I want a hamburger tonight."

"Okay. You like it well done?" he asked.

"I'm having your baby, and you don't even know how I like my hamburgers?" I laughed. "We have to be able to joke about this, amor. I like it medium, and I also want jalapeños on it."

Carlos said, "You can't eat spicy food when you're pregnant. No jalapeños for you."

"What?" I exclaimed.

"Spicy foods aren't good for pregnant women." He stood up to give the order to his brother in the kitchen.

"Wait a minute. I don't believe you. How do you know that?" I debated.

"I don't know. I just know it." His confidence was bold.

"Well, until I hear that from a doctor, I'm eating what I want to eat." I insisted. He didn't argue.

Chapter 34

I WENT TO THE PAY PHONE again to try my mom. The phone line was busy. I had been praying she was there and would answer. But as I looked around, I realized this was not where I wanted to have this conversation. I dreamed of curling up in bed with a phone and an hour to talk with my mom.

As I walked back into the restaurant, Carlos' cell phone rang. We looked at each other. My mom and I have a psychic connection, so even though it didn't surprise me that she was calling me at the same time I had been calling her, it made me happy every time it happened.

"Hello?" I answered.

"Hello? Sara?" She sounded concerned. I immediately started crying when I heard her voice.

"What's wrong, Sara? Are you okay?"

"Yes, I'm fine." I could hear her fear and didn't want her to start assuming the worst. "Mom, I'm pregnant."

"You're pregnant?" she repeated, probably to hear what it sounded like coming out of her own mouth or maybe so her friends could hear. I imagined them all sitting around her.

"Yes." I choked some sobs away and tried breathing. "I've been trying to get a hold of you. I just found out. I got a blood test, and I'm pregnant. I can't believe it."

My mom's voice was soft and calm. "It's going to be okay. I know that. Everything is going to be okay." We talked for a little bit. We talked about the clinic and Carlos' reaction and how awesome he was. I told her I needed to call Dad. She reassured me it was going to be okay.

"I know, Mom. I'm trusting in the universe. I trust that God has a plan, and I'm praying a lot."

"Don't forget to ask your angels for help, Sara. They are there for you. Everything is happening exactly the way it is supposed to. I know it is hard to believe, but it is."

I hung up, feeling lighter. Carlos brought out my food, and though the upcoming conversation with my dad still consumed my monkey mind along with all sorts of questions and unknowns, it was a relief to have told my mom. I hadn't felt many moments of peace or calm since I found out, but I knew that if I was going to find peace, it would be in prayer or meditation. I pulled out my notebook and added those two things to my to-do list.

I REVIEWED the list and was torn between everything I should be doing and everything I wanted to do. I needed to be meeting with doctors and figuring out my life. But I longed to go to a bookstore and buy all the books about growing a life inside of me, raising a bilingual, multicultural child, parenting, and childbirth. And I still needed to talk to my dad.

IT WAS LATE, almost ten at night, when I walked back up the hill, exhausted. The pay phone on my street was quieter than the ones closer to el centro. But the dogs were still loud, and I never knew when a water or gas truck would drive up the road, honking with someone yelling, "Agua." There were always random things that could ruin a whole conversation. I just wanted to get this conversation over with, that was for sure.

My dad answered after a couple of rings.

"Hi, Dad. It's Sara."

"Oh, hi Sara! How are you?" He seemed genuinely happy to hear my voice.

"I'm okay. How are you?" I asked. "Is this an okay time to talk?"

"Yeah, I'm good. Your mom is up in Door County with her friends. Me and your sister just finished a late dinner, and she's doing homework now."

"Okay, Dad. Look, I have to tell you something. It's kind of a big deal." I paused to catch my breath. "I just found out that ... um, that I'm pregnant."

There was a moment of crackly silence. I looked around at the palm trees and the dark ocean. There were a couple of clouds lit up by the moon, but otherwise, the sky was dark.

"Well, that's predictable," he finally said. "You would get pregnant in Mexico."

"What does that mean?"

"It's predictable that you would get yourself into such a complicated situation."

"I guess," I replied. I didn't know how to reply. He went on to say it was exciting that I was having a baby but that it didn't really matter since I'd be so far away. And then he tried encouraging me to elope. He had a lot of advice for having only known for a minute.

A truck revved its engine, and we waited until it was quiet again. I was sad and just wanted to get off the phone.

"I already talked to Mom. I'm going to a clinic. I'll let you know more soon."

It was done. I didn't have to make that phone call again. Ever. I went straight to my studio, crawled into the fetal position under the covers, and held myself.

IT WAS THE END of May, and I was scheduled to return to Madison in ten days. Now everything felt undecided. The next few days went by quickly as I busily arranged and rearranged details. Falling asleep came easy. I was so exhausted each night when I lay down, but I knew to pray for a full night's sleep. Waking up in the middle of the night was the worst. My mind raced, and falling back asleep was nearly impossible. Lying in bed, I listened to the nighttime noises, the dogs barking randomly, the distant waves crashing. If it were past five in the morning, I'd hear the buses barrelling down the roads, and my mind would spin in circles, jumping from fear and uncertainty to the sureness of my love for Carlos and the excitement of raising a family together. So many intense emotions, so overwhelming.

I was grateful for my morning classes. I would leave early while Carlos slept soundly, and the day started for the rest of the world. But on Monday morning, June 11, something was wrong. I was lightheaded, dizzy, and couldn't stand in the shower without holding on to the wall. Carlos was still awake, watching me get ready.

"Don't go teach this morning, Sara. You are weak and need more sleep."

"I'll be fine. I'm just really dizzy. It's probably because I'm not drinking coffee anymore."

I had quit drinking coffee and smoking cigarettes. I allowed myself to lament for a moment. Not because I missed smoking cigarettes but because I didn't get to enjoy my very last one fully. I missed coffee and was afraid my body was not handling the lack of caffeine. But I was so proud of myself, not for quitting cigarettes or coffee, but for my sobriety. I felt an incredible rush of joy for not having any alcohol in my system and wondered about the timing of it all. I had just so happened to quit drinking alcohol three months earlier, and here I was, growing a new human in my body. I took this as another sign I was meant to have this baby. It made me feel like my body was the perfect temple, even if my life and financial situation felt less than ideal.

Oh, but my body was not happy that morning. I didn't understand what I was experiencing, so I took it slow as I made my way down the hill. I left, as I always did, at six-thirty. Walking past the gas station to the bus stop, I couldn't quicken my step, as I usually did when the guys working there would catcall me. I was trying to maintain my balance. I inhaled the heavenly smell of sweet bread. I climbed the bus stairs. I always sat on the right side of the bus on the way to class so I could see the ocean slamming against the shore as we rattled down the Malecon boardwalk. A sliver of the moon shone over the glassy ocean. I normally felt invigorated by the quiet morning. But by the time I got to class, I was dizzy again and clutched the wall as I walked up the stairs.

Once I realized I wasn't getting any better, I asked Chris to sub for my nine o'clock class. I called Carlos and told him I needed to go to the doctor and then went into my seven o'clock class.

"Okay, class, you are almost ready for the exam on Friday. I'm not feeling well, so you'll use this time to review Chapters Six and Seven and work on the review questions at the end of the chapters." I sat in the back of the room and prayed. I was too weak to stand.

Carlos, on no sleep at all, arrived in a taxi within thirty minutes of me calling him. He rushed to my classroom, slowly walked me back down to the street, and helped me get into another taxi. I put my head on Carlos' shoulder and said, "No estoy bien, amor. I don't know what's wrong."

"It's okay. It's going to be okay, amor. No te preocupes." We drove in silence to Dr. Javier's home office. Carlos had called ahead; we were his first patients of the day. It wasn't even seven-thirty.

Inside, the doctor took my blood pressure. "Your blood pressure is very low, Sara." He rolled his chair back and looked at me. "What have you eaten today?"

"Nothing. I eat after I teach."

"Hija, you have to eat. You are growing a baby. You need food, sugar, and fruits. How are you sleeping?" he asked.

"Not well. I fall asleep right away because I'm so exhausted, but I wake up in the middle of the night and can't go back to sleep. I just lay there."

"Entiendo. But your body needs rest. Es muy importante. Please don't let the stress keep you from caring for yourself and your baby."

It hadn't even occurred to me that I could be harming my baby. I was already so proud of myself for being sober and cutting cigarettes and caffeine. And here was this doctor telling me I wasn't doing enough? What else didn't I know?

He sent me away with a simple prescription: Eat a healthy breakfast of yogurt, granola, fruits, and honey.

He explained what foods were best for me and coached me on how often to eat. He prescribed drinking water, frequently resting throughout the day, listening to my body when it was tired, and not allowing unnecessary stress.

Hmm, unnecessary stress. Really? My whole life was turned upside down, but I should try and keep the stress at bay? It seemed absurd. I missed the love, advice, and encouragement from the women in my life. As supportive as Carlos was, it was my body. I was the one having a baby while living in a foreign country.

I reviewed my prescription, which was literally written on a piece of paper, and remembered the last prescription, not in writing, but clear as ever: no drugs, alcohol, sex. I thought about my extreme shift in priorities—torn between two worlds.

Chapter 35

CARLOS AND I WENT straight to the internet cafe in the touristy part of Old Town, where they charged a lot for a big bowl of yogurt, granola, fruits, and honey, and I devoured it. My remorse and embarrassment at not having basic common sense quickly turned humorous. This is hard business, being healthy for a baby. Good thing I have a prescription for eating and drinking water!

The doctor was right, and the food recommendations were really helpful. I appreciated the guidance and the structure of knowing what to eat, how often, and what foods to focus on. But resting was a different story. I didn't have time to rest. I had shit to do.

The next day, Carlos made me a huge bowl of cut-up fruit for breakfast that included mangoes, cantaloupe, grapes, apples, bananas, and papaya. I ate all of it.

And then the diarrhea came. Too much fruit will do that to you. Here was the issue, though. Carlos and I were still in the romantic dating part of our relationship. I had accidentally farted once when we were laughing together, and even though I had been horrified, I was also relieved to get the first fart over with. But I had never farted a big smelly fart or pooped in front of him. That was for married people.

Now, my stomach rumbled, and I knew I had to go to the bathroom.

"Carlos, tengo que ir al baño," I said. There was no door to the bathroom. Only a colorful sarong hung as a curtain, so every sound could be heard.

"You have to go stand outside," I told him.

He laughed. But I didn't.

"I'm serious. You need to go outside. I have to poop."

"But we are having a baby together, Sara. I don't care about poop."

Thankfully he didn't argue more, and with a smirk, he went outside while I sat on the toilet, miserable. He kept asking loudly through the open doorway of my studio if I was okay.

"No. Díos mio! I am not okay." It was bad. But I survived. And never again did I eat that much fruit in one sitting.

I WISH I COULD say things got better, but they didn't. Every day was full of what felt like a million details to attend to. Where I had been unsure whether or not I'd return to Puerto Vallarta after my summer trip to Italy, I now was certain I'd come back in the fall, so I got busy finding someone to sublet my apartment.

Later in the day, I went to the bathroom, and to my surprise, there was blood again.

"Carlos, I'm bleeding." It wasn't a lot, but I didn't know what an acceptable amount was.

"You need to rest. You are too busy and working too hard," said Carlos.

He was right. I called into work and told my boss I wasn't working the rest of the week. It was the last week, anyway, and he was able to find subs. He also kindly assured me that they'd pay for my sick time.

After a nap, I went to the pay phone to call my mom.

"Mom, I'm bleeding. It's kind of like spotting but more. But not like a miscarriage. But I don't know what a miscarriage is like. What should I do?"

"What color is it?" she asked.

"Red, Mom. It's blood."

"Sometimes blood is more brownish. I'll call my doctor and call you on Carlos' cell phone later, okay? Don't worry. It's going to be okay."

I wanted my mom with me. She was too far away. I wanted to talk to a friend but didn't know who to call. My friends were all unmarried with no kids. When Carlos called Dr. Javier, he said that I should be in bed resting and not to worry if the blood was brown, but if it was red, I should worry.

I was on a pay phone talking to Carlos, who was out running errands. It was hot, and the streets were busy. I was tired and scared. "Es rojo, amor." *It's red.*

"I'll meet you at your house. And I'll bring food. Just go home and rest, por favor." He sounded worried, and I knew he was tired and scared too.

"Okay. I'll go now. Te amo."

But before I caught a cab, which was a luxury I knew was warranted at that moment, I walked to the church and sat in the back row again.

Hi God. I'm here again. So here's the deal. If this is a miscarriage, if I lose this baby, I know it is meant to be. And I know I'll be fine. But I figure there is a lesson here for me, and I'm not sure what it is. I don't know what you want, so please send me some clear answers.

I sat and listened. I got nothing. My chest tightened with fear. I felt some kind of leaking in my underwear. Worrying something bad was going to happen, I hurried out to catch a cab. I couldn't wait to lie down and cry.

IT WAS QUIET. I loved the quiet. The fan was blowing directly on me—no bra, just my tank top and some shorts under my sheet. I had a bottle of water next to me, a candle that wasn't lit but still smelled wonderful, some incense that was also unlit, and two spiritual books by my bed.

The first thing I said to Carlos when he walked in later that day was, "Oh my God, I can't lie here all day!"

"How long have you been here?"

"An hour, probably." I looked at the clock.

"Are you hungry?" He was carrying a bunch of grocery bags, and he was sweating. He hadn't taken a cab. He had walked up that hill with all those bags in the midday heat.

"Kind of."

He unpacked some groceries, and we talked. I cried, and he cried. We didn't know what was going on. I admitted that I secretly would be relieved if I miscarried. I don't think he felt the same way.

"Wouldn't I know if something was wrong?" I asked him.

Carlos looked at me lovingly. "Sara, you didn't know you were pregnant; why would you know if you were losing the baby?"

"Good point." He was so smart. "What if a miscarriage is meant to be? We aren't ready for a baby anyway. But we can't imagine having an abortion."

"But we can imagine losing the baby?"

"No, well, yes. I don't know." I was used to telling him everything, but now I hesitated. What if he had an opinion that didn't honor me and my body? I was scared to face that potential truth. I didn't know how strongly his religious background would influence our current situation, unwed and pregnant.

His sister came to the door. I wasn't expecting her.

"I made you some soup," she said. "Is there anything I can do to help?" I must have looked a bit bewildered. Carlos jumped in to make up for the awkward silence. He asked if I had any laundry his sister could take to get washed. I was so uncomfortable. I didn't know her well, but I longed for a sister friend. I longed for a woman to talk to. She came and sat by my side, and tears welled in my eyes. I don't know what Carlos thought, but he took my laundry and left us alone.

As Reyna sat with me on the bed, she told me about her pregnancies and her sister's miscarriage. She told me that Carlos was really worried, but he was acting tough. I didn't want to tell her that I had imagined losing the baby and that I had daydreamed about having my life back. I started to cry. I felt horrible even thinking the thoughts, but I couldn't tell her. She was so sweet with me.

Carlos returned. "I brought you this from the pharmacy," he said as he pulled this plastic bin thing out of the bag. It was bright blue.

"What is it?" I asked in Spanish.

"Una bacinilla," he answered.

"What is that?" I asked in English.

"It's for going to the bathroom."

"It's a bedpan?" I asked incredulously. "You want me to pee in that?" I was mortified. But before further conversation ensued, Carlos' phone rang. It was my mom.

"What did you find out, Mom?"

"The doctor says there isn't anything you can do. If you lose the baby, you lose the baby. They don't recommend bed rest. They haven't seen a difference in the percentages of miscarriages based on bedrest or not. So they tell women in the early stage of pregnancy, like you, to carry on as normal and try not to stress out. Stress is actually not good at all."

"Oh my God, Mom, how am I not supposed to be stressed out? Why does everyone keep telling me not to be stressed out?" She tried to comfort me, but I couldn't stay on the phone with her. Carlos and his sister were there, and there was this bedpan situation happening. We hung up, and Carlos looked at the bedpan in his hand again as if to remind me we were in the middle of a negotiation.

"The bathroom is less than five feet away, Carlos."

I was immediately uncomfortable talking to him in English in front of his sister. I switched to Spanish, conscientious of Reyna's presence. "El baño está muy cerca, Carlos." I went on to tell them what my mom's doctor said. I didn't want to disagree with Carlos' doctor. I didn't know the right answer, but I also didn't want to stay in bed. I mean, I had warmed up to the idea of having a baby, but I still had plenty of panic moments, too. I was trying to surrender to whatever the universe wanted.

"If we are meant to have the baby, we will. If not, we won't," I pitched. Also, I wanted them to understand that I would be super careful but would not use the bedpan. I believed my mom's doctor that if I was going to miscarry, I was going to miscarry, in bed or walking around. I also believed Carlos' doctor that rest might help and that overexerting myself didn't feel okay for me or my body. The blood was a sign that something wasn't right, and I promised myself not to ignore it and to continue to take precautions.

We agreed that I would rest but would get up and walk around slowly to use the bathroom and get myself food when it felt okay to do so. Carlos slid the bedpan under the bed. My heart slowed down a bit.

I was carefully trying to negotiate this place between cultures. What I wanted versus what they wanted, what one doctor said versus the other. I needed a nap and was happy when Reyna left. I just wanted to be alone.

Carlos was quiet. "Carlos, what's wrong? What are you thinking?"

His silence infuriated me. Why can't he just say what he is thinking?

But he couldn't put words together for himself or me. He had shut down in a way that I was going to become very familiar with, but at that time, it was new to me. I didn't understand that he needed time and space to process and that my impatience was not helpful. I finally burst into tears from exhaustion and fear of the ominous black hole between us.

Before he left, we promised we would connect later when we weren't so agitated by the unknown and each other. The bedpan remained under the bed, collecting dust and nothing else. Finally, forty-eight hours went by with no more blood. I was free to move around again without guilt.

Chapter 36

WALKING THROUGH the streets of Puerto Vallarta, I saw everything differently.

The kids on the corner couldn't tell my life had just turned upside down.

The women at the laundry place who always greeted me with warmth and compassion couldn't tell.

My students couldn't tell.

Gloria, who made me fresh-squeezed orange juice on the corner, couldn't tell. The internal shift was monumental, yet no one could see it. It made me feel isolated, lonely, and completely disconnected from the beautiful humans I normally felt connected to.

Yearning for connection, I gave myself an assignment. I decided to look for everyone's higher power in their faces. On the bus, I would make eye contact with someone and smile. Then I would glance at their third eye and intentionally connect the love of my higher power to the love of their higher power. I went to the grocery store and did the same to an older woman. *I see your divine love,* I said in my head. She reminded me of my great-grandmother, Lena. I could send her love, too. My love game was expanding and bringing me such joy. This must be what trusting in oneself is all about. It was exhilarating, and while I practiced this, I noticed how excited I was to show this new life in me such a beautiful practice. I realized, as I sat on the bus sending love to a young man who had just offered up his seat to an older man, that we were "we" now.

THE CONVERSATION about marriage came up early one evening at the restaurant. Neither of us believed we needed to be married to have a child together, and we didn't feel pressure from our families, either. But we had talked about getting married—way, way out in the future—on occasions when we were carefree, laying on the beach, or gazing at the stars. So as much as it wasn't necessary, it was on the table.

"Maybe this baby is catapulting us into marriage, and we should follow our hearts."

"Tal vez ," Carlos said. *Maybe.*

"But maybe we aren't sure. But we are sure. And if we are sure, shouldn't we get married?"

The pattern was becoming more apparent, I would vomit my thoughts a mile a minute, and Carlos would quietly process at a much slower pace.

"It's okay that we are unsure," he finally said.

"I want us to be sure we aren't getting married because we are having a baby," I said. "I know I am sure about loving you, but I'm not sure about the marriage part. And to be honest, sometimes I'm not sure you are either."

"I want to be with you, Sara. I have no doubt about marrying you. I'm also okay if you don't want to get married as long as we can be together."

"It just seems so cliché. A shotgun wedding."

He didn't know the term, so I explained, and he laughed. He reminded me that we choose our life; we create it.

"I mean, I know we created this little life," and I patted my belly. "But I know this isn't the life you planned on creating. You were so clear about not getting married until your thirties. What about you being twenty-seven and in love with a pregnant me?" I asked. I worried I was messing up his plan. I worried that he was messing up my plan.

I had replayed that conversation we had at the restaurant many times.

"It's a good thing we have time," he had said.

I remembered him saying that.

We think we have all the time in the world, and then something happens, and we don't think we have enough time, like it's something we can control, manage, or arrange. Our thoughts about time are just that—thoughts.

IT WAS FINALLY the day of my departure to Madison. I was fragile and scared. My confidence level had been higher when I arrived in Puerto Vallarta than it was leaving. Yet, I believed there was a bigger plan for me, and I had to trust it. That faith helped steady me as I braced myself to say goodbye to Carlos.

He brought me to the airport, helping me check in my extra-large backpack. We had handled so many details as a solid team since the positivo result three weeks earlier, and we were more connected than ever, but the host of unanswered questions and worries still hung between us. The intensity with which I missed my mom was pulling me back to Madison, and I hoped being with her would bring me clarity and answers.

I reminded Carlos of what we had talked about but needed to confirm it again for myself. I told him I wasn't sure exactly when I'd be back and still wasn't sure if it made sense to get married before the baby was born. Or where the baby would be born. I didn't know so much, but I promised him I wanted to be with him more than anything and that I loved him with all my heart, with all my strength, and with all my soul.

"Con toda mi alma, amor. Te amo, te amo, te amo."

We cried together. We kissed and hugged, and finally, I tore away from him to board the plane, where I found my window seat and cried some more. A sweet older English-speaking lady sat next to me, offered me a tissue, and told me, promised me, that in the end, everything was going to be okay.

She said, "If it's not okay yet, it's not over. Because in the end, it's always okay."

I sniffled some more and repeated in my head over and over again, *It's going to be okay.*

Chapter 37

LOOKING BACK NOW, it seems quite impossible that everything happened in such a short period of time. I had delayed my flight home by a week because of the bleeding and the stress, so when I arrived on June 15, I only had two and a half weeks before the family trip to Italy.

Yet, in the days after my return, I realized I wanted to marry Carlos right away. It felt important to me to be married when the baby was born. It wasn't because logistically everything would be easier with a marriage certificate, which I found out later it most certainly was, but because I was certain that this baby was a sign from God that following this path of being a family with Carlos, for this child, was surrendering to my highest good—to God's will.

I wanted to live for God's will. I didn't believe that any of my grand plans were better than what was all of a sudden unfolding for me. The love Carlos and I had tripped upon was so powerful that I believed anything was possible.

Sitting on the couch in our familiar position, my mom massaging my feet, I talked and she listened.

"I want to be with him. I love him. But I don't want to marry him just because we are pregnant. I don't think I even believe in marriage, and now I feel pulled toward it so quickly," I said.

"Marry him because you want to marry him. It doesn't matter if you are pregnant or not. If you want to marry him, and that is what your heart is telling you, listen to your heart," she said.

She made the decision sound easy. I learned later that it wasn't.

"Is it weird that I needed to talk to you to help me figure out if I should marry him or not? I've been so wishy-washy with him about it. And he is fine with whatever I want."

"No, you have a lot going on, Sara. Be gentle with yourself. All of this is normal. Especially wanting your mom at a time like this." She squeezed my knee, and I felt deeply loved and cared for. I went to my room, the guest room, where there was a box of tissues, a cute little lamp, and some books neatly stacked on the side table. My mom had taken the time to get the room ready for me. She had even curated the books with a copy of *What to Expect When You're Expecting* (the 1996 edition) and *The Pregnancy Journal, a Day-to-Day Guide to a Healthy and Happy Pregnancy*. I sat on the bed, pulled out my calling card, and listened to the foreign ringtone, hoping Carlos would pick up.

My parents had moved into their home a year earlier. It was the home I stayed at most recently between my life in Los Angeles and Puerto Vallarta. That was five months of summer fun, a firefighter boyfriend, extreme drinking, and continued drug use. It was where I lived over Thanksgiving weekend in 1999 when my best friend's eighteen-year-old sister was killed in a horrific car accident. At the funeral, I wondered why God would have taken Robin and not me. I was wasting my life, disregarding it, while Robin had been living with purpose and potential. Questioning how I lived my life, I felt the heaviness of shame. And then, a week later, with that shame still weighing on me, I was raped. It was a brief five months on Hillcrest Drive, yet the memories were lasting.

I FELT AT HOME in their house, but in a distant way, and for that I was grateful. Now I was visiting while preoccupied with my soon-to-be new family in what would become my new home base, Puerto Vallarta.

Wherever you go, there you are.

I'd missed sitting on the bed, surrounded by fluffy pillows, using the cordless phone.

The click of Carlos answering jolted me, reminding me that whatever country I was in, there would always be someone I loved in another country who I wanted to talk to and be with. I would always be caught between two worlds.

It was loud where he was, probably because he was outside at one of the markets. After some back and forth to make sure the reception was okay, I confirmed he had time to talk to me before I spilled.

"Let's get married. I know I said I wasn't sure, but I talked to my mom, and I'm sure." I paused for a second but not long enough for him to reply. "And I'm thinking August will be good. I won't have a big belly yet, and it'll be summer here, so we can get married outside." I couldn't imagine my family and friends not knowing the father of my child, my future husband, or not being able to attend the wedding. Since it'd be last minute, making it easy for them to attend was a priority. I wanted to properly and officially combine our lives.

"Umm, okay," he said.

Spouting all my potential ideas, plans, and hopes spurred just as many questions.

"You have a visa, right? So you can come without a problem, right? And what about your family and friends? Will they be able to come?" As I spoke, I knew there would be a financial stressor in all of this. I reminded him that my parents would help pay for the wedding and that it would be simple and small, nothing big and fancy.

Carlos preferred to process information slowly, so when he didn't respond with the same lightning speed I had, I got nervous and questioned him and doubted everything again. This was how our conversations went. I would spin plans quickly, and he would stay silent, and then I would get anxious. But I stayed on the phone, and he eventually opened up, and decisions were made.

Yes, he had a visitor's visa, but no one else in his family did. I made notes in my notebook, which had quickly turned into part health journal and part wedding planner:

- Get information about family visas
- Pick a date
- Confirm budget with parents
- Make a list of wedding decisions
- Confirm doctor's appointment with Mom and Brooke

IN MY MIND, the conversation went well. Carlos was on board with coming to Madison for the wedding, and he gave me the go-ahead to start planning. He had his hands full managing the restaurant and figuring out travel logistics for his family. We were back in the groove of teamwork.

Chapter 38

THE OB-GYN CLINIC was the most comforting place in the world. I knew what to expect, and from the first appointment, talking to Dr. Weber was such a relief. The whole process and all the procedures fit my experience from the little things, like scheduling the appointment, to the basic preliminary checkpoints of getting my weight and height and taking my blood, to the part that felt most important to me, when she came in and answered all my questions, told me what to expect over the next couple of months, what significant milestones to look for, and offered me a bunch of brochures. I walked out confident.

I faked excitement when we heard the baby's heartbeat at the next appointment. It felt wrong to have my best friend and mom by my side without Carlos, but I didn't want to worry anyone.

Dr. Weber called me a couple of days later. "Your bloodwork came back, and there is something we need to address," she said. I was standing in the kitchen playing with the phone cord. No one else was in the house.

"You tested positive for chlamydia."

"What? How is that possible?"

She didn't answer. Finally, she asked, "Were you sexually active prior to getting pregnant?"

What kind of fucking question is that? Yes, I'm twenty-five years old. I'm as slutty as they come. I felt myself getting defensive.

"Well, I was drugged and raped last November. Does that count?" I said. "Or maybe Carlos gave it to me. How am I supposed to know?" It was one of those moments where I could completely disassociate from the trauma and engage in a conversation without feeling my feelings. The numbness was back. I didn't mean to be snarky, but I wasn't prepared for more surprises.

"Oh Sara, I'm sorry. I didn't know." She must have been referring to the rape. I was still on the chlamydia news. She continued, "Chlamydia is a sexually transmitted disease that can go undetected for years. We will put you on an antibiotic to take care of it. This is most likely the reason you have had spotting. The antibiotic will clear it up, and it won't affect the baby. I recommend you let Carlos know and ask him to get tested."

"Right," I replied. She confirmed my preferred pharmacy, and since I didn't know what else to ask, I said goodbye and hung up the phone.

"Fucking chlamydia," I said out loud after slamming the phone down. What else do you want to put on my plate, God? I went to my room and cried. Crying came easily.

After letting the tears flow for a while, I pulled myself together, reached for the phone to call Carlos, and then burst into tears and hung up the phone. Before I dialed again, I looked up chlamydia in my Spanish dictionary. Clamidia.

"I'VE GOT A LOT to update you on, Carlos. Do you have time to talk?" I asked. The phone reception seemed good. Sitting on the bed again, I was mesmerized by the full green trees out the window. The leaves were dancing with fervor. It was so different from watching palm trees sway. I loved them both.

But at that moment, I missed Carlos and the palm trees more than anything. I wished I could sit with him on my bed in my studio apartment with the fan blowing on us and the palm trees standing tall and certain outside. I longed to be in his arms as I processed this horrible news and all the feelings it brought up in me.

"I am at home. I don't have to go to the restaurant for a while because Reyna is opening it up for me tonight. Como estás, amor?"

"I'm so tired. But I'm good. And I'm burping a lot."

"Me too!" His voice lifted and we laughed.

"Okay, but here is the news." I got serious quickly. "I had a bunch of tests done, and they found out I have chlamydia. You either have it, or you don't. I don't know. You should get tested and take something just in case."

I felt this sick feeling in my stomach. I felt dirty. I felt angry, and I was worried about what he would think. But at this point, I was too tired to do anything but pray and trust the process.

"Also, Carlos," I paused, "are you still there?"

"Si," he said.

"I think we should get married on August 5. It's a Saturday. You could get a one-way ticket, fly in a week early, and then we could drive my car down to Puerto Vallarta with all my stuff after the wedding."

How about that for a phone call? I have chlamydia, you might have it too, and let's get married in less than six weeks. Oy vey. But my to-do list had both of those things on it, and I was on a mission.

We talked more about the chlamydia situation. He said he'd get tested, and he said he'd check about the August 5 date. He still wasn't sure who in his family could come, but he had more information to give me about the visitor visa process, so I took notes, and we got off the phone after a lot of "Te amos."

I would be lying if I didn't admit to feeling weird every time we talked about getting married, which made me worry.

Chapter 39

AFTER MANY MORE conversations with my family, Carlos, and friends, we all agreed on the August 5 date. Carlos started looking for flights. I started arranging the details. My friends jumped in. We had six weeks to plan the wedding, and we'd spend two of those weeks in Italy for my Grandma Harriet's family reunion dream trip.

We made as many arrangements as possible before we left for Italy. My mom used her political connections from her previous job as a lobbyist to contact someone who could write a letter on behalf of Carlos' mom and sister to expedite their visitor visas. We enlisted the help of my friends to get the invitations mailed out since they wouldn't be printed until after we were already in Italy. There wasn't a phone number to give them if they ran into any issues, but they had my email address, and I promised them I'd find internet cafes so we could communicate.

With as much as I had on my plate, I kept thinking about being in Italy sober. The emotions were all over the place at any given hour. Pissed, happy, excited, and scared out of my mind. How does one go to Italy and not drink wine? But now I was pregnant, and the focus was on growing a healthy baby. It helped.

WALKING INTO THE Borders Book Store on University Avenue made my heart happy. I picked up a wedding magazine, paged through it, tucked it under my arm, and headed straight to the Parenting/Family section. After browsing for a bit, I had three new books, and I found an armchair in a bright corner by the second-floor window. Flipping through the wedding magazine again, I tried to find some inspiration, but I was distracted by a wave of baby excitement. I had so many questions. My thirst for learning the scientific stuff and the "what to expect when expecting" literature had been handled by my mom already. But what had been missing was access to all of these new books specific to raising a multicultural, bilingual baby and living in a mixed-race family. My imagination and curiosity were tingling. I put the magazine down and contemplated which book to jump into first: *I'm Chocolate, You're Vanilla: Raising Healthy Black and Biracial Children in a Race-conscious World* by Marguerite Wright; or *Raising Nuestros Niños: Bringing up Latino Children in a Bicultural World* by Gloria Rodriquez; or *Raising Bilingual Children: A Parent's Guide* by Carey Myles.

THERE WAS ALREADY a designated area in my bedroom for the books I intended to take with me to Mexico. Having been starved for books in Puerto Vallarta, I had pulled a stack from my boxes in the basement soon after I arrived at my parents' house. Thinking about the growing stack, I tensed up again. How was I going to learn everything I needed to know? What about the books I had hoped to read about addiction and alcoholism and the twelve-step books? What about my dream of traveling all around Mexico and learning about the cultures of different areas? What about the spiritual books I had on my wish list?

What business did I have bringing a baby into the world when there was still so much I needed to know, understand, and read about? As my brain raced, I felt uneasy, small, and unsure of myself. My hand automatically moved to my belly and rested there.

"Hey there, little person. I love you." Deep breath. "It's going to be okay." Another deep breath, slower. "I'm not sure why me, why Carlos, but please know that I'm so glad you picked us. I love you more than everything in the whole world."

I was trying to ground myself back into the present moment, aware of my heightened anxiety, so I focused on surrounding the little bean-sized baby with love. Then, slowly, I allowed the love to fill me up, extending through my first chakra at the top of my head. I immediately felt calm.

It's all okay. Everything is exactly the way it is supposed to be. I closed my eyes and felt the presence of something bigger. I deepened my breath, and the anxiety disappeared as quickly as it had come. *I can do this. I can do this. I can do this.*

Feeling relaxed again in the comfortable chair, I reached for Gloria Rodriquez's book. The rollercoaster was real and exhausting. After a while, my eyes were tired, and my stomach rumbled. I stuck the magazine back on a rack and paid for all the books.

THE NEXT MORNING, as I read a book about angels, I felt the desire to journal. Prayer is like talking to God, so meditation must be the listening part. And the conversation? How did that work? I scribbled in larger letters: practice doing prayer work with a goddess.

Wow, notice how I say "with" and not "to"? I think I am really integrating this higher spirit and my own inner light with God—the idea of God—of the divine. I am one with God. I noticed this the other day when I had a hard time thanking God for my sobriety. I ended up thanking us and our teamwork. We aren't separate; we are one.

Journaling helped me understand what I believed, find clarity, and grow deeper through writing. As I circled around, I realized I could incorporate spiritual growth while growing a family. I didn't have to learn one thing before starting to learn other things. Yes, there would be a wide range of books on our bookshelf, and that was perfectly wonderful.

Chapter 40

IT WAS JULY 2001 when my mom, dad, sister, and I arrived in Italy and were transported to the castle my grandma had rented for the family reunion. It seemed unrealistic for us to be here during such a busy time. When the tension and voices would rise, I quickly reminded my parents that a small, simple wedding was fine, and I didn't want anyone stressing out. I didn't understand the sheer amount of work I was asking from my parents. But I don't remember them ever making me feel guilty. They must have known how scared I was and wanted me to be happy and to feel supported, which I did. Being with my mom's side of the family—Grandma Harriet, who I was very close with, aunts and uncles, and my younger cousins—was calming but being the outlier in the family didn't help my feelings of not belonging. With the majority of the grandchildren being ten-plus years younger than me, I was used to feeling out of place, but the fact that I also felt out of place in my own life made it more intense.

I didn't want to sit at the kids' table, and I didn't want to sit with the adults. So I wandered on my own, read my books, and journaled. I said no to the wine. When out driving on the winding roads, we pulled over so I could throw up. At night, I would lay awake listening to the noises of the mysterious castle, trying to imagine what my life would be like in a year, in five years. When anxiety gripped me, I pulled out the AA phrases "One day at a time" or "Easy does it."

After finding out I was pregnant, I hadn't gone back to an AA meeting. Pregnant people don't drink. I thought it would be weird. But I hadn't been to enough AA meetings to learn that AA isn't just about not drinking; it's about finding a new way of living. And support is always needed for that.

I longed to talk to Carlos, but the time difference made it challenging, so we relied on email. One afternoon the family was going to a wine tasting or some tour, and I opted to be dropped off in town for the afternoon. My heart was the happiest it had been in a while as I strolled the magical streets in my flowy flower hippie dress, tennis shoes, and movie star sunglasses. Finally, I found a spot where I could check my email.

The internet cafe I found was not air-conditioned. In fact, the front was open to the street, and the July sun made me sticky. I sat at a tall table lined with computers, and my legs dangled. As I opened my Hotmail account, I couldn't help but smile. Communicating with Carlos via email was a treat. He typed in all capital letters. His updates were full of details and logistics, and he'd always end with lots of amor de mi vidas and sweet words like carinosa, te quiero, te extraño, eres preciosa, y más.

His newest email notified me that one of his friends (who had a visa) could be his best man at the wedding and that he was still in the process of getting a tourist visa for his mom and his sister Martha. Those were the only two family members that would be able to come, mostly because the others had to work or couldn't be away from family that long, or it would cost too much, even if we helped with the plane tickets.

Carlos also notified me that he had arranged for Reyna and his niece, Claudia, to take care of the restaurant. He could come to Wisconsin for two weeks. He was coming ten days before the wedding. His mom and sister would arrive two days before the wedding.

It wasn't until I hit reply and began to type that I realized the keyboard was meant for writing in Italian. *Challenges can be fun,* I reminded myself, and I kept it short.

Then, I read through the next email. It was from my two best friends, Haley and Brooke, who were in charge of the invitations. But the email was not an update as I expected. It was a long note asking me to cancel the wedding. They had thought about it a lot, discussed it in depth, and wanted me to know that it was okay to have the baby without being married. They would support me in that decision. They were sure I was moving too quickly and making a big mistake. My heart raced, and sweat trickled down the side of my face. I was shocked. I wiped the sweat away and allowed the betrayal to clump up in a ball in my stomach.

Fuck them, I thought.

They were supposed to be finalizing the invitations and mailing them out. Only five weeks remained. My chest hurt. I looked around the café. Where am I? What am I doing? How can I settle myself?

I checked in with my senses. The fans blew humid air all around. The bored-looking woman behind the front desk was reading a book. An older man with blond hair and thin round glasses was sitting at a computer. He didn't look Italian. Where was his home? Was he happy to be traveling, or was he missing his family while on a mundane business trip? My heart started to slow down.

It helped me to get out of my own dramatic world and imagine what life was like for others. Grounding myself in the present moment settled my anxiety, but the sick feeling in my stomach still reminded me of my distant friends who were telling me not to marry this man I loved so much.

Within that second, the cord tightened between Carlos and me while the cord to my friends loosened. I was meant to be with Carlos, to have this baby, and start our family together. Of course, it didn't make sense to anyone. Of course, it felt too fast. But I felt more certain than I had ever felt.

I didn't reply to their email. I left the café and walked the streets of Florence, Italy. There was a peace inside of me that felt warm. I was more alone than I had been in days, yet for the first time, I didn't feel alone at all. This sense of love, protection, and companionship swirled around and inside of me. People walked by, and I smiled at them like they were old friends. It felt sensational to add some swing in my walk and ooze with confidence, love, and an electric sexual energy. I was going to live on my own terms, and it wasn't my job to prove anything to anyone.

Chapter 41

MY PARENTS REMAINED steady and supportive through the push and pull between external messages, internal confidence, and friend drama. There were hints of understanding; they remembered meeting, marrying, and having a baby (me!) in a whirlwind that shocked their friends and family. They believed anything was possible, especially love.

Days passed, emails were exchanged, and the invitations went out. It was a lopsided guest list. One hundred of my family and friends were invited, plus Carlos' mom, sister, and a best man I didn't even know. One hundred and three people would witness our marriage. It felt like my wedding, not our wedding. My parents stepped in and made many decisions, allowing me to focus on my health and well-being. We were all navigating stress as best as we could. My parents had two houses—one in Madison, where I had been staying, and the other an hour west of Madison, in the hills of Richland County, on sixty-plus acres. We called it their country house, where they would go on weekends and where they hoped to spend more time once my sister graduated from high school. Since we only had six weeks to plan a wedding, it was the best and only choice for our location.

The minute we arrived back in Madison, my dad worked overtime getting the country house fixed up and ready. My mom worked overtime getting family members booked into lodging. I coordinated travel plans for Carlos and his mom and sister. My mom's connections had worked;

tourist visas were secured, and plane tickets were confirmed. We were all attending to the many details and anxiety. Still, my intense anticipation of Carlos' arrival remained steady and strong—to hug him, to snuggle my face into the crevice of his neck and shoulder, to inhale, and feel his hand wrapped solidly around mine. Every day was one day closer.

There were moments when paradox and opposing experiences and emotions swarmed me, and all I could do was turn the music up loud and dance it out.

Money was another inconsistent narrative. It was and was not an issue at the same time. That was how it had been all my life. I had the invisible net below me. I could fall into the worst place, and someone would catch me and help me up. Between my layers and mixture of privilege and family members who valued helping family out, there would always be a place to land. That privilege wasn't verbalized, but I could feel it.

Growing up, there were subtle (and loud) reminders that we weren't rich, and money doesn't grow on trees. Making money takes long hours, grit, getting dirty, and sometimes sweat. And then when you make that money, save a lot of it and spend it wisely. Don't spend more than you make or spend frivolously. Always, always live within your means. Know your expenses, know your income. Growing up, money advice was offered up constantly. I'm grateful for my moneywise father and the uncomplicated ways I learned about money. He kept it simple and repeated these beliefs over and over again:

- Save ten percent of what you make.
- Make more than you spend.
- Work hard.
- Invest in your values.

My dad worked hard his whole life, made smart, practical (and sometimes complicated and brilliant) decisions that didn't always make sense to the outside world, but on the inside, at the dining room table with his spreadsheets, his life goals, his values clear, his decisions were spot-on.

My wedding was going to be cheaper than he had anticipated. Yet the looming baby created an extra load of pressure and concern. In his mind, my health and well-being were his responsibility as the provider of the family, and if, for some reason, Carlos and I were unable to support ourselves, he would be there. He was one of the many safety nets, and between extended family and friends, I would never worry about being on the streets. None of that crossed my mind, though.

The conversations leading up to the wedding were about how we could be cutting expenses here and there. Then, my dad would suddenly overhear something we were debating and offer the more expensive option. The messages were mixed. Don't spend too much, but wait, this is your wedding. It is a worthy investment, and we have money to spend on it.

Having a perfect wedding day was not really a concern of mine. I knew it would be a nice wedding, but I saw it as a day to honor our love and commitment, not a day that needed to be the most perfect or extravagant. In fact, I strongly believed that spending a fortune on a wedding was irresponsible. I thought I'd be able to find a dress I'd like for one hundred fifty dollars, and maybe I would have, but my mom and friends convinced me to visit a fancy wedding dress store, where I fell in love with a five hundred dollar dress. It felt absurd, but my heart sang as I twirled around in it, and my mom insisted we buy it.

Looking back, it makes perfect sense that I was preoccupied with my new life in Mexico after the wedding. My Pisces self might have wanted to be more absorbed in the romance of a wedding, but I was consumed with preparing for the next stage.

Or maybe I was more focused on life post-wedding day because I was still doubting something. Unable to shake my hesitation, I blamed my childhood and trust issues with men.

Chapter 42

IT WAS THE SPRING of my senior year in high school, 1993, and I had already been admitted to the University of Minnesota in Minneapolis. I was counting the days to get out of my house and be on my own. On this particular sunny afternoon, my two girlfriends and I were hanging out in my sunroom, stoned again. Since we all were set on the colleges we would attend for the next year, high school didn't matter much anymore. I picked up a book from the coffee table and started leafing through it when I found a piece of paper being used as a bookmark.

My mom's handwriting.

Maybe a poem.

She was always leaving her writings around the house, so it didn't seem like a breach of confidence to read it out loud to my friends. It started with, "I first met you ten years ago ..."

Oh, this must be about my sister, I thought.

I was eighteen, my sister almost nine. She would have been unborn but perhaps growing in my mom's belly if I had the timing right. I kept reading, and as I flipped the page over, it became clear that this was not about my sister. It was a letter to a grown woman who had betrayed my mother.

Her words were daggers of anger, blood dripping from the open wounds. This unnamed woman was someone we knew who went to our temple.

"What the fuck is this about?" I said to my friends as I tried to piece things together. I reread the letter. Later that night, after my sister was asleep and my dad was still at work, I confronted my mom in the kitchen. Holding the letter up, I asked her what it was about. She was confused by my question.

"But Sara, you knew about the affair. What are you asking me?"

"I don't know what you are talking about, Mom. What affair? What is going on?"

I had no idea what she was talking about. She must have realized that I genuinely had no recollection and went on to tell me the whole story. I was scrunched in the corner of the couch, probably with my arms crossed, while she sat with her back straight, close to the edge, with her small feet planted firmly on the floor. Her voice was soft and gentle, like her personality. She didn't seem nervous. If anything, she had a professional sense about her, like she was fully aware of the importance of her every word.

"In 1983, you were in second grade, and we were living on the near east side of Madison, right in front of Orton Park. Dad was doing well in real estate and partying a lot. He had an affair and told you that he was leaving. And then he told you not to tell me. I don't think he told you about the affair, only not to tell me he was planning on leaving. You told me later when we were at the park. He didn't end up moving out, but there were a couple of times when he didn't come home at night, and we fought a lot, so I just assumed you remembered. You certainly could hear us fighting, and we talked about it in front of you more than we probably should have."

My eight-year-old self drew a picture of my parents and me in front of a house with a shining sun. At the top, in the sky, I wrote, "Please don't leave us." It was the kind of crayon-scribble drawing you might see in a Hallmark movie. I wouldn't believe I drew something so cliché, except my parents saved it and gave it to me when I was in my thirties when they were cleaning out some boxes.

There were fights—loud fights—and crying.

I don't know why he told me not to tell her. Maybe he was planning on telling her later, but for whatever reason, that mistake, which he has since apologized for, severed a trusting bond I had with him. I must have felt terrified of being abandoned.

The closing on the new house in the fancy new neighborhood was fast approaching. Then moving day. According to my mom's story, my dad went out on our first night in the new house and didn't come home. My mom was devastated. There were more fights.

Then my dad got his shit together, apologized, promised it would never happen again, and wanted to be forgiven. At some point, she must have agreed to forgive him. But I don't think forgiving was enough for him. He wanted us to forgive and forget, to move on and not look back. But my mom couldn't. Maybe she tried. I don't know. Years later, she had not forgotten. Forgiveness is complicated. It's messy. It seemed like my dad wanted to be fully forgiven in a way that was unrealistic.

I still don't recall this time of my life, but because the body remembers, I understand the impact better now. I am all too familiar with the coping mechanism of erased memories (disassociation). They didn't forget the time their marriage was likely at its worst, but they never talked about it around me, either. Not until I was eighteen years old. In their minds, I knew and remembered because I was there; I was one of the players. But as I moved into third grade, then fourth, fifth, and beyond, all I knew was that I didn't like my dad anymore. I felt like I needed to protect my mom, but I couldn't remember why. I didn't know that I knew things I shouldn't know.

It all made sense as I sat with my mom, listening to her tell me about this significant chunk of my life. Oh, this is why I hated my dad so much. This is why I was Daddy's girl until we moved to this house, and then I hated him. This is why I always fought with him and tried to convince her to divorce him.

I did remember things from third grade, like the new friends I met, a favorite teacher, and our dog, Koko. I also remember my dad coming home drunk a lot. He was loud and sometimes funny but mostly angry. I knew that even after he quit drinking, I was scared of him and worried about what he would be like when he got home. I knew to turn off the TV and pretend I had been studying when his car pulled into the driveway. I knew to brace myself for what kind of mood he might be in. I knew that when I pretended to be doing something important, like homework or reading a book, I was safe from his criticism. I knew that watching television was bad, and reading was good. I knew I needed to quickly put away the ice cream if I heard him coming downstairs. Eating ice cream was bad. Eating apples was good. Being lazy was bad, and going to work was good.

I had to figure out what he would be okay with to stay out of his line of attack. If he was stressed or irritated, we knew immediately that our evening would be rearranged based on his day. Our world revolved around his moods.

In the same way no one ever talked about the affair, we also rarely talked about his drinking problem after he quit. It seemed to be a good thing that my dad replaced alcohol with work and exercise. It was admirable how hard he worked to provide for our family and how well he cared for his body. But the high value placed on making money and staying fit meant that my mom was inferior because she didn't work as hard, make as much money, or exercise enough, and she loved sweets.

"You're not going to eat that, are you?" he would say to my mom as she reached for a piece of birthday cake. I cringed every time he criticized her. I hated the look of scorn he gave her, and I hated the way she responded to him. There were two ways it would go: Either my mom would lower her eyes, ashamed, and not eat whatever he was scolding her for, or she would snap and righteously remind him she could do whatever she wanted. Then she would eat two pieces. Both responses were reactive, from where I sat, and reeked of dysfunction.

It wasn't until a few years ago, when I was in my early forties, that I learned about the drama triangle and could see how my parents, our whole family, would interact based on the three roles of dysfunction: the perpetrator, the victim, and the rescuer. We all moved around the triangle based on the situation. Mostly my dad was the perpetrator, my mom the victim, and I, the rescuer. But sometimes, as I would take on the rescuer role—to save my mom from my mean dad—my dad would treat me like the perpetrator, and then I would fall into the victim role. Poor me, my dad was horrible. Poor Mom, he was so mean to her. And my mom would turn my dad into the victim. "But, Sara, you don't understand. His childhood was very hard, and he suffers, a lot too. He is doing the best he can." The "poor dad" thing didn't resonate with me. I wanted my mom to be strong enough to stand up for herself, and I wanted her to realize the harm he was causing. I daydreamed of her leaving him.

My mom loved my dad, and I imagine she wanted to forgive him more than anything. I doubt she wanted the fear and doubt that surfaced when he was late for dinner or missed it altogether. I say this because she was always quick to defend him when I relentlessly pointed out that she deserved better. It wasn't until I was eighteen that some of these pieces came together for me.

AFTER MY MOM shared the story, I went to therapy with my dad a couple of times. I told him things I would never have said outside of that space. I was angry. I was full of disdain. I blamed him and shamed him and couldn't find a place in my heart to forgive him. It was like I had just learned it all over again. It must have sucked for him.

Trauma has consequences. I can see now, looking back, that I desperately sought love, security, and an escape, so I abused alcohol, drugs, and sex. I was caught stealing numerous times, starting when I was in third grade, and I didn't stop until I almost got caught in a music store my sophomore year in college, and I faced the realization that, as a nineteen-year-old, I could have ended up in jail. I wish I had seen how the other destructive outlets impacted me, but I didn't.

I'm not blaming my dad. My dad has his own story, with his own wounds and coping mechanisms. We all do the best we can. I don't think he ever had an affair again, though I don't know. This isn't that story. My parents have their own love story. There was love and pain and suffering and more love. They committed to each other in a way that worked for them. I acknowledge and honor their stories and am grateful for the lessons I've learned as their daughter.

I was insistent that I didn't need help from anyone, ever. My strength was an asset, a survival tactic. It wasn't until my mid-forties, after hundreds of hours with helpful therapists and self-exploration, that I started to see how my extreme independence was really a trust issue. By not relying on others or allowing others to support and help or love me, no one could let me down or hurt me. My job was to take care of myself, all on my own, and that was how I could protect myself from disappointment and harm.

Chapter 43

ON JULY 27, 2000, ten days before the wedding, I drove three hours to the Chicago O'Hare airport to pick up Carlos. The past six weeks had felt like an eternity. We planned the wedding, arranged for his family to get their paperwork, and attended to dozens of details like dresses, tuxedos, food, cake, music, tents, chairs, invitations, flowers, and more. We had gone on a ten-day family trip to Italy. I had heard the baby's heartbeat at the doctor's office and found out I had chlamydia. I had finally gotten my brochures about being pregnant, along with a stack of books that I coveted. So much had happened in six weeks. So much had changed in seven months.

The rape felt like it had happened years ago. I hadn't even known Carlos. Or Puerto Vallarta.

As I drove down I-94, the sun was bright and hot but knowing the heat in Mexico gave me pause before complaining. The blast of cool air from the vents reminded me of the luxury of my silver 1992 two-door Toyota Celica. I stroked the dashboard like I was petting a beloved cat and turned up the music. TLC's *Crazy Sexy Cool* was on, and everything felt right in the world. I didn't have much more time with this car and wanted to make the most of it.

My idea of driving my car to Mexico after the wedding had been thrown out quickly. It was an extremely sporty car with front lights that raised up when you turned them on and tinted windows in the back. It was hot. It was also unrealistic. I bet a car seat wouldn't fit in it. When my dad offered to sell it for me after the wedding, I inhaled sharply. Grief washed over me as the reality of what my life would look like flashed in front of me. A married woman with a boring four-door car, if we got a car at all. I tried again. A married woman with a baby on a bus? Was this my future?

Panic crept up, so I quickly diverted my focus to Carlos. I was up for any challenge and adventure with him. I could do this. I was ready to hand over the sports cars, the binge drinking, and the spontaneous travel for car seats, cribs, and baby bottles.

MY STOMACH CHURNED as I stood in the waiting area in front of the international arrivals for my future husband. I ached to hug him, hold him, and be with him. I wanted his presence desperately. The doubt and fear of not remembering him, of not knowing him well enough to marry him, tugged one side of me while the other shook with happiness, certainty, and overwhelming love.

I saw him before he saw me.

I was struck by how much shorter and skinnier he seemed. Is that him? Do I even recognize him? Is he shorter than me? How do I not even remember this? I instantly regretted the heeled sandals I was wearing.

I started to freak out inside but kept my calm. I watched him as his eyes locked on me and his brilliant smile lit up his whole face. The room blurred out as we moved quickly toward each other, without running, and then fell into each other in the tightest, warmest, most desperate embrace.

This is what I had been waiting for. Us.

I inhaled the moment and felt the weight of him around me as I breathed in the smell of his too-strong cologne. He held my face with both of his hands, and we looked at each other, smiling, giggling, kissing, and hugging again.

Instead of driving straight back to Madison, we stopped at a cheap highway hotel. I didn't want to share him with anyone the first night we were together. I didn't want the pressure of family quite yet. I wanted him all to myself. And I wanted to give him a breath before the rush of the wedding swept us up. He showered, and then, naked, we crawled into bed together. He stroked my belly. He whispered hello to our little human that we had created together. He gazed into my eyes. I couldn't wait to say what had been pulling at me for weeks.

I inhaled and then blurted it out. "I need to ask you something. Don't take it the wrong way, okay?" He stayed steady and calm, waiting for me to continue.

"Is it okay if I decide I don't want to get married? I mean, I love you. But I need to know that you'll still love me, and it will be okay if I cancel the wedding." I was propped up on my elbow, looking into his dark brown eyes. He didn't respond right away, but he also didn't take his eyes off me.

Finally, he said, "Yes. I will still be here for you, and I will love you, even if we don't get married. I want to be with you. Married or not." With deep confidence, he reassured me that I wasn't rocking his world with this inquiry.

I was finally able to open up about what had been bothering me. "It's the overall concept of marriage and the 'death do us part' vow."

I explained that it wasn't him or us that I was unsure of; it was putting a vow before my own sovereignty. "I can commit to being the best mom I can be for our baby for the rest of my life," I said. "But I am not on board with committing to you, no matter what, for life. People change, and if someday you and I don't have the same respect and love for each other as we do now, I want us to be able to choose differently. Basically, what I'm saying is that I believe in divorce."

It might have been a weird thing to say before getting married, but it wasn't until we talked about it so openly that I fully understood my discomfort in putting a cultural norm before my best interest. The fact that he got it and was in agreement gave me confidence. I couldn't wait to marry him.

"Let's be the kind of couple that is willing to make changes for our highest good as individuals, as a couple, and as a family. Let's choose each other every day." It felt like our secret, another way we were breaking toxic outdated cycles.

The next morning, we lounged in bed, reconnecting. As the time got closer for us to get on the road, we both admitted to being nervous about him meeting everyone and the wedding being only ten days away.

Every time we practiced saying the hard thing out loud to each other, we saw how quickly the hard thing became less hard. Squeezing his hand calmed me instantly. It still does to this day.

As nervous as I remember being, my nerves were probably nothing compared to his. He was about to meet my dad—my scary dad—for the first time.

Chapter 44

WE ARRIVED AT the house and, clasping hands, walked through the front door. My mom wasn't home. My dad welcomed us and then immediately said, "Carlos, come with me. I am going to pick Kathryn up from the pool."

"Should I come along?" I asked.

My dad said no. I nervously unpacked our stuff and putzed around the house, waiting for them to return, praying for Carlos.

Later that night, after a comfortable reunion with my mom and not-super-awkward dinner for the five of us, we escaped to my room, where Carlos reported the details. My dad started with a list of interview-like questions, and when they got to the pool where my sister was waiting, she was quick to ease any tension. She was sweet and loving to Carlos immediately. My dad must have seen the warmth in Carlos' eyes like most people do when they first meet him because there was acceptance, respect, and love from that moment on.

My girlfriends had been asking me about my plans for the bachelorette and bachelor parties, but I was dodging them. It seemed like a better idea not to have one, knowing I wouldn't have the one I had always dreamed of. It wasn't long ago that I explained to John from AA how problematic the concept of never drinking again was based on my bachelorette dreams. If it weren't for that "one day at a time" thing and my ability to leave the door open for my killer pre-wedding party, I might not have tried AA—that's how excited I was for the bachelorette party I had been planning for years.

It had never occurred to me that I'd be planning my wedding four months later or that I'd be knocked up. There would be no trip to Las Vegas, no bumps in the bathroom stalls, no dancing on tables, no shots at the bar, or champagne for breakfast at three in the afternoon.

Damn, I wanted that bachelorette party.

Sitting on the floor in my parents' living room with my girlfriends, looking at the ultrasound image of this alien-like human living in my body, I wasn't in the mood to talk about a no-booze bachelorette party. If it couldn't be everything I'd dreamed of, then I didn't want it at all. Their ideas sounded boring. I hated boring. I wanted bright lights and high-heeled boots up to my knees. But I really didn't. I liked being considerate of my body and my health. I couldn't imagine not taking care of this baby with the utmost care, but this state of mind felt foreign, and I couldn't imagine what a new kind of bachelorette party would look like.

My friends were being incredibly supportive and tolerant of my mood swings. They had accepted my firm stance on wanting to marry Carlos. It hadn't come up since my return from Italy. But I would be lying if I said I didn't care if they were talking about it behind my back.

I felt like I had let them down when I left seven months ago, after Haley's sister died, and I worried I was letting them down again by choosing marriage and putting a guy first. My friends must have sensed my anxiety and reassured me the bachelorette party would be fabulous. And it was. Okay, it wasn't fabulous, but it was really great.

On a sticky, hot, and sunny afternoon, we gathered at a local pottery shop, got creative, and painted flower pots, coffee mugs, and vases—all sober. Afterward, we met Carlos, my dad, and some guy friends at the local pool bar, the Great Dane, where they were having their version of a quickly thrown-together bachelor party, celebrating the groom they had all just met for the first time.

That morning we found out Carlos' best friend wasn't going to make it for the wedding. Danny, one of my best guy friends, stepped in to be his best man. Awkward, for sure, but also incredibly gracious and sweet. When we got to the bar, we found Carlos and Danny playing pool, joking around, and sipping Wisconsin beer. I was in awe of how calm Carlos was through all of this. He was at ease, charming, and lovable. Combining these two attempts at traditional bachelor and bachelorette parties felt natural to us.

If I had the energy to question everything traditional about a wedding, it would have looked a lot different, but everything moved so fast during that time. My friends, some of whom were meeting Carlos for the first time, pulled me aside randomly to gush about how good-looking he was.

It was true. I didn't know he had been running every day and that he had lost weight and buffed up. I was just as surprised as they were. I had always bragged about my catches, although not for the right reasons. But I had fallen in love with Carlos' heart first and his looks second. In the beginning, I was so focused on not having a boyfriend that by the time I realized I really liked his heart and his mind, I was already completely charmed by him for reasons beyond his appearance. His handsome face and beautiful smile were a bonus.

At first, he seemed wrong for me. His responsibility, work ethic, warmth, kind, vulnerable heart, and consideration for others were exemplary. I didn't see myself as all those things or deserving of those characteristics. Yet, I shared those characteristics too, and with time, I was able to see myself that way.

I wasn't turning in my wild, spontaneous side. I was allowing it to show up in different ways. I could be fun and extravagant without drugs and alcohol. I could live life vivaciously and be a wife and a mother. I hoped.

My friends loved him immediately and were quick to tell me.

"He is so kind, Sara. Really, the nicest guy."

"His smile is the most beautiful smile ever."

"He looks at you with such adoring eyes."

"Sara, he's hot! Why didn't you tell us he was so hot?"

"You are both so in love!"

Finally, my family and friends met him and approved. I knew they would, but I also hoped I wouldn't care if they didn't. It was my life. It was our life together, and that is what mattered the most.

After more than twenty years of marriage, I now know that is far from the truth. When families clash, problems that seem minor become insurmountable. My attitude that it was my life, our life, and no one else mattered was naive and lacked experience. It was wrapped in righteousness and the fear that we wouldn't be accepted or approved as a couple. I used righteousness and independence as a way to protect the fear and hide from it. I was scared to show my insecurities.

Thankfully, I had experienced enough therapy and healing spaces to see the value of opening up and sharing my vulnerability. My mom was a social worker, and her brothers were psychiatrists. Growing up, we had a family therapist, and I had gone to a support group for sexual assault survivors in college. I knew the value of therapy, and at that point, I was open to being vulnerable with Carlos, but not everyone.

Trusting in the universe helped me realize I could trust Carlos and our relationship. And thankfully, Carlos was also courageous in sharing his whole heart with me. We started our relationship with trust in ourselves and trust in each other, and that also meant respect for oneself and respect for each other.

I wish there were ways to bottle that up. Trust in oneself is complicated and hard. The messages we grow up with are a combination of parents know best, which translates to they know better than you and respect your elders, which can be interpreted as they deserve more respect than you do. One example of this is when we tell our children to hug a family member, as an order, as a thing one must do. We don't ask the child if they want to hug the family member. And later, when a boyfriend tells us he wants to have sex, we don't always think to ask ourselves if we want it. Many people aren't raised to check in with their own preferences. Girls are raised to obey the rules, not question authority, and not challenge parents or teachers. Listen, be good, sit still, reach for perfection.

What I loved about having my mother as my mother is that she loved me for all of me, not in spite of my shortcomings. Unconditional love meant she loved my entire being with adoration and care, no matter what, even when I was bitchy, rude, or impatient. She also practiced self-love, and her love for everyone around her was so abundant that it was hard not to be infected. In the grocery store, my mom was friendly and kind to strangers. She made friends wherever she went. My friends and I felt lucky to know her.

As I sat on a high stool near the bar, surrounded by my closest people, my mom brought me water and squeezed my hand. It wasn't my dream bachelorette party, and she knew it, but I was happy, and she knew that, too. We shared a strong sense of gratitude for this uncertain path before me.

"I am happy to see you both so happy," she said.

I smiled. "Thanks, Mom. Me too! I still can't believe this is all happening."

"Keep taking deep breaths." She rubbed my back and allowed me to lean into her. The warmth of her softened my already-tender heart.

THE WEDDING MAGAZINES full of inspiration for flowy dresses, flowers, and fancy cakes were of little interest to me compared to exploring the different ways we might create our own ceremony. I pored over prayers, vows, and ways to integrate our two languages and this precious human growing inside me.

The combination of religions, traditions, and cultures in our families could have made it daunting, but instead, it strengthened my opinion that this wedding was all about us—our love. Pregnant, not religious, marrying a Mexican Catholic man, and standing on the shoulders of my two powerful and religious grandmothers and a strong Jewish lineage, I was not confused one bit. I was ripe with a sense of openness, a freedom for us to unite in love.

Bursting with love, connection, and harmony, I imagined our union as the opportunity to bring our full spiritual selves, our families, and our different worlds together and then mix them all up in a creative endeavor to expand the love in the cosmos.

It didn't occur to me that in honoring this gushy, idealistic kind of love, I would be robbing someone of their hopes and dreams for me, for us. It didn't occur to me that my mother-in-law would squirm uncomfortably as I walked down the aisle, outside in nature, far away from the traditions and comfort of her church. It didn't occur to me that my Grandma Harriet would long for a rabbi, the traditional broken glass, and the comfort of knowing that her great-grandchildren would be raised with her Jewish traditions.

None of these scenarios entered my mind. All I focused on was what I wanted, what we wanted, and how to create a unique combination of spiritual openness with a Spanish-speaking translator. Language felt more important to me than religion or tradition. It was non-negotiable that the ceremony be performed in Spanish and English to bridge the families and clarify that our marriage and family would value bilingualism. I secretly hoped it would turn the attention away from the religious barriers. For me, religion couldn't be an integral part of the wedding since it wasn't integral to our relationship. Carlos wouldn't have minded centering his mother's Catholicism out of respect for her, but he also didn't mind rejecting the notion of a "proper" wedding either. Yet to our other family members, what was a wedding without the religious aspect?

Now, I can better understand how much my mother-in-law would have preferred an English-speaking wedding with a Catholic Mass, even without understanding a word spoken, compared to the outdoor wedding in Spanish of mumble-jumble love and a commitment to honor each other versus honoring Christ our Lord.

Chapter 45

THE WEDDING LOGISTICS were going smoothly. Carlos stayed with his mom and sister at the neighbors', and I went to the country house. The chaos wasn't unsettling; I allowed myself to go with the flow.

The next morning, I wandered around in my plaid flannel shirt unbuttoned with my corset-style strapless bra underneath and sweat shorts. It was a gorgeous morning with no clouds in the sky and a warm breeze. I strolled across the yard, focused on the angel my mom had placed amongst the bright black-eyed Susans and purple coneflowers. This is where I sat and meditated in the way Alfonso had taught me. Looking far out across the valley, I found a spot to gaze at. I breathed deeply and listened to the birds, voices coming from the house, cicadas, a car slowing around the curved road. I felt the breeze against my face and the ant crawling on my bare foot. Allowing my mind to relax and my heart to open, I thanked God for my life, for Carlos, my family, and this magical day.

I found myself back in the house as my friends started to arrive. People were bustling about. No one expected anything from me. My friends updated me about the disgusting motel where they were staying. Brooke was concerned about bugs and the potential rainstorm coming our way and shared this all in the same excited breath. Champagne was poured as we moved on to the next stage of makeup and hair. I wasn't jealous. I kept focused on my baby belly and rejected any enticement to get sucked into worrying about the details.

Sitting in a comfortable armchair with sparkling water, I watched the bustle. Barefoot and ready in my elegant, white, simple, strapless wedding dress, I peered outside at the rain coming down and the guests rushing to get under the tent. Yet the rain didn't worry me. The logistics of the day didn't worry me. I had made it here. I knew this was what I wanted, and I was happy to be here. How it unraveled or came together was not of concern to me. I trusted that everything would turn out exactly as it was meant to. My heart was happy. And then, without warning, I felt faint, and my stomach growled. I urgently called out for food. Someone passed a granola bar, and I scarfed it down. With a bit of food in me, I was ready to go, but the wedding was delayed due to the downpour. With the extra time, we turned Madonna up loudly and danced in a circle to the song "Like a Prayer," singing as loud as we could.

Grandma Harriet popped into the bedroom to see how I was doing. "You're sure you don't want to wear shoes?" she asked.

"It's beautiful out, Grandma. Why would I want to wear shoes?"

We both laughed as the rain poured down, and I put my hand on my belly. I wanted to be barefoot. If I was getting married pregnant, I had to be barefoot. I loved being barefoot anyway, and with an outdoor wedding and a rebellious spirit, it felt like the perfect way to walk down the aisle. I showed her my white Puma tennis shoes with a silver stripe and promised her I'd wear them for the reception.

The rain had eased up. Someone knocked on the door to tell us it was go-time. The couple of girlfriends who had been hanging out with us slipped out to find their seats. Brooke and Haley were in matching outfits, a dressy tank top and knee-length pencil skirt in hot pink satin. I was vehemently opposed to the classic bridesmaid dresses, especially for this outdoor country setting. They started out with little baskets of rose petals that they sprinkled across the ground. My sister followed, looking so graceful in a long, buttery-yellow chiffon dress and a bouquet. The harpist began, and then it was my turn, with my parents on each arm and my dad holding a purple umbrella over us until we ducked under the tent. The wedding song played, and we walked down the aisle.

As I stood with my back to my family and friends on our wedding day, I looked up at the two people marrying us—one was stating our vows in English while the other one translated them into Spanish. We were in the United States. I was in my country, with my culture, and this was my language. Your language, mi esposo, is important and valued ... and secondary. The ceremony was translated because it was important but was not led in or by anything of Mexican culture. I had been so focused on the spiritual meaning of this union for Carlos and me and the importance of the language of our love, which at its beginning was in Spanish, that I failed to see how my perspective, with my white culture, was dominating the wedding plans.

But my twenty-five-year-old self felt enlightened and proud of our bilingual wedding. It seemed, from my perspective, that I had incorporated our dedication to both the English language and the Spanish language into the beginning of our marriage. How could I know that the language was just a sliver of the deep cultural thread woven together as we joined our lives? There was so much more than the language we would need to integrate and navigate.

TWENTY-SIX YEARS EARLIER, my parents stood before a rabbi and a priest at their wedding. The two religions seemed united at the beginning of their marriage and were equally honored. What was unseen was the depth of the differences in bringing two different religions together in marriage and the cultures, beliefs, traditions, and a socioeconomic clash. Carlos and I would soon learn how the diversity of thought, heritage, religion, tradition, finances, and values would come to the forefront as we joined our families.

What we did know was love.

My mom and Marcelina held hands and laughed together as they tried to understand one another. Marcelina spoke in Spanish, my mom in English, and their eyes sparkled with joy while I, Carlos, or his sister attempted to translate what the other one was saying. This happened throughout the day as Marcelina talked to my grandmas, my dad, my cousins, aunts, uncles, and friends. She was open and loving, and her kind eyes and beauty mesmerized and charmed everyone. Marcelina and Martha were the best dressed of anyone at the wedding in their formal satin gowns and glamorous updo hairstyles. Martha's warm smile and friendly spirit put everyone at ease. I cherished their presence and the love and delight in their eyes.

Even as Marcelina shivered and pulled her wrap tightly around her, she refused to change into warmer clothes. The evening air chilled her while the other guests sweated on the dance floor, more accustomed to the Wisconsin weather. The rain had stopped after the ceremony. It had been a quick and heavy downpour. I hadn't minded. I loved rain.

Both of my grandmas were fashionistas. Their lipstick was always applied perfectly, their elegant jewelry matched their outfits, and they'd spent many years navigating uncomfortable heels. Marcelina was the same way. My mom followed suit to an extent but also encouraged comfort and didn't go all out on hair and makeup. Her inner hippie appreciated beauty with a natural look, wearing soft-colored lipstick and makeup that was less pronounced but still applied diligently. As she got older, she leaned into comfort a bit more while still showing up at the salon to color the grays. I admired these women, and I brought my flair, having no problem lacing up my cute white tennis shoes, making sure they peeked out beneath my elegant wedding dress for photos, and letting my hair loose as the evening progressed.

"You get better service when you wear lipstick," Grandma Harriet would say. And even though my mom assured me I was gorgeous without makeup, she was always quick to offer me her lipstick before posing for a photo or walking into the grocery store. Beauty and our attention to it were passed down by lineage. Manicured nails, hair appointments, shoe shopping, and the perfect eyebrows were frequent topics of conversation. The difference between my two grandmas was that one would criticize my sloppy outfit or uncombed hair, while the other gushed over my beauty no matter how disheveled I was.

I got my confidence from the women in my family, without a doubt. I know now that is a rare gift. Perhaps it was because my grandmother, my mom's mom, was so adoring and because my mom grew up in the sixties, embracing feminism and challenging the patriarchy. I don't know all of the influences on my mom, but I know that even as a human being with her own self-doubt and moments of low self-esteem, she embodied a love of self and radiated confidence in how she walked and how she experienced the world. And because she was my model and constantly challenged me to look in the mirror with love and adoration of my own self, I embodied a self-confidence that radiated when I walked into a room, too. And because she questioned my critical self-talk and reminded me, over and over again, that it was my job to remind myself that I was enough, I was beautiful, I was smart and capable, and most importantly, I was loved, I grew up noticing negative messaging and boldly rejected it. My mother chose to embody self-love as her aspiration in life, and she succeeded. And I have inherited her gift in abundance.

WE HAD GOTTEN through the day and were enjoying the lights that twinkled inside the tent and lit up the dance floor. Carlos and I were close, grasping each other's hands as often as we could, trusting that God had a world waiting for us.

What I didn't see at that time, I see so clearly now. It takes courage to question and challenge culture and tradition. I didn't do that for our wedding. And yet, wasn't that what our marriage was all about? Questioning and challenging our different cultures and traditions as we joined together to raise our own multicultural family? Our wedding had all the essential white midwest cultural and traditional pieces and none of the Mexican traditions. Maybe there was some overlap, but not because we were aware of it. The traditions specific to the U.S. that we incorporated without thinking about it included the groom not seeing the bride in her wedding dress before the wedding, bridesmaids in matching outfits, a maid of honor and a best man, me carrying a bouquet and then throwing it to a crowd of single ladies, feeding each other the first bite of cake, a cheesy cover band and some first dances, a registry at the local Macy's, removing the garter belt and tossing it to the single men, and the toasts before the meal.

I remember questioning the meaning of "something old, something new, something borrowed, something blue," but I never got an answer. Turns out, the rhyme is from the 1800s in England. At that time, the "something blue" was usually a garter, and the "something old" was passed down from an elder. Both the blue and old items protected the bride against the Evil Eye, a curse passed through a malicious glare that could make the bride infertile (didn't need that). "Something borrowed" was preferably the undergarment of a woman who already had children. Legend says that wearing this would confuse the Evil Eye into thinking the bride was already fertile, and the curse would be thwarted. Apparently, the meaning has changed with time. Now, something blue represents purity, love, and fidelity; something borrowed symbolizes borrowed happiness; something old stands for continuity; and something new shows optimism for the future. I likely would have laughed and not played if I had known all of that. But I was along for the ride and took to the cultural norms like a good girl.

But I insisted both my parents walk me down the aisle so as not to play into some patriarchal indication that my father was giving me away to another man. I was sober the whole day—no champagne, no celebratory drinks with friends at the bar, no glass of wine under the stars by the bonfire. I remember thinking, *Who am I? How did I get here?*

As the night passed, I watched family and friends change under the influence. I saw the small group of friends huddled in the darkness by the big trees, the lighters sparking as they got high. I heard that a couple of my friends were sharing some coke. I felt detached, but I didn't feel alone. I was as close as I had ever been to my own higher power, this growing baby, and a new husband. The detachment was odd, though. Would I lose all of these friends? Was it possible to stay friends with them as my life took a hard turn? If my life was so different now, on August 5, 2000, than it was on August 5, 1999, what would my life be like on August 5, 2001? I would have a six-month-old baby. I couldn't comprehend the immensity of it all, so I shoved the feelings down. Suddenly, I became acutely aware of how tired I was. I had danced, I had laughed, and I had marveled at how well the day had played out. In the same way that stabbing hunger had hit me before the ceremony, I felt an urgency to attend to this blanket of exhaustion. Growing a baby was no joke.

We said our goodbyes, and Carlos drove me to a cabin in my little Celica. His confidence and caretaking nature were stronger than his insecurities about driving the unfamiliar country backroads. We were exhausted but couldn't resist the tradition of lovemaking on our wedding night. And then we crashed hard.

The next morning, Carlos and I met back at my parents' house, where there was brunch and a small gathering of our closest family and friends from out of town. I was more dazed than I was present. I enjoyed the love of my family and friends around me, but my mind kept wandering to what would happen next. I was already planning the trip back to Puerto Vallarta and trying to comprehend how it would all work, not just logistically but as this new person. I had surrendered to God's will, but now what?

The wedding had always been about the ceremony of our union and the opportunity to have a party, bringing together our loved ones (more accurately, my loved ones) to celebrate our new beginning and to gather their prayers and love for us and the new life we were introducing into the world. I wanted that, for sure. And I also believed that the marriage was where the magic was, not the wedding day. Learning to be married in a way that was aligned with our values was more important than an extravagant wedding and not as easy to define or execute. I was up for the challenge. And the challenge of being in a marriage that fulfilled me and becoming the kind of mother I'd be proud to be was invigorating and, at times, overwhelming.

PART THREE

Chapter 46

CARLOS FLEW BACK on his own, and I boarded a plane a week later with a mixture of excitement, anticipation, and trepidation. I didn't want to leave my mom, but I desperately wanted to start my new life. At the Chicago airport, my mom held my face in her hands and wiped the falling tears with her gentle touch.

"I'm scared, Mom."

"I know. It's okay. I promise it'll be okay."

"Come visit me, okay?"

"You know I will."

"Write me letters."

"Of course."

"I love you, Mom."

"I love you, too, Sara." She smiled and added, "Don't forget to eat."

We laughed and I cried more. Gathering as much courage as I could muster, I walked myself to the gate.

Four hours later, as the plane descended, I could feel the shift inside me from fear to excitement. I wanted nothing more than to step off that plane and feel the rush of heat hit my face, smell the ocean breeze, and get busy creating a new life for Carlos and me as a married couple and soon-to-be parents.

It was mid-August in Puerto Vallarta, which meant the heat was stifling, with no hope of an ocean breeze. With the sun burning down, I played a new game of finding the shadiest side of the street to walk on or a bus stop that was near an awning to stand under. Where I used to seek out the sun, I now hid from it. This was my first time experiencing such heat. I avoided walking home up the hill in the middle of the day and learned to rub ice cubes on the insides of my wrists and shower (multiple times a day), without washing my hair, to cool down. I learned to dress comfortably in lightweight clothes and carry a little washcloth to wipe away the sweat. I had been so curious about what it would be like to live in heat like this that it felt more like a fun experiment, which kept my complaints at bay, although that wouldn't last. I wasn't working yet. The next round of classes started early in September, so I had a couple of weeks to settle back in.

There was a lot of settling in that needed to happen. My friend who had sublet my studio during the summer moved out a couple of weeks earlier, so when I arrived at my apartment, it was closed up and musty. The smell struck me, and I couldn't open the windows and turn the fans on fast enough to try and move the air. A good project energized me. I went to work cleaning, unpacking, and arranging items, knowing this was our temporary landing place until we could find an apartment together where we would learn to be married and welcome our baby.

I could hear Carlos coming from half a block away. His keys jangled from his belt, and I peered out the window, taking a welcome moment to pause and wipe the sweat from my face and between my breasts. How could he wear jeans in this weather and not be soaking wet? He walked through the door with a big smile and handed me a large styrofoam cup full of ice and horchata water. I slurped it down.

"¡Amor, mira, mis libros!" *Look at my books, amor!* I grabbed the plastic bag full of books I had stored while I was gone over the summer. Pulling them out, one by one, I showed him the darkened edges, thrusting them close to his face so he could smell the mildew, and I dramatically made a pouty face to clarify my pained heart.

"I'm not sure why you stored books in a plastic bag like that," he said.

"What was I supposed to do?"

"I don't know, but keeping them in a plastic bag just collects moisture."

Right. Of course. "I can't throw them away. I love them so much."

I cradled one of the books in my arms.

Carlos laughed as he took the book and brought it over to the kitchen counter, where he proceeded to clean off the mildew with a soft cloth and instructed me to leave them out in the sun. He worked on it a little bit before I grabbed his hand and pulled him to the bed.

"I can do that later. How are you? How was your day?" I asked.

We sat on the bed with the fan blasting at the highest level. He had brought the *Mano a Mano* booklet, which I had used when looking for apartments eight months earlier. I pulled open my notebook, and we talked through what to prioritize. We needed an apartment ASAP, but we both decided we needed a queen-sized bed first. We would get the bed for us in this studio and then move it when we found a new apartment.

"Let's go now," he said.

"Now?" I asked, thinking about my sticky skin and unkempt self. It was six in the evening, and the day was winding down.

Except it wasn't. Stores were open late. I had never bought a bed before, but there I was, sweaty and giggling as we tried out the different beds at the shop down the hill, within walking distance of my apartment. Some things were so easy to cross off the to-do list, while others were painstaking.

Chapter 47

I WAS IN CHARGE of the apartment search. Eight months earlier, I had been searching for an apartment as a single, carefree traveling woman. Now I was searching for an apartment with my husband and our soon-to-be baby. It floored me, and it made me laugh too. Of course. Of course, this was my life.

The plan was that I would go for the first viewing, and if I found something I liked, we'd go back together. It was a strategic plan but a disheartening one because I couldn't find anything I liked. They were either too dark, which now indicated high mildew potential, too far of a walk from a bus stop, too small, or too cramped. I toured one that was high up a hill in the jungle area, and I envisioned bugs, lots of bugs, falling on me while we slept. Every Friday, a new edition of *Mano a Mano* came out, and I would sit at the restaurant with a limonada, guacamole, and my pencil, circling potential listings and praying I would find us something.

Now that it was the beginning of September, I was settling into a new routine that felt calming, even though we were still cramped in the small studio. I taught a couple of classes at the school and tended to the apartment, my body, and my spiritual practices. I also ached for my mom. I missed my friends. I missed my sister and my dad. I longed for authentic bagels and good pizza. The heat reminded me how much I missed the cooler weather. And I missed blending in.

Out and about in the city, I was constantly checked out, whistled at, and talked to like a tourist or sex worker. Some days were better than others. On the more challenging days, I felt stuck and isolated. In a letter to my mom, I wrote:

What really bothers me about tonight, as I sit here alone in our apartment, is my lack of choices. I have created this world, and there aren't a lot of options in it right now. I do what I can to keep the house in order, then I go to work and afterwards, to the restaurant. I get so tired, and I come home, alone and exhausted. I'm always tired. And alone.

I WASN'T USED to loneliness and isolation and wasn't sure what part of this new life was contributing to it. My teacher friends from the school liked to go out drinking more than I wanted to. They were all single, too, and I had returned from the United States with a ring on my finger and a growing baby in my belly. They couldn't comprehend my new life, which I understood because I couldn't comprehend my life either. They planned weekend getaways while I searched for an apartment with a nursery. I missed my friends back home, but I also knew that I was moving farther and farther away from their reality, and we would likely not be as close if I were back home, anyway. I missed having friends who I had something in common with.

Then there were better days when I was really tapped into my spiritual practices. It was mid-September, and I was about five months pregnant and had been expecting to feel the baby kick. I had been patient in an anxiously excited way. One afternoon I was alone, reading *The Four Agreements* by Don Miguel Ruiz, and found a love prayer that I decided to use for meditation. I filled my lungs with a deep breath and imagined I was inhaling pure love. I let it fill my body, and then I released it with a slow exhale, letting it surround me, in and out. I sat up in my bed with my legs crossed and my back propped against the wall, breathing love in and out. Then I imagined a tunnel of energy and light swirling above my head, entering my seventh chakra through the crown of my head, traveling down, surrounding my baby, and flowing out of my first chakra, at the base of my spine. I imagined my heart was fully open, and the light, energy, and love flowed through me. The top of my head tingled from the energy as I continued breathing. After several minutes, I lay down and put my hand on my belly as I continued to feel the energy swirling around. As I held my hand on my stomach, I felt a distinct kick. I jolted. The baby kicked!

I had my doubtful moments and challenging days, but I had begun to create a toolkit to help me stay on my desired path of living a spiritually inspired life and to build a trusting and fun relationship with a higher power, God, and my spirit guides.

After years of sexual trauma and numbing out, my body and heart were not well connected, most notably during sex. It was like I could tuck my heart in bed, lovingly, turn the light off, lock the door, and then I could face the world. I was skilled at protecting myself and thinking I had control. Carlos and I talked about it frequently. We wanted to experience the love we knew existed when all energies were open and trusting. And we knew I was capable of shutting down. He was also capable of shutting down, and shutting down was not the kind of intimate relationship we wanted.

Chapter 48

I WOKE UP CRYING on September 15, 2000, the night before Día de la Independencia, Independence Day in Mexico. Between missing my mom and missing Carlos, who was always working, and feeling lonely and scared about my life, I allowed myself to cry until I couldn't cry anymore. Journaling helped as I poured my emotions onto the page. Feeling lighter, I showered while Carlos slept soundly. My to-do list was calling me.

After grabbing the newest edition of the *Mano a Mano* for apartment listings, I ran errands. Then midday, hot, exhausted, and weak with hunger, I went to my suegra's house to rest and eat before my evening classes. Mi suegra, my mother-in-law, always had food on hand. When I arrived, the house was bustling. Carlos' sister, Reyna, and her daughters were already eating a strange-looking meatball soup, and they giggled as I tried to understand what was being offered to me. These were the moments I felt like an outsider, even though the family was so welcoming. Well, except for his sister, Judith. She was nice enough but stared at me silently. Constantly. Her eyes always followed me like I was a caged animal that might escape.

My mother-in-law graciously let me use her phone to schedule apartment showings and allowed me to hide out in the back room of the house, where I would nap, grade exams, or sit in gratitude. Sometimes I just needed a quiet place to think in English and rest my brain. Marcelina could have judged me harshly for retreating to the back room or breaking unspoken rules, like putting my bare feet on her coffee table, curling them underneath me on her couch, or, Gforbid, turning down her food. And maybe she did, but she didn't show it. When I left to teach, kissing her cheek, she blessed me with al Padre y al Hijo y al Espíritu Santo. Her love was potent. After class, as the sun set, I joined the other teachers in the plaza for the Día de la Independencia celebrations. The streets seemed empty of tourists and buzzing with energy and noise as Mexicans poured into the plaza.

Mexican flags, red, white, and green balloons, and rainbow-colored papel picado were strung from the balconies decorating the streets and the plaza. Around eleven, the crowd started El Grito (the Cry), a traditional shout of "¡Viva Mexico!" I had learned that just before midnight on September 15, 1810, Miguel Hidalgo called for a revolution, and his speech ended with the now-famous cry "Long Live Mexico!" That triggered an eleven-year war leading to independence in 1821. It was now 2000, and the energy was electrifying as some of the crowd shouted different Mexican heroes' names, and everyone yelled in response, "¡Viva."

¡Hidalgo!

¡Viva!

¡Morelos!

¡Viva!

¡Allende!

¡Viva!

My body tingled with goosebumps, and I put my hand on my belly. I imagined my baby feeling the powerful energy and connection to their Mexican culture. Suddenly, I realized my baby had Mexican blood, meaning I had Mexican blood in me at that very moment. There I was, far away from anything I had known, yet feeling a part of something much bigger than I could comprehend. My baby chose this mingling of cultures, languages, and religions. And now I was receiving the gift of deep connection in a way I never dreamed of. I am carrying a life inside of me, with Mexican blood and a strong ancestral connection to this land and these people that I can never have in the same way. But I can witness and experience the love and power of it all. After waking up sad and lonely, my day had certainly ended differently.

Chapter 49

THE NEXT MORNING, I finally saw an apartment I liked enough for Carlos to see. Not surprisingly, it was a place he had found out about from someone at the restaurant. His restaurant connections were constantly proving helpful. This was also how he managed to buy a whole apartment's worth of used furniture from someone leaving town, including a coveted washing machine. It saved us a lot of time and money to have it all delivered as soon as we got the keys.

Once we decided that the apartment was the one, it happened fast. Within three days, we had moved in. And then, three days after that, we were completely out of the studio, and both places were spotlessly clean. Carlos and I worked well together.

The two-bedroom apartment on Calle Colombia was on the second floor of a two-unit residential flat. A private wrought-iron door led up the side stairs to the front door. The tiled floors were cool and easy to clean. The main room was like a big square that housed a spacious living area with high ceilings, the kitchen with a large counter where we placed wooden stools, and a dining area we ended up using as an office. There was a front patio for outdoor space with big plants in the corners. The back half of the apartment had two large bedrooms, each with its own bathroom. The guest bedroom offered access to the back patio, where the washing machine and water heater were, and a spiral staircase led to the rooftop, where we hung the clothes to dry. I loved the natural light and the spaciousness. It was unusual for something this nice to be within our price range, three hundred dollars a month, but not unusual because the location was less than ideal. On the one hand, it was a short walk to the ocean, close to the bus stop, and not a far ride to the restaurant, but there was no neighborhood. To get to the ocean, we had to cross the main throughway—four lanes of fast-moving cars and mopeds. The area was very commercialized. The property was right next door to a mechanic named Hugo. It was basically an empty lot that he filled with car parts, broken motorcycles, and an occasional car. There was a welding shop, a car wash, and a high school within one block. There were no other homes or apartments on the street.

As a loud banging noise rattled the window, I said to Carlos, "We can't get everything we want, amor," I walked over and shut the window. Our budget was tight. The restaurant brought in roughly a thousand dollars a month, and our rent was three hundred. The goal was for the restaurant to cover us because I wasn't going back to work after the baby was born. I still had money saved from my grandma's gift, and we had received a good amount from the wedding, so we felt solid in our plan. We would use the savings for the pregnancy appointments and birth, which would be out-of-pocket expenses, and hopefully not need to touch Carlos' savings, knowing we would need to buy a car at some point.

AS MUCH AS I loved our apartment and its energy, the light, the spaciousness, and the rooftop for hanging our clothes to dry, it didn't take long to realize that domestic duties were incredibly time-consuming and not that much fun. The dust that accumulated called for daily, or every other day, floor sweeping and mopping. I was grateful we had a washing machine. No one else in his family had one. It was hooked up next to the cement sink bin, which I would've used to wash the clothes if it weren't for the machine. With the clothes washed and wet, I would climb the spiral staircase and hang them to dry with clothes pins. The expansive view from the rooftop of the mountains to the east had a crisp outline that shifted with the light and was multi-dimensional and mesmerizing. They were covered in palm trees and other jungly plants and trees. I could also see them through the small window in the shower and marveled at them every day. There is a mountain view from my shower! I could see other houses and rooftops in the distance and often found myself humming as I hung the clothes in a particular way so as not to require a lot of ironing. Carlos taught me some tricks, and I took mental notes when visiting other homes. I knew there were particular techniques, and I wanted to do my job well.

Cooking was also something that I wasn't used to. The food I cooked was pretty terrible, but Carlos never complained. He mostly ate at the restaurant, but on occasion, when he was home for lunch, he kindly ate the food I made. On Sundays, his only day off, we always went out for dinner.

As much of a feminist as I was, I took on these domestic duties, not because I thought it was my job, but because Carlos had a full-time-plus job, and I didn't. It was a strategic move, which meant I didn't experience any resentment until much later. If the restaurant supported us financially, then I would support us domestically, and I would learn to wife and mother like it was a job, even if being a nurturing homemaker was never part of my dreams.

After a few weeks in the new apartment, I created an altar under the window in the dining room. I set up a long wooden coffee table and dressed it with a brightly colored sarong. I decorated it with candles, photos of family, a framed image of La Virgen de Guadalupe, two little buddha statues, and my angel cards. I kept my spiritual books and the prayer notebook I had created on the table. I wrote down my gratitudes and what I would later call my spiritual evidence list. The list contained encounters I deemed magical or synchronistic to remind me that signs were all around when I paid attention.

It was almost October, and my baby belly was showing. I hadn't gone out with my teacher friends in a while, so I said yes to the Saturday night invite. We started on the Malecon boardwalk, where most of the group sipped forty-ounce beers, and we got street tacos at Parque Hidalgo. Then we went to Roxy's dance club. This was my first time dancing as an obviously pregnant person. Maria and I didn't waste any time getting on the dance floor while the others needed a couple of drinks in them first. I wore a short, flowy, red baby doll dress with small white flowers, and my belly popped out. At first, it was fun watching the people watch me, and I swayed innocently. Then the band played "Maria Maria" by Santana, and I couldn't help but dance a couple of sexy moves. It was wrong. Maria burst out laughing with me, then other people started laughing, and I immediately stopped. I probably could have kept dancing, but I was self-conscious and terrified of being seen as an inappropriate mother. It was another moment where I didn't know how to be in my body or the world.

Back at the table, Diane, another teacher from the United States, drilled me with questions. What weird things was I experiencing? How was my body changing? How was I dealing with fitting into my clothes? She asked if it was hard to sleep, how exhausted I was, what I was looking forward to, and what I was scared about. So many questions and so very interested in the details. It was the first real conversation I'd had in a long time, and she wasn't even a close friend. Her inquiries felt sincere and honest, and I opened up to her in a way I hadn't opened up to anyone in a long time. I went home happy.

EARLY IN THE MORNING, when Carlos climbed into bed, I told him all about my night out. He had his head on my stomach, listening intently.

"Sara, the baby is swimming!" My heart exploded with his childlike enthusiasm. I was so in love with the moment that I never wanted to leave our bed. But the reality was we had very little time together, and even these moments couldn't make up for the long hours apart.

Chapter 50

ALMOST IMMEDIATELY after the wedding, Carlos decided to return to get his high school diploma. With so much going on, I didn't see why he needed to do it right away, but I wanted to be supportive. What I didn't realize was how time-consuming it would be and what kind of strain that would put on us. It was an eighteen-month program. He had class every weekday afternoon from four to six-thirty, meaning he woke up at ten, ran errands for the restaurant, came home for lunch around two, rested, and then went to class at four. He went straight to the restaurant from class and worked until four in the morning, sometimes as late as six.

I called my mom to cry about how much I missed Carlos. Now that we were in our new apartment, we had a phone line, making it easier to talk to my mom more often. But it cost a dollar per minute, so we mostly emailed. She wrote me the most beautiful, poetic, loving emails. I had never missed her so much in my life. It surprised me how I ached for her. My mom listened and consoled me and reminded me that I needed to find friends with whom I could talk.

I REACHED OUT to Lupita, my past student, who was Mexican and a young mom. We scheduled a coffee date and jumped right into the tough stuff, conversing in Spanish while surrounded by mostly English-speaking tourists.

I opened up to her. "Marriage is hard. I knew it would be, but I am surprised that it's the little things that are hard, not the big stuff." The ocean was three blocks away, and I had angled myself so I had a glimpse of the water. I felt my energy boost sitting outside for a midday coffee with flip-flops, sunglasses, and a friend to gush about the intimate details of pregnancy, marriage, and family. But when Lupita started complaining about her husband, I shifted uncomfortably in my chair. I didn't want to be the kind of wife that complained about her husband, but I also didn't want to be the person that pretended everything was always fine.

I went along with it for a while to try it on. I told her about how sick I was of picking up after him and complained about him constantly watching soccer. Lupita listened and vigorously shook her head in agreement. Her anger intensified as she ranted about her husband. I flashed to five years from now and worried that I would become resentful. I hoped this was just a moment in time and wouldn't be forever.

"At least we are on the same page with this baptism argument," I told her, trying to lighten things up. I explained how his mom was relentless about us baptizing the baby while my mom was incredulous at the possibility. Carlos and I had already decided we were not choosing a religion for our child. We didn't want to sign our child up to be part of an institutional system of religion without their consent.

"The big things are easy. We talk openly, and I love how we process and respect each other," I said.

"Si, si! Talking makes it better. Pero, my husband, just gets mad when I disagree, so I usually end up agreeing with him so we don't fight in front of the kids. I wish we could talk more." She had tears in her eyes. I squeezed her hand. I stayed quiet and let the sadness sit on the table between us.

It was a lovely coffee date, but it also left me worried about what I had signed up for. I didn't think I wanted to be a stay-at-home mom, but I was in Carlos' world, trying to make this new adventure work, and there weren't many options for me in the career department. Teaching English was the perfect job while traveling around as a young, spirited woman. But it wasn't something I imagined myself doing as I looked into the future. Was Lupita's life my future?

On my way home that afternoon, I gazed out the bus window, ignoring the stares, while holding my belly to protect it as we rattled down the road. I hated being stared at all the time. But that was unrealistic. Any pregnant woman, anywhere, knows that. We are gawked at, smiled at, stared at. I was not enjoying the moment.

The bus was packed, and it was hot. The windows were open in hopes the breeze would give us all some relief from the midday heat, but there was none. We screeched to a stop, and I instinctively grabbed my stomach and the seat in front of me at the same time to steady myself. The standing riders who didn't have seats shuffled back to more balanced positions while people rushed to get off and more people got on.

That's when I remembered my love burst trick. I picked a person on the bus, softened my gaze, conjured up all the love inside of me, and sent it directly to the older woman sitting a couple of seats away. I wondered about her life, the pregnancies she might have endured, the fears she wrestled with, and the people who loved her. My heart rate settled, and my breathing slowed down. It was going to be okay.

My energy must have shifted, too, because the woman seated next to me smiled and started talking to me. She acknowledged my baby belly with enthusiasm. Mexican culture has a strong reverence for expectant mothers and young children.

She asked me if I knew if it was going to be a girl or a boy. I said no. She looked at my belly with a fixated stare and then told me it was a boy. I laughed.

"That's what most people say," I told her.

Walking home from the bus stop, another woman kindly told me I was having a boy, too. It was becoming a common part of my days.

That night, talking to my mom on the phone, we listed all the myths and rules I had been told:

- If you dream the baby is a certain sex, it's the opposite.
- If you are skinny all over except your lower belly, it's a boy.
- If your baby "rides high," it's a girl. (I didn't even know what that looked like.)
- If it's a round belly, it's a girl. (But what belly isn't round?)
- Don't stand in front of copy machines or microwaves.

- You can't carry anything or bend down when you are pregnant unless you have children or a house to care for, then you are an exception to this rule.
- Eat a lot, but don't eat too much.
- Don't exercise too much, but don't get fat.

"Now you're just making things up," my mom said. I was literally writing these down while we were on the phone talking. She was making dinner.

"Maybe I'm getting a little sarcastic. But Mom, it's true. Everyone says I'm having a boy, so I guess I should prepare for a boy. And everyone is so nice to me. Except not always. Sometimes I get on the bus, and it's packed, and I just assume someone will stand up and offer me their seat because usually they do, but like yesterday, no one did. On two different bus rides!"

"Maybe they couldn't tell you were pregnant," she said.

"Mom, I was sticking my stomach out and holding my hand on my lower back dramatically, so they HAD to know."

"You and your drama, Sara." She was smiling. I could hear it.

"What are you making for dinner?" I imagined her in the kitchen and wished I could be there setting the table and eating her comforting food. Kathryn grabbed the phone and started telling me about tennis or her friends. She sounded happy, and that made me happy. She gave the phone back to my mom.

"I learned how to make black beans yesterday, Mom."

"What do you mean, you learned how?" she asked.

"Like, not from a can. Carlos showed me, and they do taste different, better."

"Oh! Fancy." Growing up on mostly canned food, it was hard for either of us to imagine making beans from scratch, but in Mexico, it was unheard of to make beans from a can. And here I was.

I had told her everything and some things twice already, so we got off the phone. It started to rain, and I rushed up the back spiral staircase to the roof to save the clothes I had left out to dry.

Living in Puerto Vallarta during the rainy season meant I had to learn some lessons the hard way, like how hard it was to dry laundry between downpours. Leaving the windows open was another hard lesson I learned one afternoon as I rushed home in the pouring rain to find my altar soaked, including my framed photos and a photo album. It had been so sunny and dry that morning that I would never have guessed the rains could have come on as suddenly and violently as they did. I cried. I learned.

I WOKE UP in a sweat in the middle of the night, not because of the heat but because of the coke dream I was having. I immediately took inventory of my surroundings, holding my baby belly and remembering my new life.

I'm okay. I haven't done anything stupid. It was just a dream.

Except it felt too close to my old life, the memories too fresh. The one-year-ago-today moments were still full of my old life. I didn't even know Carlos a year ago. I grabbed my journal and wrote:

But time is ticking, and I don't have the luxury to learn slowly. The books stacked on my bedside table, on the living room coffee table, on the kitchen counter are proof that I don't feel like I know enough. Not yet. What does motherhood need from me? How does this child need me to be? What do I need to know to be the best I can be? Can I find a strong thread of responsibility, routine, and steadiness?

No, the negative, diminishing self-talk is not helpful. I have my mom. I experienced a loving mom who also wasn't ready when she gave birth to me. I have that real-life evidence; I can tap into that when I feel insecure.

THE NEXT DAY I went to the ocean alone. In my bright blue bikini, my full breasts filled out the top, and my beautiful belly made it impossible for me to see my toes in the sand. I waddled into the ocean and dove in. The water was cool and refreshing. I imagined my baby in my womb of water and fluids as I held my breath underwater and listened to the quiet, active sounds of the ocean. I floated to the top, on my back, and my belly bobbed up and out of the water while the rest of me was right below the water.

The peace and oneness opened my heart up with wonder. *I love you, little baby. I love you so much. I promise to be the best me I can be for you.*

Chapter 51

WHEN CARLOS ARRIVED home from work around five in the morning, he would shower, washing off the smell of the restaurant, and no matter how quiet he tried to be, I'd wake up, grateful to snuggle into his clean scent. He'd recount his day, report any chismes, *gossip,* and since I missed him immensely, I took what I could get, even at such odd hours. One particular night, about a month after he had started school, he came home bursting with energy.

"You know what, Sara?" he said. "I'm proud of you." He went on praising me for all the things I'd been doing with the apartment, making it a beautiful home, and how well I was feeding the baby and taking care of myself. He told me he was proud of me for being so strong and always having a positive attitude.

The soft light lit up our purple room when he turned on the bedside lamp. I propped myself up, interested in his reflections.

He went on, "You know what else I'm proud of?"

"Dime, amor."

"Myself." And we talked about his hard work in school, navigating the restaurant, homework, and our new apartment. I was happy to see him on such a high. I really was. But I also felt a stab of invisibility. I had been struggling with my own emotional ability to be positive and proud of myself. I always felt like I fell short when I compared myself to him and everything he was doing. Why was I so conditioned to compare myself to others?

AT THE BEGINNING of October, we booked a trip to the Midwest for Thanksgiving. I couldn't imagine my family not seeing me pregnant, and my mom wanted to host a baby shower. The excitement of knowing I'd see my mom soon kept me going through October. I also decided to find a birthing class. Maybe I could make new friends.

Lupita recommended I call Tere, a Spanish-speaking midwife who offered affordable birthing classes, so I signed up.

At the first class, I met Stephanie and knew we'd be friends. She was from Chicago, light-skinned, blonde, and blue-eyed. Stephanie's husband, Alberto, was from Mexico, and they had met during his residency, where Stephanie was a nurse at a hospital. Part of Alberto's doctorate program in the United States was conditional upon him returning to practice in Mexico upon graduation for no less than two years. That's how Stephanie, who never planned on living in Mexico, ended up in Puerto Vallarta, where she still lives today, with her husband and four children.

Stephanie didn't speak Spanish very well, so I helped her. She was amazed by my fluency. It confused me why it was such a big deal for an American to speak Spanish while Mexicans were expected to speak English in the United States.

"Oh, you learned it from your husband." I often heard this when people were trying to figure me out, which didn't make any sense. My husband wouldn't have been able to "teach" me Spanish, in the same way I didn't know how to teach English when I arrived.

There were six or seven women in the birthing class. Most of them attended with their husbands. Stephanie and I did not. Both of our husbands were always working, and without Alberto there, Stephanie struggled with the language, but it never seemed to bother her much. Her carefree and confident spirit was refreshing. It also reminded me how much I loved my competency in the language. I took notes, like a good student, and what I didn't understand, Stephanie did. The mixture of the two languages, Spanish and English, and medical and non-medical, made us a great team with an abundance of giggles. My new English-speaking, pregnant, boisterous, loud, and friendly amiga gave me hope. Maybe I can do this. Maybe I can meet people, create friendships, and find joy here in this new life.

Most of us were in mixed marriages, and the group's makeup included Mexicans, North Americans, Portuguese, Italian, and the scuba diver couple who had lived all over the world and spoke numerous languages. Many were like Stephanie and me, without close friends, family, or much of a community. We all bonded quickly, hoping for friendship. After the second class, Adriana invited us to her house on Sunday night. I was excited to get to know them better and that they picked a Sunday so Carlos could join me.

Driving into Gaviotas, I gawked out the window. It was like a suburban neighborhood, almost a gated community. All the homes were large, with yards and garages. I hadn't seen anything like it since moving to Puerto Vallarta.

"Wow, this is a nice neighborhood," I exclaimed. It was like my regular glasses had been replaced with different lenses that had me seeing a new set of socioeconomic differences around me. I typically felt more economically privileged than the people I interacted with regularly, but driving into Gaviotas that night, I realized I was looking up the ladder. I felt out of place as we sank into the oversized couch in their spacious living room with low lighting, candles, and a Spanish jazz album playing. I remember living in Beverly Hills and going to fancy parties where I would make up stories about who I was and what I did for a living. But at those parties, I wasn't looking for real friendship; I was having fun trying on pretend identities. Here I longed to feel comfortable being me with friends I could trust, but truthfully, I wasn't even sure who this new me was. I squirmed uncomfortably on the couch and reached for a pillow.

We all exchanged "how we met" stories and chatted about pregnancy, births, and babies. As first-time moms, we were excited, scared, and nervous, and the evening was full of laughter and camaraderie. But driving home in the dark, I declared to Carlos that I didn't foresee us becoming close friends with any of them except Stephanie. I adored Stephanie's unpretentious personality and our instant sisterhood connection.

Unfortunately, Stephanie left for Chicago before the class ended. She couldn't believe I was going to deliver my baby in Puerto Vallarta, and I couldn't believe she was going to leave her husband to deliver hers in the States.

"But millions of women have babies in Mexico, Stephanie," I said to her, not having done any research about the millions of Mexican women and infants who also lacked access to good health care in the overcrowded system.

She knew more about Mexico's medical limitations, but neither of us knew how to talk about it very well. I was naive. I liked my doctor. The hospital seemed clean, and it was private.

It hadn't taken Carlos and me long to agree on the hospital or the doctor. We didn't know what we didn't know. The payment plan was agreed upon upfront—one thousand dollars for a natural birth and one thousand five hundred for a C-section. Tere had warned us repeatedly that the doctors in Mexico were C-section happy—more money, easier to schedule, and less time. Listening to her advocate for a natural birth had me motivated and determined not to be one of the C-section statistics. I took on unwarranted confidence in planning my baby's birth.

Stephanie promised we'd connect when she returned so our babies could be friends. They were due within two weeks of each other at the end of January, and we both assumed all would go well and we'd see each other soon.

Chapter 52

OUR MIDWEST THANKSGIVING 2000 trip was successful and stressful, as I'd known it would be. My mom and I packed it all in: a baby shower in Madison, a shopping trip in Chicago, a weekend in Minneapolis, a lot of belly rubs, and a classic Thanksgiving meal at their country house. Carlos graciously went along with it all.

We were also able to go to Haley's sister's memorial service, remembering her life and her death a year earlier. Carlos sat next to me in the church, squeezing my hand as tears flowed down my cheeks. My mind wandered to my life one year earlier, sitting in the therapist's office, with no tears whatsoever. And yet, in the past six months, I had cried a lot. Ever since I found out I was pregnant, I cried tears of fear, anxiety, love, loneliness, awe, and whatever other emotion visited me. Once, while sharing in an AA meeting, I apologized for crying. Afterward, a woman graciously sought me out to tell me how much she cried after she quit drinking because she could finally feel her feelings, and it was perfectly normal. My hormones contributed, too. How was I to know where the tears were coming from? I didn't know; I couldn't know. I could only accept the emotions and allow the tears to flow when they did.

Before flying back out of Chicago, we visited my grandpa, my mom's father, who was in a nursing home in Evanston, suffering from Lewy body dementia. This visit meant the world to me. I wanted Carlos to know Grandpa Milt. My Grandma Harriet, who brought a banana to the nursing home every morning for my grandpa (extra potassium, she said), guided us to his room, hoping he'd be in a good mood. With Lewy body, you never know. Seeing him this way as the disease progressed and his mind deteriorated was heartbreaking, but I wasn't scared. We briefly stumbled around conversations, and then, when my grandpa put his hand on my belly, he softened as I introduced him to his great-grandchild. I imagined a depth of understanding, and the connection to our lineage, ancestors, and spirit guides mingled together in the room with us. This baby was loved beyond this world in ways I would never understand, yet I could completely sense it at the same time—the pure love, the continuity of life and lineage, the power of family.

AT THIRTY-FIVE WEEKS, my stomach bulged, and sleep was difficult. I was exhausted most of the time, which made me think it was reasonable to skip the family Christmas party at my mother-in-law's. From what I could gather, the party wouldn't start until eleven at night, meaning it wouldn't end until four or five in the morning. I couldn't imagine being up that late. But I shuddered at the thought of what everyone would say if I skipped it. I was already worried about how they perceived me, so I put on my stretchy leggings and an oversized top. The days were sunny, warm, and usually in the eighties, while the nights dipped into the low seventies, but up at Marcelina's house, the ocean breeze was chilly in the middle of the night. I welcomed the opportunity to wear socks and tennis shoes while my sisters-in-law were decked out in sexy party dresses and high heels, with heavily applied and glittery eyeshadow, thick mascara, and bright lipstick. I stood out in my casual clothes and natural look, with light mascara, lip gloss, and air-dried hair falling long over my shoulders. I felt pretty even next to their glamour and enjoyed complimenting them as much as I enjoyed being comfortable. To my delight, no one made me feel out of place, and my beautiful belly was adored and celebrated by all.

"It's going to be un niño, Sara!"

"What are you going to name him?"

"When is the due date?"

"How do you feel?"

I fielded all the questions and enjoyed the attention and excitement. For two hours after arriving, we devoured the delicious pozole Marcelina had been preparing for days. Eating together wasn't the same as it was for my family. Here, with so many people to feed, we rotated in and out of chairs in the dining room. When it was our turn to eat, we sat at the table, and one of Carlos' sisters brought us a plastic bowl. Mostly, Carlos' seven sisters served and cleared. The one constant was Marcelina. She was in the kitchen the whole time, serving her family. It was her joy. Salsas, limes, tortillas, onions, and jalapenos were frequently refilled in the center of the table. There was always agua fresca, and the flavor changed regularly. I don't remember what it was that night, but my favorites were horchata, limon, and Jamaica.

It was my first time at a posada, a traditional Mexican Christmas celebration where the family reenacts the pilgrimage of Mary and Joseph seeking shelter. The traditions of Carlos' family at Christmas were so touching, meaningful, and fun. How did Carlos not tell me what it would be like? Likely, because it wasn't a novelty for him. It was what every Christmas was like for him growing up.

Marcelina directed half of the family to stand outside with candles lit and printed copies of the song they all knew by heart. I took a printed copy and stood outside. Carlos was with the other group on the inside. Outside, with the front door shut, we were pretending to be Mary and Joseph, asking to come inside, begging for shelter. Finally, the door opened, and they welcomed us all through song. Then, we packed in the small living room, with some people sitting on plastic chairs and others standing or leaning on the edge of the couch, and went around in a circle sharing something we were thankful for and something we wished or prayed for in the coming year, with the oldest of Carlos' siblings going first and then passing the large candle to the next sibling. After that round, the spouses were included and shared, too. Everyone gave Marcelina a present, hugging before the presents were opened (not afterward, like we did in my house growing up), and we exchanged Secret Santa gifts. Maria Felix had picked my name and gifted me a beautiful statue of an indigenous woman breastfeeding her baby. I knew exactly where I was going to place it on my altar. The laughter, love, and drama that came with a large family filled me with so much happiness. There were probably fifty family members there that night. I appreciated the lack of materialism and could see what future traditions were possible for Carlos and me.

It was also exhausting. We got home just before the sun started to rise. I imagined the children in the United States waking up to gifts under the tree, and I was glad to be where I was. My fingers were swollen, and my feet hurt, but I had weeks and weeks of free time ahead of me to rest. I hadn't signed up for the next teaching session, as it would have overlapped with my due date, so I planned to enjoy my life as much as possible in the next month leading up to welcoming baby love into our home.

Giddy with excitement, my mom arrived on January 23. I was sure the baby would be born on January 27, the day I walked into the restaurant one year earlier, but that day came and went. Having my mom with me to go on long walks and marvel at the beauty of the ocean, the mountains, the palm trees, and the love from the people all around us was calming and peaceful.

"Everything that needs to get done will get done, Sara," my mom reminded me. I was anxious. "Go make a gratitude list." So I did.

"Everything will work out exactly the way it will work out. Let go and let God."

Oh, sweet, Mama. "You're so wise," I told her.

Chapter 53

THIS CHAPTER IS THE BIRTH STORY—the whole damn chapter! If you aren't into birth stories, I'll save you the gory stuff and tell you the short version: It was horrible. But we all ended up healthy and home within four days. My dad flew into Puerto Vallarta early on January 30. We had scheduled his flight thinking he would arrive after the birth, but our baby waited until the last day in January. Mom and I went on an extra long walk that day. She reminisced about the long walk she went on the day my sister was born in 1984. We soaked up our time together, walking as a way to bring a new life to our lineage.

Later that afternoon, the contractions started. I showered, got my bag ready, and we lounged around the living room with mounting anticipation, my notebook on hand to track the timing of contractions. Carlos called his sister for backup at the restaurant, and then I called someone. Maybe the doctor or the clinic. I don't remember, but there is a photo of me talking on the phone, fresh out of the shower with a towel on my head and a long, flowy bohemian skirt pulled up over my chest, with my giant pregnant belly.

Since the contractions were still far enough apart, we decided to walk to the corner taco stand. While we waited for our large order of tacos de pastor, I was hit with an extra intense contraction. I quickly made my way to a pickup truck parked close to us, put my hands on the bumper, and leaned forward to ease my back pain. It looked like I was trying to push a parked Ford F-150. I was calm but not for long.

Around ten that night, we left my dad at our apartment, and my mom, Carlos, and I went to the hospital. As I clutched my belly in anticipation of another contraction, the receptionist told us that no birthing rooms were available. It was a full moon; they had all been taken.

"Wait, what?" I asked.

"When women go into labor at the same time, we can't control that."

"So what am I supposed to do?" I was stunned and outraged. "What are my options?"

"You can go to another hospital," the nurse said.

"What about my doctor?" I asked.

"He can't help you unless you deliver here."

"How am I supposed to deliver here if there isn't space?"

"We have beds set up in the waiting room. And as soon as a room becomes available, we will move you into it."

"A waiting room?" My calmness had disappeared. My scared and privileged self was showing.

I took Carlos aside. My mom was waiting patiently, but she didn't understand anything. Carlos listened to me rage about things for a bit. The pain was overwhelming, and the time between contractions became shorter and shorter. We didn't even know what other hospital we would have gone to.

"Why didn't they tell us we needed a plan B, Carlos? We don't have a plan B!"

So we opted to stay.

Someone brought us to a waiting room that was set up with three individual hospital beds, separated by sheets hanging from the ceiling. The bed in the middle was empty. The closest bed was occupied by a woman resting after a C-section and the birth of her twins. They gave me the bed on the far end, next to the bathroom. The woman in recovery had to walk past me and my bed to get to the bathroom. She also had to be in the same room as me while I labored, and she tried to rest. It was far from ideal.

There was no button to call a nurse. There was barely any space for my mom or Carlos. They brought a bench in for our stuff as well as a chair. This was not the beautiful birthing room they had sold me on. But I was in too much agony, and there wasn't anything I could do, anyway.

It was back labor, and the pain was beyond comprehension. A couple of times I asked my mom to go find a nurse. I refused to let Carlos go. I needed him right next to me at all times. She did her best, but the language barrier was a problem. The nurses were all busy and kept asking my mom questions. No one else spoke English.

After about five hours and such intense pain, I vomited all of the tacos, and everyone insisted I get an epidural. I didn't want one. But I also didn't think I could go on, so after an hour of resisting, I let them give me an epidural. The instant relief was welcomed and then followed by grief and more fear.

I was also pissed. I had this all-natural, no-drugs birth plan, and it was not working out. After the epidural kicked in, the suffering subdued, and because I was only dilated to six, they wanted me to rest as much as possible, so I tried. My mom lay on the middle bed, and Carlos rested in the chair next to me. I went in and out of sleep.

At one point, a nurse came in quietly, and I was sitting up, awake. She didn't say anything to me. She went up to the edge of my bed, took my left leg, and lifted it to check me. There she was at the bottom of the bed with my leg up in the air, and I couldn't feel a thing. It was the most unsettling, upsetting experience.

I gasped. "¡Por favor, dime si vas a mover mi cuerpo!" *Please tell me if you are going to move my body!*

She looked at me with surprise, and I instantly knew why.

"Yo hablo español." I told her I speak Spanish. I felt like I did when I went to get the ultrasound months earlier, like I wasn't there or didn't deserve to be communicated with directly. I wanted to cry. This isn't the way it was supposed to be. I felt alone and scared and wished it could all be over. How was I going to get this human out of me?

By eight in the morning, I had dilated to eight centimeters, and the nurses were happy with the progress. They kept me drugged up and not able to feel much. By nine thirty, they announced I had dilated to ten and were ready for me to go into the operating room to push. While my mom and Carlos were in a different room getting dressed in scrubs, a nurse left me on the hospital bed in an empty hallway. Alone and terrified, I started calling out in Spanish, "Is anyone here? Am I all alone?" and then in English, "Is this some kind of a sick joke?"

Finally, a nurse came and wheeled me into the surgery room with bright, blinding lights. That was the first time I saw my doctor. I don't know why I thought having an English-speaking doctor would help. The doctor only shows up at the very end anyway.

For the next twenty minutes, I pushed. Then my doctor got a phone call and went out into the hallway to take it. I was told to wait. I looked at Carlos, bewildered. "What is happening?"

Carlos calmly kept telling me it was going to be okay. I had to believe him. He was the only thing that made any sense to me.

After a couple more pushes, the doctor returned to the delivery room and declared I needed an emergency C-section. It was just me, my mom, and Carlos with the doctor and two nurses. We had no idea how to advocate for me, so we told him to go ahead.

My mom confessed to me weeks later that she was mortified when the doctor started pulling surgical instruments from a vat of alcohol, like they did even before her time. She felt like she was in a nightmarish scene and was terrified for me. I was behind a large blue disposable sheet and, thankfully, couldn't see anything. I held Carlos' face close to mine and prayed to God everything would be okay.

Everything was fine, technically speaking. The doctor was a C-section pro. I vividly remember violently shaking and barely remember holding my sweet, healthy baby after he was born. At some point, we were rolled back to the waiting area, traumatized by the whole eighteen-hour experience, to begin the recovery process.

Let's talk about expectations, lived experience, and high standards. My ignorance showed with my declaration that "Millions of other women have babies in Mexico, so why can't I?"

Those millions of women who have babies in Mexico also grow up in Mexico and have an understanding of the healthcare system and how unjust it can be; I didn't. My nurse friend, Stephanie, back in the States, was astonished that I delivered our baby in a hospital that didn't have a NICU. Many Mexican women might not have been surprised by what transpired the night I went into labor, but I grappled with feeling entitled to better treatment and incredulous at the lack of resources for everyone.

I DON'T KNOW how long we remained in the waiting room before they brought me into a birthing room. I know it was long enough for me to welcome many visitors to our cramped space. I know it was long enough for me to start to adjust to the reality of the situation and surrender.

I did it.

We did it.

Here was this little human I had waited so long to meet. Ten fingers, ten toes. And such pink, pale skin.

"I thought he'd be brown," I said to Carlos and my mom.

"Maybe he will be. Maybe his skin will get darker, like the way their eyes change," my mom said. She might have been looking at me as she spoke, but I wouldn't have known. I couldn't take my eyes off the baby. Carlos leaned over to smell him, and we all took turns kissing his precious cheeks.

We named him Alexander and called him Alex.

There were visitors nonstop all afternoon. Carlos' oldest sister, Maria, came by in the evening when I was sleeping. When I woke up, she was quietly sitting on the bench across from me. I talked to her for a little bit; she was so kind and concerned. But my brain was too tired to speak, and even more so in Spanish. I was exhausted beyond anything I had experienced. I stayed quiet for a while, trying to avoid small talk, hoping she would get the message that I wanted to be alone and rest, but she didn't. Finally, I asked her to leave so I could sleep, and she quietly and quickly left.

The following day, I woke up in the private birthing room where I should have been all along. It was a beautiful, spacious room with flowers, a comfortable couch for Carlos, a lounge chair for my mom, and still plenty of space for the bassinet where Alex slept. It was the room where I tried walking for the first time after the surgery, where I first showered, where Alex learned to latch, and where I could relax and enjoy our time together without worrying about random people walking by or squeezing more people into the small space. We stayed another three nights, and then they said I was ready to leave. I didn't want to, but it was time.

Right before we were released, we received the bill. Six months earlier, we had agreed on either a thousand dollars for a natural birth or one thousand five hundred for a C-section. They charged us one thousand five hundred dollars. It was a C-section, but I was irate. And then I was devastated.

"There is no way they can charge us full price when I was in active labor in a waiting room. Hell no. This is ridiculous, Carlos."

But Carlos didn't want me to be upset. I didn't want to be upset. I wanted to enjoy being a new mom, and it felt trivial to argue the cost of successfully bringing this new life into the world. But the injustice was too much for me, so I fought it, and they resisted, which meant I yelled and felt horrible. They finally gave us a discount.

"I wanted to pay full price, Carlos. I wanted to be in this room the whole time. I didn't want to have to ask for a discount and argue with them about it. But it wasn't fair." Carlos tried to calm me as I cried, unsure if it was the hormones, exhaustion, or the actual dispute. My parents weren't around for the confrontation but heard all about it later, allowing me to be as irate as I wanted. They didn't really care; they were so in love with their new grandbaby. We were finally home.

Chapter 57

HOME WAS WHERE I could be in my own love bubble with Alex.

Home was where I could heal.

Home was where we could be comfortable together as a new family.

Home with our new baby would mean my loneliness would go away, I would feel fulfilled in my new life as a mother, and things would fall into place.

It seemed to me that seeking a new way of living without escaping in the party scene and meaningless sex was what propelled me into this new life I was supposed to live as a wife and a mother in Mexico. But that didn't mean it was going to be easy. That didn't mean I wasn't going to continue to question everything. And it certainly didn't mean I would feel any sort of confidence.

I wish I had known that.

Home was where we landed after the traumatizing birth, and I had no problem allowing my mom to help with most everything while Carlos took care of me and my healing incision with great care. He changed the dressing and bandages in his gentle, thorough way.

Carlos went back to work soon after Alex was born, and when he wasn't working, he was home with us, attentive and doting on me in every way. He barely slept but was never crabby. I, on the other hand, didn't handle the lack of sleep as graciously as he did.

Ten days after Alex was born, I insisted we all go to the beach on a Sunday afternoon since it was the one day when my mom, dad, and sister would all be there. Carlos was hesitant. My mother-in-law got word and scolded me, asking why I wasn't abiding by the forty-day recovery period. I admitted I didn't know anything about it.

She shook her head in a critical but loving way and gave me a quick overview. After forty weeks of pregnancy, Mexican mothers take forty days where their only job is to rest, recover, and take care of themselves and their new baby. It is a time to bond, heal, and be vigilant with a bland diet and no responsibilities. I acknowledged the benefits and promised that this outing was part of my recovery, for my well-being, and that I would be very careful. She was most concerned about the fresh air and the wind that could make baby Alex sick. So I also promised her I would keep him covered the whole time. I knew better than to argue with her. It was a moment in our relationship when we got to practice honoring each other and our different beliefs and listening with love.

Over the next two weeks, my family members came and went at different times, which felt overwhelming and disconcerting when I wanted to feel calm and steady. But I was insistent on focusing on breastfeeding Alex, healing, sleeping, eating well, and drinking a lot of water. My only job was to keep this little human alive and stay healthy. The nights were tough. All I wanted to do was sleep, but that was clearly irrelevant to Alex.

One morning, a couple of weeks after Alex was born, he was inconsolable, and I found myself consulting one of the ten books I had on pregnancy, birth, and babies, in search of the section that explained how to care for the umbilical cord stump. His little belly button area protruded angrily with each cry. It was scary looking and gross. I begged him to stop crying. He didn't listen. I couldn't wait for it to fall off. But it looked like it might be getting infected, so I read the section which told me very clearly that I should not submerge my baby in water or cover the umbilical cord until it falls off. The book directed me to sponge bathe him to keep him clean and to give the umbilical cord stump as much air time as possible to avoid infection.

Unfortunately, I hadn't read this section before and had already given Alex baths. I called our Spanish-speaking pediatrician and asked to come in.

I walked Alex to the clinic by myself. I wasn't going to wait for Carlos to come with me. The doctor was very stern. I told him about the contradictory information I had read in my book, and he waved his hand. In an irritated voice, he told me to keep the umbilical cord wrapped tightly, and to prove his point, he grabbed some gauze from the counter and wrapped Alex's tummy quickly and not so gently. I told him my book also said not to get the stump wet. He shook his head at me again and told me that the water would assist in helping it fall off.

I went home, pulled between two cultures, and called my mom, sobbing. Exhaustion from lack of sleep and the mental work of keeping this baby alive was too much for me. I told her I couldn't deal with these conflicting instructions, that it all felt impossible, and that I wanted to give up. I didn't care who was right; I just wanted an answer. I just wanted clear, simple directions, and if it wasn't asking too much, I wanted someone else to do it for me.

"Do what? What are we talking about again, honey?" my mom asked.

"His umbilical cord stump, Mom! Something is wrong with it, and I don't know what to do. My book says one thing, and the doctor says the opposite!"

"Oh, honey. I'm so sorry. I'm so sorry. I wish I were there to help you."

She went on to tell me I should take a rest before making any decisions. She said she understood that it might seem easier for an outsider to give me an answer, but learning to trust myself would make my life easier.

I didn't believe her. How would I know the answer to an umbilical cord stump question? And I couldn't rest when there was ooze coming out of my baby's belly button. She was offering profound wisdom, and I was being unreasonable.

"You might not know the answer, but you know how you feel when you contemplate the two different perspectives, right? Which one feels right for you?"

That made it easier for me to calm down and think differently. The next decision became straightforward. I didn't like how the pediatrician treated me, which made it hard to trust him, so I followed my book's advice and vowed never to return. Within a couple of days, the stump fell off.

For a moment, it got easier.

Learning to trust myself was incredibly challenging. My mom's insight helped me through that specific crisis. But at that point in my life, it was more comfortable to look for the answers in everyone else and not trust my own intuition.

Chapter 54

AFTER THREE STRAIGHT WEEKS of visitors, my dad left, and it was nice to have some space for us. I was tired of people, but I was also lonely for connection. I had no idea this would be so hard. Two days after he left, on February 20, my glamorous eighty-year-old Grandma Harriet, my mom's mother, came to visit on her own. Her eyebrows were perfectly and dramatically arched, her lipstick freshly applied and bright, and her hair dyed and salon-styled. She stayed at a hotel nearby, and Carlos arranged for her to visit us daily. She could have stayed with us, but she loved her independence and the luxury of a hotel.

I sat on the floor by her feet the first afternoon she was over. She was on the couch, and I was propped up with the feeding pillow, leaning against the other couch while Alex breastfed. I told her everything: all the pain and hardship of having a newborn, learning to feed him, keeping him alive, trying to get sleep. I remember her loving, kind words. I remember the softness in her eyes, her gentle touch. I remember the energy of her stepping into her role as my grandmother and great-grandmother to my child. She radiated the presence of a queen.

"Honey, Sara, my love. It's hard. I get that. It is really hard. Here's what I want you to know: it'll get better."

I sighed and looked desperately up at her.

"And then it'll get worse. Then it will get better again. And then it will get worse again. And better. And worse. And so on and so forth. Forever."

No. No. No, that's not what I wanted to hear. Yet it resonated deeply.

I could see the ups and downs within a day. I could see it being months or years at a time of better and worse—cycles of life. I was experiencing it. This wisdom was beyond the hardship of a newborn. This wisdom would come back to comfort me in the toddler years, the teen years, and beyond. This was hard, but there will be worse moments someday. And there will be many better moments too.

I didn't want the afternoon to end. Her presence was everything I needed. Her love and adoration of me, Alex, Carlos, and acceptance of our life was a tremendous relief. I didn't know someone could love my son like I did. But my mother did, and her mother did, too. My grandma's love and delight showed in her eyes, which she constantly dabbed with tissue as they filled with happy tears. She seemed almost giddy. I could feel a new connection to her, to our lineage, with the birth of this child. The experience of this profound love was healing for me.

I LOVED BEING Alex's mom—more than anything. I took my job very seriously. I consulted the books and asked people for advice, yet I didn't care if my way of being a mother wasn't how other people thought I should be. Once I decided what would work for us, I was confident until I changed my mind, and then I was confident in that decision. I was open to different ways and wasn't rigid unless I thought being rigid was the best way. The problem with motherhood is that you can't take a break to fill yourself back up, and mothering on empty is a different kind of mothering; it's not as graceful.

After finally having a week alone with Alex and Carlos, I felt grounded for a moment. The absolute awe and exhaustion had me in a constant state of feeling overwhelmed, emotionally and physically.

I was healing. Thank God, I was healing.

But I was also still a mess.

My milk squirted out and nearly choked him every time he ate. The apartment was scattered with boob pads, books, and spit-up towels.

I didn't go out, yet I changed my clothes multiple times a day. The laundry was a constant chore that, thankfully, I didn't have to do. Gemma, my precious, feisty niece, came over three times a week to mop the floors, help with the laundry, and wipe down the bathrooms and kitchen. Not a deep clean, but enough to keep things manageable. Some days I couldn't wait for her to come because I was bored out of my mind. On other days I was so exhausted I didn't want to see or talk to anyone. She was respectful either way.

One morning, I was feeling extra energized. I had showered and slept okay, and Alex had eaten and napped well. I had my groove on. He was sleeping when Gemma came over. On that day, I wanted to know about her hopes and dreams. I wanted to know when she was going to learn English and when she wanted to visit the United States. I just assumed she would.

Everyone does, right?

Wrong. Millions of people have no desire to move to the United States. Gemma is one of them. When I asked, with assumption in my tone, about her going to the United States someday, I was surprised when she laughed at me and said no. She told me she was scared of flying, and there was no way she'd ever get on an airplane.

I was shocked by this. Mostly because I couldn't comprehend how the fear of flying could be such a strong barrier to seeing the world.

THE CONVERSATION clarified that Gemma had no desire to learn English or travel the world. I couldn't feel more disconnected from someone. As she started to clean and laugh with me about other things, I quietly considered what it would be like to live such a simple life. Not simple in that there weren't complications or complexity to her future life. She'd have setbacks, illnesses, and hard decisions to make. But still, there was a simplicity that I hadn't considered.

Alex woke up, and as I sat on the couch breastfeeding him, I thought about what it would be like not to wonder where I'd be in five, ten, and twenty years. To know I'd be here, in this town, maybe even in this apartment, raising humans, being a wife, maybe working, maybe not. The simplicity of knowing—this is it. This is where I am, where I belong, where I'll be—forever.

I loved the wonder of my life in front of me. I loved the idea of being able to go anywhere and do anything. Getting on a plane never registered as an obstacle. That was part of the fun.

Then Alex was full, and I was jolted back to reality. I remembered there was no going anywhere or doing anything right now; I had a baby. I had a husband. I was a mother. My joy faded. How am I going to do this mother/wife thing? What am I doing with my life?

I looked down at this tiny baby in my arms and couldn't believe he was all mine. He was so perfect. I loved him so much. But loving him wasn't going to ensure I loved my life.

Chapter 55

ALEX WAS ALMOST SIX WEEKS OLD when it became clear that my grandpa was near the end of his life. There was nothing easy about getting the three of us to Chicago. The paperwork to get Alex's U.S. passport and birth certificate stating he was a United States citizen born abroad included a trip to Guadalajara, numerous trips to a government office in Puerto Vallarta, translated documents of our marriage certificate and my birth certificate, and what felt like an unnecessary amount of notarized and certified copies of so much paperwork. But we did it. And during that time, it became clear that my life, our life, would be easier if I legally took Carlos' last name. So I did that too.

Being in Evanston, Illinois, for the end of my grandpa's life was healing in many ways. All of my extended family was there, and the sorrow of losing the family's patriarch overlapped with the joy of a new generation that was lovingly passed around and still smelled like a delicious newborn. Funerals are a special time to reminisce, tell stories, and share our memories while also creating new memories and reconnecting. We hadn't booked the trip for more than a couple of days, and since my grandpa hung on longer than anticipated, Carlos had to leave the day before the funeral, having been away from the restaurant too long already.

It was at the services that one thing became clear about how this international lifestyle thing was going to work—funerals needed to be prioritized. Carlos' void was like a shooting pain in my heart all day. I needed him there for me, my family, and his own connection to our new shared family.

That's when we agreed that we would attend all funerals and weddings of our close family—no matter what. We agreed that might mean we would have to make a fast decision to get on a plane, and it might mean expensive plane tickets, but if we were going to combine our families, we needed some non-negotiables.

We talked about our willingness to budget for international family travel to ensure we could live in a meaningful way for our family with our own set of rules. It was part of the book we were writing for our marriage and our family, where we made sure to clarify what mattered, what we would sacrifice, and how we would prioritize and budget. Money was one of the first things we learned to negotiate as a team because it was sensible. We didn't know that prioritizing my mental health would come a close second and sooner than we could have imagined.

Chapter 56

GOING TO THE GROCERY STORE was the most exciting thing I did on a regular basis—a far cry from jumping on a plane in pursuit of a new adventure. Carlos was never home. I was lonely. I wanted to go out, but every day was long, and everything took forever, and as time went on, it became clear that Alex wasn't going to be a good sleeper. He was attached to a boob all the time, and it was hard. It was so fucking hard. My sister-in-law, Martha, came over one afternoon to visit us. Alex slept the whole time. He only slept when I wanted him to be awake and never slept when it was time to sleep. I told Martha to take him home with her.

Then I changed my mind.

I had never felt such an extreme paradox of emotions in my life. I felt infinite, gushy love for this baby. I didn't know I could love the way I loved him. I would get teary-eyed listening to him coo and smile at me. He was precious and perfect in every way. And then, an hour later, or maybe only minutes later, I'd want to throw him out the window. Like, literally throw him out the damn window.

Even now, twenty years later, I hesitate to admit this in writing. I'd say it to your face easily because I know you would see how much I loved him. But typing it out makes me nervous that you might not understand that I would never do anything to harm my baby, but oh my God, there were times I just couldn't deal anymore.

I know not everyone will get this. But I'd bet millions of moms will.

HERE IS AN EXCERPT from the journal I kept for him from when he was two months old:

I got mad at you this morning. I still might be a little mad. This eating and pooping thing is out of hand. In the middle of your eating sessions you start to poop, and it distracts you, so you bite my nipple. Then you quit eating because you are sitting in your own shit. I changed your diaper. You'd only eaten for ten minutes, but you were done. An hour later, you were freaking hungry again. You are supposed to be eating every three hours, not every hour! But it makes sense because you only ate for ten minutes. So you needed to eat again, and I'm pissed about it. I yelled at you, and you thought it was funny. Which made me laugh. Anyone looking in from outside would think I've lost my damn mind.

Another one:

Tonight you ate on and off from 6–10:30 p.m. Then you drove me to tears—no, not you, your babyhood—and finally after I called Papi twice, in tears, you fell asleep at midnight. Glad you are asleep now. Glad I can call Carlos crying when I need to. I love you. Please sleep all night. I know you won't, but it doesn't hurt to ask.

THIS WAS ABOUT the time when I started thinking it was a good idea to drink again. I would wake up from a dream where I had been smoking cigarettes, snorting coke, and slamming shots, only to find myself torn between that life—the one that I hated and had struggled to give up—with this new life that I also hated yet couldn't dream of giving up.

I felt confined, stuck, exhausted, lonely, and desperate for a drink.

A drink would make it better.

It would take the edge off. It would be something I could look forward to at the end of a grueling day.

I started daydreaming about a night out with friends and shots of tequila. I didn't want one drink to ease my mundane life; I wanted to escape the whole damn thing. I could go out, get drunk, and then come home to this life and maybe handle it better. I attempted to justify drinking again in my journals, right next to the entries about the exhausting mood swings and my concern that I was losing my mind.

I AM ALMOST certain that this type of journaling and a new understanding that I could have a love-hate relationship with my baby and not be a horrible person came from the book that I claim saved my life, *Operating Instructions: A Journal of My Son's First Year* by Anne Lamott. I'm not exaggerating when I say it profoundly impacted me, kept me on my healing journey, and got me back to AA meetings.

Anne Lamott was a recovering alcoholic and also had a surprise pregnancy. The book conveys her journey through the first year as a single mother struggling in even more ways than I was with the never-ending crying, breastfeeding, diapers, and the journey of self-reflection and recovery. Reading her story helped me understand that I wasn't alone or a terrible mother for wanting to escape.

Sometimes Carlos would come home from the restaurant drunk. I could tell when he had been drinking by the clanging sound of his belt as he loudly undressed. Even after he showered, I could smell the booze oozing from his pores as he crawled into bed. I always pretended to be asleep because he was gross when he wanted drunk sex. These were the nights I contemplated asking him to quit, too.

But within a couple of weeks, I went from disgusted by his drunken nights to jealous. My desperation for life beyond breastfeeding, sleep training, and laundry was something I could name. The loneliness, depression, and fear were something I could barely admit even to myself but were becoming undeniable. I certainly couldn't explain it to Carlos. Guilt hijacked all emotions when it came to acknowledging the internal turmoil that racked me.

A couple of months after Alex was born, Carlos and I went out for our Sunday date night to a dimly lit Italian restaurant with candles at every table, a formal waitstaff, and a hushed air.

I was relieved to be out in the world without a baby on my boob.

I was relieved not to have to deal with bedtime.

I was relieved to be waited on for the night.

I had made it through my grandpa's funeral and traveling with the baby, and I wanted to celebrate. I deserved a reprieve. The waiter brought us the wine menu, and as Carlos motioned that we didn't need one, I gently put my hand on his and said, "Wait. I want to look at it."

With compassionate eyes, Carlos asked me, without using any words, if I was okay.

"I don't think it's a big deal for me to have a glass of wine," I said.

He replied with a simple, "Okay." And we looked at the menus and out the window at the beautiful vista of a charming street with walls covered in luscious plants and vibrant flowers. Dimmed street lights highlighted the cobblestone streets and swaying palm trees.

I was tired of doing everything right. One glass of wine would help me relax, and then I could stop wondering how Alex was doing with the babysitter and maybe enjoy myself. I deserved it. It's not like I would start drinking again and hitting up the clubs. I had a baby. That would be impossible. One drink every once in a while would be fine.

I ordered a glass of wine. The first sip was like a mini fantasy world coming to life in my mouth. The heat of the wine trickling down to my stomach was even better. The aroma. The feel of the glass in my hand as I tilted it to my lips.

I had finished most of my glass by the time our dinner came and felt slightly buzzed. I caught the waiter eyeing my glass and knew what was coming. "Si, uno más, por favor," I answered, avoiding eye contact with Carlos.

Yes, one more. I was giddy, knowing another was coming.

Midway through dinner, I excused myself to go to the bathroom. Immediately I felt unsteady on my feet. Fuck. I'm drunk. How did I get drunk off less than two glasses of wine?

On the way to the car, I wobbled on the uneven cobblestone street, and my face flushed as Carlos instinctively reached out to make sure I didn't fall. I laughed and did a silly, sexy dance to show him I was fine.

I don't remember the drive home. I don't remember the conversation we had. I do vividly remember how good I felt being me, finally.

Chapter 57

THE NEXT MORNING, as I breastfed Alex in the rocking chair, the scene might have appeared quiet and even peaceful. But the noise in my head was loud. I bounced between self-criticism and scheming about where to hide the bottles of wine I planned to buy.

Later that afternoon, I left Alex with Carlos at the restaurant to attend my first AA meeting in months. As I rode the bus to the meeting, I noticed the warm sense of familiarity and comfort. I looked almost the same as I had ten months earlier, back to my pre-pregnancy weight, with my long wavy hair in a messy bun.

It felt nourishing to listen to the opening protocol, the reading of the serenity prayer, "God grant me the serenity to accept the things I cannot change, the courage to change the things I can, and the wisdom to know the difference." Then someone read from Chapter Five, "How it works," and the regular announcements of new meeting times, and I relaxed even more in the sticky plastic chair.

During that first meeting back, instead of just listening to everyone else share, I was quick to open up about my experience as a new mom in a foreign country, my loneliness, my desperation of not knowing what I was doing or how to be a good mom, and my desire to drink. The words gushed out. The tears flowed. I wanted to drink, and I was terrified.

IT IS RECOMMENDED that new AA members not make any significant changes in the first year of sobriety. I had moved to a new country, quit drinking, gotten pregnant, married, and had a baby—all in a year. I had silently acknowledged my one year of sobriety, but I didn't think it counted because I had been pregnant most of the time. A huge sense of relief overcame me as I shared with a room full of strangers. All around me, heads nodded with compassion and understanding. A woman brought me some tissues and squeezed my shoulder.

That woman was Faith. Faith! She found me immediately after the meeting. If I had been trying to sneak out, which I wasn't, she likely would have run after me. She was determined to make sure I knew how much she could identify with everything I shared and how grateful she was that I had come to a meeting. She didn't ask me if I wanted her number; she just wrote it down on a scrap piece of paper and shoved it in my hand.

Faith was older, maybe in her early forties. She had a deep tan, like she had been in the sun her whole life, and a short, spunky haircut on her petite, fit body. She reminded me of my cousin Toni, who made everyone feel welcome, comfortable, and seen. Faith insisted on meeting Alex and encouraged me to bring him to any meeting, anytime. As I left, feeling like I belonged, I made a mental note of the meeting times she attended. I wanted to see her again. I had no doubt that my angels were sending me a loud and clear message. I gave a nod to the dark sky. I was going to be okay. I was loved and cared for, at least for today. I needed to keep coming back to these meetings. I wanted to be sober.

"How was it?" Carlos asked as I scooped Alex into my arms.

I wondered if he thought I was losing my shit as surely as I felt like I was losing my shit. I wondered if he worried I would do something stupid with our baby. I wondered if he regretted marrying me.

"It was really good. I'm glad I went. I'll for sure go back again," I said. "How was Alex?"

Nothing else mattered as Alex snuggled his face into my neck. He smelled so good. I had only been gone two hours, maybe less, but I had missed him with all of my being. My breasts had started to fill again. As we got comfortable at a corner table, Claudia offered to bring me chicken quesadillas and a limonada while I nursed him. The wooden chair creaked underneath us, but I had gotten better at being able to nurse him anywhere, even when my milk aggressively shot out at him the minute he got close.

APRIL 20, 2001:

You are funny as shit. You have these over enthusiastic smiles and you squeal. You squeal! Like I wasn't already madly in love with you, and then you flash me one of those gummy smiles and it's like being hit by a lightning bolt of pure love.

APRIL 21, 2001:

Why don't you like sleeping more than two hours at a time, you punk ass? Is it the exhaust from the car mechanic next door seeping through your bedroom window? Or the banging across the street? Are there mosquitoes in your room? Or do you just hate me? I seriously don't know why you won't just sleep longer than two hours at a time. I. AM. SO. TIRED

I WOULDN'T SAY I was getting the hang of mothering a baby at all, but I was reading all the books, and I had joined an online mom's group. I felt completely inept most of the time, and being in chat rooms with other struggling moms eliminated the isolation. Meeting other women at the AA meetings who told me about how hard it was for them was also helpful. But mostly, people would coo at my perfect little baby, who really was perfect, and tell me to enjoy it because it goes by so fast.

Oh, the comments we would get when we were out in the world. Everyone wanted to pinch Alex's cheeks, touch his head, and exclaim, "¡Mira, el guëro chulo! ¡Que bonito, tu bebe!" Which basically means, "Look at the cute, fair-skinned, beautiful baby!" Everyone complimented his fair skin, and I cringed every time. It felt so inappropriate to gush over how white his skin was. Didn't they know we weren't supposed to talk about white skin being more beautiful, better, and desirable?

Yet, it never occurred to me how inappropriate it was for me to make comments about having brown babies. I noticed colorism in others but hadn't learned to see it in myself yet. I would later learn about how harmful the fetishization of mixed-raced babies and children is and how much I needed to learn about raising mixed children beyond my colorblind and idealistic way of seeing the world. At that time, I knew what made me uncomfortable, but I couldn't always understand why. I was endeavoring to raise a bilingual child without understanding the challenges of being a mixed-race person.

During my pregnancy, I read a couple of books about raising bilingual, multicultural children, and both were more celebratory and instructional than thought-provoking regarding systemic racism. The book I used as my guide offered a model where each parent speaks to their child in their native language. That way, the child would hear both languages regularly in the native tongue.

I took this recommendation very seriously. I would speak Spanish to someone and switch to English when I turned to Alex. If, on occasion, I spoke to Alex in Spanish because we were with non-English-speaking family members or friends, I would repeat myself in English. I was disciplined in my practice.

If Carlos spoke to Alex in English, I would give him the side eye or flat out remind him to speak our native language to Alex. This model made sense to me, and because we were living in a Spanish-speaking world, and I was the main caretaker, Alex was likely getting a little more English at home but a lot of Spanish out in the world.

This changed later. I wish I had been able to correct course, but life was busy. We don't know what we don't know until we do.

Alex and I stuck out in the crowd. We constantly heard how he was the most beautiful baby in the world, with the most beautiful white skin, and how brave I was, and what great Spanish I spoke. The praise and adoration for both of us was sickening. We were mostly treated like we were special for no reason at all. People love babies in general, but Alex's fair skin and me being a gringa raising a baby in Mexico and speaking fluent Spanish threw people off.

I couldn't blend if I tried. And I tried—all the time.

I continuously sunned myself to be as brown as possible and refused to speak English. I didn't want to be seen as a tourist or an exotic American mom. I mostly failed, but I never gave up trying. Being treated better than others made me uncomfortable and skeptical of how the world worked. I lacked much education and understanding of what I was experiencing and had no idea how to communicate my unease.

ONE AFTERNOON, Carlos came home from running errands, and as he wiped sweat off his face and stripped off his shirt, he told me about an encounter with his sister, Maria. He had seen her leaving a party store with big bags full of party supplies. They talked for a bit, and then Carlos asked if there was a party he didn't know about. Between nervous laughter, Maria admitted that there was. I don't remember what specifically he said about the rest of the conversation because I was so shocked. I only remember Carlos telling me that Maria was upset with me for asking her to leave the hospital room after Alex was born.

I couldn't imagine that all this time she was upset with me. Carlos shared the surprise and hurt as Maria was one of his most beloved sisters. Seeing his hurt, I made it my mission to make things right with her. I didn't want to be the rude American girl who creates family drama, but mostly, I wanted them to like me.

The following Sunday, we went to Carlos' mother's home, knowing there would be other family members visiting, and I prayed Maria would be there. She was. And I was surprised at how she pretended everything was fine. If Carlos wouldn't have told me she was upset, I would have never known. I didn't grow up with covert communication, so this was new territory for me. After salutations and the oohing and aahing over baby Alex, I asked Maria if we could talk in the other room.

We sat on the edge of Marcelina's bed. The room was dark and cool. I told her that I knew she was upset with me, and she told me that indeed she was. She told me how much it hurt her feelings when I asked her to leave, and that family is supposed to be with family. After a pause, I asked if I could tell her what it was like for me. She nodded and listened as I told her how different my culture is from hers.

I told her how hard it was to bring that baby into the world, how horrific the labor was, and how exhausted my brain was from navigating it all in Spanish. I wanted to be alone, not because I didn't want her there, but because I needed to honor my body and my experience. I apologized for hurting her feelings. Then I told her that I wanted us to be honest with each other and that I loved her and hoped she would tell me the next time I did something offensive.

"Because I'm sure there will be a next time. There is so much I still don't know," I said.

I said it all in Spanish, and she heard it all. She told me she was sorry. I told her I was sorry, and we hugged. Later, I explained to Carlos that as much as I hoped there wouldn't be continued drama behind my back—behind our backs—it was likely unavoidable, and we should prepare for it.

PART FOUR

Chapter 58

ON ONE OF OUR SACRED Sundays in May, while Gemma was babysitting, Carlos and I went to dinner and dove into a brutally honest conversation about how things were going. I was relieved to have AA meetings to keep me steady and offer new friends. And I was relieved that Carlos had decided, on his own, to quit drinking to support me. I didn't realize how much it helped. But I still felt like I was failing miserably, and Carlos was frustrated because he was working so hard, yet money was always tight. The restaurant was not bringing in enough money and required a lot of him. It would be one thing if it were busy, but for hours at a stretch, he'd be at the restaurant with no customers, wishing he was home with us. I could see the pressure, fatigue, and concern in his eyes.

I went right into fix-it mode, not wanting to see him struggle. "I can get a job," I said. "Or we can move and get a less expensive apartment."

"What would it be like if we moved to the States?" he asked.

I had not seen that coming. But I had wondered the same thing. We spent the next couple of hours talking about it. We laughed as we imagined Carlos golfing with my dad's mom, Grandma Bette. We cringed as we thought about the winters. And I got really sad thinking that maybe we wouldn't raise our family by the ocean in Mexico. Moving back to Madison had never been part of the plan, yet here we were talking about it. We'd be moving toward something new for Carlos and back to something old for me. Could I reframe it and see it as moving toward something new for us and not backward for me?

I missed my mom so much. I couldn't help but get excited thinking about us gushing over Alex together. I wanted her to know him and him to know her. It surprised me that I was more open to the idea than I thought I would be.

Maybe I could go back to school and get my master's degree.

Maybe I could have a real career.

Maybe I wouldn't be as lonely.

Maybe it would be easier.

Carlos' shoulders seemed to relax after opening up about the financial pressure and the frustrating hours he was putting in. He still wanted to try and make the restaurant work, and I wanted us to be a real team.

I didn't want him to feel like he had to take care of me. I could participate in the growth and stability of our family, too. Our next step was for me to explore getting a job and for us to think about maybe moving to Madison at some point in the distant future.

The next day I called my AA sponsor, with whom I had started working the steps, and spilled all sorts of scenarios out to her. She stopped me quickly and instructed me to get my ass to a meeting.

The conversation with Carlos had overwhelmed me and resulted in a restless night. I was glad for the assignment and went later that day to a meeting. My sponsor, Nora, and I met at a coffee shop the next morning. Alex was sleeping in the stroller, and I anxiously checked on him throughout the hour. She was an older, frail woman with sharp opinions, challenging physical disabilities, and a passionate love for the beach, the sun, and the Mexican way of life. It was midday, and the heat was intense as she guided me through the exercise of listing my faults: fearful, insecure, distrustful, judgmental, critical, righteous, controlling, demanding, snappy.

We talked about noticing them when they came up. We talked about the risk of making a move when I still wanted to drink and hadn't worked through the program completely.

We discussed my need to look at the past and find where I was at fault. We talked about whom I needed to apologize to and make amends with.

And we talked about the ways I would try to repair the damage.

There was a lot of blaming the disease for my actions and seeing myself as broken and weak. I came to believe that the only way to stay sober was to do exactly what AA told me to do. I had to follow the system like everyone else. It didn't occur to me to question who created AA and for whom AA was meant to serve—white men. AA was good to me, but I'm glad that today there are many other ways to explore how alcohol is abused and how to break free from addictions.

DURING THE FOLLOWING WEEKS, I began exploring getting a job. Mostly, this entailed finding someone to take care of my baby, who was now almost five months old. Again, I went down a path of discovery that opened my eyes once more to the differences in our cultures. The daycare centers had a student-teacher ratio of twenty-five to two. That spread was unfathomable to me. As I discussed daycare criteria with my online mom friends, I realized I wasn't going to find the same options in Mexico that they had in the U.S. unless we could afford the expensive private options, which we couldn't. I didn't mind that we couldn't afford a full-time nanny or an expensive American school, but that didn't mean I would enroll Alex in an overcrowded daycare center. It was apparent to me how privileged I was and how much I missed having a community with relatable problems. Carlos' family didn't understand my concerns or why I wanted to work outside the home. The birthing class moms couldn't relate to our financial situation. My online mom friends in the U.S. couldn't relate to my life in Mexico.

Even with the multiple disconnects I was experiencing, Stephanie was one bright light amidst the darkness. Even if we were in different socioeconomic places, I felt comfortable with Stephanie at a core level. By this time, in May, she had returned from the States with her healthy baby girl, and we had reconnected. Looking back, I'm sure I had postpartum depression, but that wasn't discussed. I did the best I could, but mostly I was miserable. I was sure I wasn't cut out to be a stay-at-home mom, but I also couldn't imagine leaving Alex with anyone, and we were still breastfeeding. I cried about all of this to Stephanie, who also cried to me about her hardships. And we laughed a lot, sometimes together and sometimes at each other. She laughed at me as I complained about my milk squirting all over the place, and I laughed at her stories about her language mishaps with her house cleaner.

One night she called me in tears. It had taken her longer than usual to get Ali to fall asleep, but finally, with leftover frustration and a gnawing stomach, she went to the kitchen to tear into the pizza that had been delivered earlier. She stopped in her tracks when she saw the trail of tiny ants in a perfect line across her counter, straight to the pizza box. She opened the box to find the pizza swarming with ants.

You should have heard the drama in her voice as she sobbed, trying to explain to me through her tears how absolutely tragic it was. I knew her frustration and desperation, but I could barely contain my giggles. It was like the ants had a personal vendetta against her. I'd experienced similar incidents. This was life in Mexico. The sound of a scurrying cockroach in the middle of the night. Waking up to find an almost dead one, still twitching from whatever poison it had ingested, in the middle of the bathroom floor. Stephanie made that time in my life a little less lonely. Still, no matter how long it's been since we've talked, we pick right back up with loud laughter and dramatic tales.

Being able to cry to Stephanie about the most mundane details of my life and trust her with my most intimate thoughts without feeling judged still didn't make me feel comfortable about our financial differences. She was married to a doctor, and they had a nice apartment with a pool and a full-time house cleaner who also cooked for them. I was jealous. Seeing how they lived made me wonder what it would be like if I were to get a job that paid well. I wondered if we could stay in our apartment, even though the fumes and noise were assaulting at times, instead of moving to a less expensive, smaller apartment. I didn't want to live on Carlos' income alone. Struggling with money and lack of time together made me ask who I was in this equation, who I was supposed to be, and how to fit into this new life.

Chapter 59

CARLOS AND I MIGHT have been struggling with money, but my side of the family had an abundance of it. They didn't act like they had a lot of money, but it's all relative, isn't it? We determine value by how much money we have and how much stuff we accumulate and rarely question the capitalist economy that benefits from a scarcity mindset, imagined or real.

At age twenty-six, I didn't understand what I do now about systems of oppression; I could only see the surface view. But I could sense the tension around money and the false narrative that money and happiness were tied. And I was aware that my side of the family offered a security net, making it hard to imagine not having a safe place to call home each night. A lifetime of socioeconomic privilege comes with a lack of understanding of poverty, the distress it causes, and the impact of that experience.

GRANDMA HARRIET had spent months planning the annual family reunion, and Carlos and I were excited to go on an all-expenses-paid trip to the Outer Banks of North Carolina for a week at the end of July in 2001.

Prior to the trip, I was in charge of ensuring all our travel documents were in order, which was no small task. Carlos would be traveling as a Mexican citizen with a visitor visa, which he had obtained before our marriage. I would be traveling as a U.S. citizen but needed to make sure my FM3 work visa was up to date so I could exit and return without any issues. Luckily, I had stayed in close contact with my old teaching job at the university, and they wrote a letter confirming I was still working. Alex would be traveling as a U.S. citizen with a U.S. passport we obtained in Guadalajara. Then we needed copies of both his birth certificates (the Mexican one and the born-abroad one), our marriage certificate (which was in English), and a certified copy of the marriage certificate in Spanish. I might have been organized and efficient, but I was also flabbergasted by all the requirements. Learning how the systems worked made me wonder why I had never questioned them before.

Travel and immigration status were constant conversation topics. One night, Alex and I were at the restaurant with some of my friends from AA, and the discussion turned to travel. Stories flew around the table. Carlos and I were new to this world of navigating the systems, and we listened intently as my friends shared their tips and tricks to get around certain rules and advice on traveling safely between the two countries. That was a benefit to having friends with dicey backgrounds; my AA friends had incredibly dicey backgrounds. (When Carlos had traveled to Wisconsin for the wedding, he had been instructed to tell a very specific and brief story to the immigration officers that most certainly did not include a trip to get married!) We had to graduate from the notion that because we were married, we shouldn't have issues traveling back and forth as a family. Now that we knew more, our fear of being separated became undeniable.

When Carlos first applied for his visitor visa, before we had ever met, he, like millions of other Mexicans, had to prove to the U.S. embassy that he had enough of his own assets in Mexico to show that there wasn't a risk of him not returning. Having a girlfriend or a wife with U.S. citizenship status was a red flag, as was any potential job opportunity. The shorter the visit, the better.

We put together our plan for our family reunion trip. He would say he was traveling alone to North Carolina to vacation with friends for a week. I would say I was traveling with my son for a family reunion. To pull this off, we had to agree on a couple of things. On the actual flight, we would sit together, but we wouldn't be overly engaged as a couple. We also weren't going to pretend we didn't know each other; we were told the flight attendants don't get involved. But the minute we walked off the plane, we had to embody our stories and not deviate. Carlos told me that if anything happened and he was pulled aside or detained, I must continue forward. He told me it would be worse if they found out we had been lying. He didn't need to tell me that. But I only agreed half-heartedly because I just couldn't imagine anything going wrong. I felt righteous rage bubbling up at the mere mention of immigration status. I was a hippie at heart and didn't believe in borders.

I couldn't tell that Carlos was nervous. He hid it well. I tried to get nervous because I thought that would help me stay in my story, but I walked confidently to the line for U.S. citizens. Carlos walked to the line for non-U.S. citizens. I sailed through, keeping an eye on him. I was supposed to be making my way to the baggage claim, but Carlos was still talking to the immigration officer. I stopped to fuss with the baby and kneeled down, pretending to be searching for something in the diaper bag, waiting for Carlos to pass through. But he didn't. Two officers escorted him to a nearby room and closed the door. My mouth dropped open, and I stood up abruptly, my heart beating rapidly. He had told me to keep going, but I couldn't. *They can't take my husband. We belong together.* What was happening? We were just going on a weeklong vacation. His documents were real and current. What was the problem?

Instead of going to baggage claim, I walked to the elevator right in front of the room he was in and paced back and forth until he finally came out. He walked right past me like he didn't know me. I tried my hardest not to run to him. He was playing the game too well. I tried talking to him at baggage claim, but the dirty look he gave me shut me up.

It wasn't until we were on the plane from Dallas to North Carolina that he shared his frustration.

"Sara, you made it worse. I saw you pacing by the elevator."

"But why did they take you?"

"I don't know. They probably wanted to make sure I was telling the truth. I'm not good at lying. I was so nervous. I'm sure they could tell something wasn't right, but it was fine. I stuck to the story, and finally, they had to release me."

I was upset that we had to lie in the first place. From my perspective, the system lacked common sense and compassion. I was appalled that I couldn't have just walked in there, grabbed Carlos' hand, and marched out. He was upset that I had put us all at risk. We didn't have the history together or the communication skills to understand each other. We dropped it and didn't talk about it again for many years.

WHEN IT DID come up thirteen years later, in 2014, I brought it up, and we stepped into some hard conversations. I had been learning about my whiteness and was doing the ugly work of examining my privileges. Understanding that the system was meant to protect and work for me, not against me, was apparent in how I showed up throughout my life and had been on full display that day, long ago, at the Dallas airport. I had the right to be in an American airport without being questioned or hassled, and if someone wronged me, I had the power and privilege to call a manager or an attorney. I was a white woman. And my whiteness, like my femininity and damsel in distress act, all played into a privilege I had never learned about, talked about, or fully understood until I was close to forty years old.

Carlos acknowledged that he hadn't liked my attitude, but he didn't know how to confront me about it. His childhood in Mexico hadn't included conversations about racial profiling, white supremacy culture, or systems of oppression, and neither had mine. We were unsure how to be in these conversations but knew they were important.

AFTER THE AIRPORT INCIDENT, I paid more attention to policies, procedures, and laws. I saw how the systems in place could harm our family, not protect us. I was raised to feel protected, and now I questioned who was really protected and at what cost.

And the rest of the trip in North Carolina? Lovely, thank goodness.

Chapter 60

I WAS HAPPY TO RETURN HOME to our normal routine: going to the grocery store and the beach and finding shade from the beating sun. It was incredibly hot. It was the kind of hot that required a couple of outfit changes and three showers a day. It was the kind of hot that made it hard to do anything and kept me hidden inside our apartment, specifically in the one room with a window air conditioner. Trapped. Even so, I managed to continue my search for childcare and a job in real estate, where the money would be better than teaching. It didn't take long to realize I wouldn't be able to find a daycare that fit my high standards, so I started interviewing nannies in hopes that some future job would cover the cost and then some.

AFTER SEARCHING for a couple of weeks, we hired Marisol. She was in her late teens and, like many young Mexican women, already had a lot of experience with babies and young children, between younger siblings, cousins, nieces, and nephews. Her role was to help around the house and hopefully become Alex's nanny when I started working. It had been recommended that I make sure we had reliable help for a while before I found a job; apparently, it was hard to come by. I was following directions, and even though it made me nervous paying for help without having a job yet, I hoped we were on the path to a different way of life, with me earning a decent income.

I liked Marisol right away. She was kind, caring, and respectful. She loved Alex immediately, and watching her play with him and enjoy him as much as I did gave me the greatest pleasure. It meant Gemma wouldn't be helping anymore, so we promised her she would be our designated babysitter for our Sunday date nights. I was excited to have more time to explore work opportunities. I can't say I didn't worry about what it looked like to Carlos' family. Here I was, a very healthy and capable woman with only one child who had hired help. Carlos' mom raised eleven children without help. In fact, she had to walk to a river to wash the dirty laundry and then carry wet clothes back home to hang dry. I had a washing machine! Knowing what I knew, I never complained to her or my sisters-in-law. But an hour later, you could find me in a ranting conversation with Stephanie about how hard things were even with help—the exhaustion, the puke in my hair that morning, picking up after our husbands, the ants in the kitchen again.

Even though I didn't always know where or how I fit in as a mom or a wife in this new life I was living, I started feeling more confident, with fewer moments of anxiety and panic about what our life was supposed to look like or what the future would be. I wasn't as sleep-deprived as I had been, which helped me stay steady. I trusted that we would find our way even though I didn't know which way that was. I still felt so lost. I'd thought that things would make sense once becoming a mother and wife.

I haven't found my way because I'm looking outside of myself for the way. The way is inside, Sara.

I needed to tap back into my spiritual practice with myself, God, and prayer. I needed to surrender to God's will and look for the ways of co-creation by acknowledging and following the signs. Oh, how easy it was to forget and delightful and reassuring to remember.

When disconnected from spirit, I was a nervous wreck, worried, and certain I was doing it all wrong. Noticing this radical difference in how I felt at different times throughout my day or during the week helped me use the tools I was learning in AA meetings and the books I read. Staying grounded in trusting myself and trusting God—perhaps the two were the same—offered me moments of peace, confidence, and faith that everything was exactly how it was supposed to be. Divine timing was working for me, not against me.

Learning to surrender was a constant practice, yet, I had specific moments I could pinpoint that offered massive impact. I surrendered when I saw Lupita at the church and told her I was pregnant. I surrendered when I declared to Carlos that we were getting married. I surrendered when Maria told me about the AA meetings. There was a practice of daily surrender that would serve me, too. I wanted that. A daily or more regular practice meant consciously staying open to synchronicity, seeking human connections on a deeper level, being present, meditating, and practicing mindfulness throughout the day.

I practiced by pulling angel cards, wearing beaded necklaces (or prayer beads, as some people call them), and reaching for them during the day as a reminder that I am God and God is me; we are in this together.

I practiced by offering love to strangers, silently and intentionally.

I practiced by receiving love in the not-so-obvious places, like a breeze at the same moment I stopped to smell a flower or a child's concerned smile after I stubbed my toe.

I practiced by turning the music up loud and dancing with Alex in my arms, twirling in the living room, feeling the joy and exhilaration of music and movement rush through me.

WHEN ALEX WAS seven months old, we maintained our Sunday date nights to stay connected and strong in our love and commitment. Alex was now consistent in going to bed early and waking up early. I had my favorite grocery store, gas station, fruit and veggie store, lunch spot, and regular AA meetings throughout the week. I usually left Alex at the restaurant for the Thursday evening AA meetings and always brought him to the women's meeting on Sunday mornings, where he received an abundance of attention as he was passed around.

I had some solid friendships but still missed my mom all the time. We had just seen my parents in July at the family reunion, and I was already scheduled to fly to Madison for a visit at the end of September. But early in September, the unexpected happened. While I was in Mexico, where the heat continued to be unforgiving, the excessive sweat uncomfortable and embarrassing, my family was in Madison, where the cool evening breeze reminded them that summer was ending and fall was around the corner. Like all Americans who are able to remember, I can tell you exactly where I was on September 11, 2001, and what it was like living abroad as my country took a quick inhale and then held its breath for what must have felt like months, and for some, years. My teacher friend, Gillian, was over for coffee that morning. We were hanging out in my living room. Alex was on the floor playing, wearing only a diaper to stay cool, when the phone rang right before nine. I scooped Alex up, swung him on my hip, and picked up the phone.

It was Melissa, a friend from AA. "Sara, are you watching the news? Turn on the news."

We had cable TV, which included CNN in English. With one arm holding Alex, I propped the phone under my chin and flipped it on. The first plane had already hit. I had either dropped the phone or hung it up already because as the second plane hit, I clasped both hands around Alex's head and buried his face to my chest.

"Oh my God. Oh my God."

Time passed. The towers started to collapse. The shock silenced us.

Gillian and I reached out to our other American friends, and some stopped by throughout the day to be in the same space together, eyes on the TV screen. At some point, I excused myself to put Alex down for his nap. Alone for the first time, as I rocked him and sang our favorite song, "Somewhere Over the Rainbow," I cried. I worried. I wondered. And I cried some more.

Over the next couple of days, when I went out in the world, local people asked how I was. Their eyes were sad and concerned, and we both knew what they meant when they asked. The disconnect was immediate and noticeable. This was happening to me, not to them. These were my people, my country, not theirs. It didn't occur to me that maybe they were also worried about family members and friends in the United States. I only saw what separated us.

This was tragic for everyone to imagine, yet, suddenly, and at a cellular level, I felt a distinct and profound connection with other Americans that I had never felt before. Ever. There was a look exchanged between other Americans and me at the grocery store or the bus stop that was new to all of us. A desire to hug each other even though we were strangers. I had always wanted to separate myself from the other gringos. But now, these were my people in a new, weird way. After a week, the local news moved on. But in the United States, no one had exhaled yet.

I hear stories, and I've read accounts, essays, and interviews of what it was like for people living in the States during and after September 11, but I can't relate to most of it. It was a time when I felt more American and connected to my roots than ever, yet I also felt more disconnected and far away at the same time. The grief was a deep well that kept pulling me in. I kept resisting it. I wish I had allowed myself to feel the grief, but I was scared. I worried it would consume me, and I would lose myself in the sadness. I didn't want Alex to have a sad mom. I wanted to be happy for him. I clearly lacked a deeper understanding of grief and the ability to experience opposing emotions at the same time. It wasn't something I had witnessed in my family, so I navigated it as best as I could and stuffed it down.

Travel plans were delayed and then canceled. Fear was around when we woke up, it stuck around for most of the day and made itself known before bed. I was not going anywhere without Carlos, so that meant we stayed in Puerto Vallarta until close to the end of November.

THE HEAT SUBSIDED a bit as we rolled into November. I could breathe easier, and life seemed a little more gorgeous without the stifling heat. The rainy season was almost over. Even though I lived in constant negotiations with the downpours and our laundry drying on the roof, I relished the rain. The smells were earthy of damp cement, and the flowers grabbed my attention as their vibrant colors glistened from the raindrops. The rainy season captivated me, sparking poems in my head that tumbled into my journals.

I reflected on my current life, the colorful dahlias in the warm sun, and my sweet little boy sleeping with his angel face next to me. I reflected on the life I had been living a year earlier, daydreaming by the beach with my big pregnant belly. And then I reflected on life two years earlier and could barely remember the girl in the back of the Jeep on the cold November night. The anger in me about the rape felt unreachable and elusive. Even if I could have accessed it, I would have diminished it, knowing it was the anger that had brought me here. Expertly, the anger went into the locked steel box in my heart, not to be opened for many, many years.

Anger wasn't a common emotion for me, but emotion generally showed up daily. I cried easily. Listening to a friend tell me her birth story or details of a recent wedding brought unfamiliar tears to my eyes, and sometimes I would have to choke back a sob. I was constantly riding the emotional roller coaster of being newly sober—from glamorizing the old party days and the memories of the empty, devastating times to my newfound freedom and pride coupled with the shame of who I was before and my harmful behavior. So many contradicting feelings.

Similarly, I felt the contradicting feelings of being a new mom, from the pure love and awe of this new life to the unbearable responsibility and pressure to do it all perfectly. I experienced the frustration that comes with profound exhaustion, small joys, and large traumas. I was starting to realize it might always be like this.

Chapter 61

AFTER ALL THE HOLIDAY VISITORS had left early in January, life calmed down. One afternoon, I skipped into the restaurant all by myself. Marisol was taking care of Alex. I shouted as I skipped in, without a care in the world as to who was there. "¡Tengo trabajo! ¡Tengo trabajo!" I got a job! Carlos was behind the bar stocking alcohol and barely had time to put the bottles down as I rushed in, bursting with excitement.

"¡Dime todo!" *Tell me everything!*

It was a part-time job working at a small real estate office a block from Los Muertos Beach in the heart of Old Town—the Romantic Zone.

I'd interviewed with Lorraine, the eccentric American owner. She had lived in Puerto Vallarta for years, and liked doing business her way. My job was to answer the phones and keep the office doors open while she and the other agent, Sasha, showed homes and met clients. The hope was that I'd get some walk-in business and learn how to lease and sell units to help her business, which would, in turn, help stabilize Carlos and me financially. This position was quite the opposite from the one I had applied for at the Coldwell Banker office in town. The vibe at Lorraine's office was easygoing, informal, and less stuffy than other real estate companies.

Maybe we wouldn't move to the States. Maybe I could grow a successful real estate career in Puerto Vallarta, earn some financial freedom, and live happily ever after with our little family, a house, a yard, and maybe even a view of the ocean. I envisioned making enough money to ease the pressure on Carlos and help support the growth of his restaurant.

My nighttime fantasizing spread to daydreaming. One morning I happened to leave for work earlier than normal. My pace was slower as I walked to the bus stop, and I practiced being aware of the smells and sounds around me while listing my gratitude for the beauty of the palm trees and bougainvillea. I inhaled the smell of the bleach water as the woman on the corner splashed the bucket onto the front concrete steps, and I memorized the sound of her plastic broom sweeping away the dirty secrets from last night. I added to my list: I'm grateful I don't have dirty secrets to clean up from the night before. After the bus ride to work, instead of rushing the four blocks to the office, I grabbed a coffee and headed to the beach, where I slipped off my sandals and walked along the ocean, astounded that this was my life. The beauty was remarkable in every way, especially in the cool early mornings while the tourists still slept in their hotel rooms. My Pisces heart had found a new source of happiness, and all I needed to do was leave fifteen minutes early for work to enjoy it.

AS I ALLOWED myself to imagine this new possible life, I faced a twinge of discomfort. I didn't want our kids to go to the American school in town, but the more I knew about the public education system in Mexico, the more I worried that wasn't an option either. If we stayed, would we send our kids to private school? I shuddered at the thought. The socioeconomic difference from Carlos' family made me worry that they would treat us differently, that we would be different. I didn't want us to be different. But I was already different, and deep down, I liked being different; nothing I could do would change that.

I knew I didn't want my kids growing up among entitled rich kids. I had a negative bias against wealthy people, and even though I had some wonderful wealthy friends, I thought the risk was too high. I was consumed with what others thought of me. I was worried that a disconnect in financial situations created a perceived barrier I didn't want, and I didn't know how to reframe it. Just as soon as I started imagining a beautiful life in Mexico, I was overwhelmed by obstacles. I prayed it would all become clear. *Grant me the serenity. Give me a sign, God.*

Within a month, I had gotten the hang of what was needed of me at the office. Sometimes after work, I would go grocery shopping by myself (which felt like a luxury), and sometimes Marisol would stay late to help with cleaning. This was a glimpse of the life I wanted. I didn't want to be the only one taking care of Alex. I didn't want to be a stay-at-home mom. I wanted a fun day at work, to run errands by myself, and then to come home and play with my baby, take him on adventures with friends, and not worry about folding laundry or changing the sheets. Yes, I wanted my cake, and I wanted to eat it, too.

One afternoon, when I arrived home with the grocery bags, Marisol slipped out of Alex's bedroom, having just gotten him down for a nap. I loved having Marisol around to help. She was loving, kind, confident in her abilities, and had a strong voice. As she helped me put away the groceries, she uncharacteristically started asking personal questions about my life in the U.S. I carefully picked details to share with her. Then, knowing better than to assume, I asked, "Have you ever thought of visiting the United States?"

She quickly exclaimed, "¡Claro que si! I would love to go to the United States." Her eyes were a bit star-struck, and I felt a pang of sadness about it. Marisol and I talked freely that afternoon because we could. No baby was distracting us; we were waiting for him to wake up so I could drive her home. As we chatted and laughed, she helped me cook rice and taught me the trick of adding chicken bouillon powder to the water with a little diced garlic and three slices of onion.

Alex woke up all smiley. We both gushed over his cuteness. We genuinely had missed him while he was sleeping and were both happy to be the ones to greet him as he woke up. She cooed at him while I changed his diaper.

"¡Oh, qué asco!" *Gross!* I was dealing with mushy poop and scrubbing his butt fervently.

"Señora Sara ..." Marisol had stopped kissing Alex's face. She looked concerned as she watched me. She knew I didn't like being called "Señora," but from time to time, she forgot.

"Eres muy brusco. Puedes ser más suave."

I stopped wiping his tush and looked at her with his legs still in the air in an expert hold with one hand. She had just told me to be more gentle. I could tell she wanted to switch places with me, so I offered her his little feet.

"A ver," I said. *Let's see.*

This could have been an awkward moment of power dynamics, but it wasn't. She was offering me the gift of her experience and her perspective. I didn't feel threatened or righteous. I felt grateful. She was right. I could see it. I had been cleaning his little butt like I cleaned a burnt pan. *Gentle, Sara. Be more gentle.*

It was the first time I could see the benefit of being more gentle, and I knew instantly that it would make me a better mom and human. I wanted to be more gentle in the world, too. I wanted to go easy, breathe deeper, and slow down to enjoy and be present in the moment more often. There was no rush. Why was I wiping his bottom like someone was outside honking for us to hurry up?

I laughed as she showed me how to care gently for this precious little human.

"¡Tienes razón, Marisol! Puedo ser muy brusco y no es necesario." *You're right, Marisol! I can be very rough, and it isn't necessary.*

After that, I continually reminded myself to be gentle and more loving. There was a time to push through, and there was a time to slow down con calma. Yes, the message had come from Marisol's mouth, but it felt like a clear message from the universe. I had asked God for help, and here it was.

I hadn't pursued motherhood. I never had the opportunity to decide if I was ready or not. But I was certain of my capacity to be the best mom, exactly as I was, even if I knew I could be better. Wanting to be better didn't mean I wasn't already wonderful. It meant I could grow with humility, self-love, and abundance and not let shame get in the way.

LATER, driving Marisol home, she admitted that she had been nervous to tell me to be more gentle, but she could see I was trying so hard and wanted to help. We talked about how challenging it is to speak our truth sometimes but how important it is, and I thanked her. I never wanted her to be scared to tell me what she thought. I didn't have to agree with it, but I knew it would create a more meaningful relationship.

At her house, Marisol asked if I would bring Alex in to meet her mom. As we walked through the front door, I realized I hadn't prepared myself for Marisol's reality, and I did my best to hide my surprise.

Her home was in the countryside. The roads weren't paved, and chickens wandered around like the hungry, dirty street dogs in the city. The home was made with cement walls, dirt floors that were meticulously swept, and a tin-like roof that clearly leaked. There were bars on the windows but no glass, and I envisioned what it was like when it rained.

I had been invited in as the necessary means to the main attraction, baby Alex. This gave me a chance to glance around. There was a single bed in the corner that looked like someone had just gotten out of it and a mattress in the other corner with stacks of clothes and boxes on top. The room was dark and fairly large, but there was only one other room with more beds. We stayed for fifteen minutes or so. Marisol's mom offered me flavored water, and I was grateful for how cold and refreshing it was. With no breeze, the heat was suffocating. No one else seemed to mind. Alex continued to entertain the smiling faces around him, and I watched like an outsider, benefiting from the glow of love and sharply aware not only of my unearned privilege but of the loving support system Marisol had in her family, giving her the courage to voice her opinion.

Chapter 62

ALEX BROUGHT MY PARENTS a ridiculous amount of joy when I called on Saturday mornings to fill them in on all the details about how he was growing and what he was doing. I would pick the best photos of the week and email them, sharing the cuteness and bragging about how smart Alex was and how big he was getting. One Saturday night, Alex and I were having a pizza dance party, and Carlos was at work. I had treated myself to delivery, which added an annoying component because, like always, I had to explain how to get to our apartment. There was no GPS then, so giving my address wasn't good enough, and with my American accent, people either questioned me, making me repeat the name of my street over and over, or they annoyingly tried to practice their English with me, delaying the whole process.

Later, sitting on the living room floor, surrounded by toys and eating pizza, Alex started coughing, and it became obvious that he was choking on something. I didn't know what to do. I panicked. I didn't freeze, but my adrenaline jacked me up so much that I might as well have frozen because I was useless. I was yelling at him to cough. I didn't want to push his stomach too hard because I hadn't been properly trained to do the Heimlich maneuver, but I also didn't want him to die.

Do I call 911? Is there a 911? Is there enough time?

I held Alex and begged him to cough harder when he abruptly choked up the piece of food that had been caught in his esophagus. It was over. I rocked him gently, but he wiggled out of my arms and continued running around the living room like nothing had happened. He was fine.

I, on the other hand, was not fine. Not at all. He could have died. He almost died right in front of me. As I sat on the floor with my back against the couch and my head in my hands, I tried to regulate my breathing—the most precious thing, our breath.

What if I needed to call 911? How does that work here? How do I not know this?

I found the phone book and flipped through it. I found a number for the police and a number for an ambulance. It was a regular phone number. I called Carlos at work.

"Is there a 911?" I asked.

"A what?"

There was no such thing as 911. I imagined myself calling the number for the ambulance and asking for help. I thought of my phone conversation earlier when I had given the pizza guy my address and then proceeded to spend four or five minutes explaining how to get to my apartment because he couldn't understand me. Four to five minutes! Alex would have been dead.

How was I supposed to keep Alex alive without 911?

I was fully aware of my American perspective and didn't care one bit at that moment. I wanted to move back to the United States the very next day. It was as clear as clear could be. As I put Alex down for bed that night, I prayed. I thanked God for keeping him alive. Over and over again. And then I went to my bedroom and cried myself to sleep. I couldn't stop imagining the worst, and it was awful.

When Carlos got home from work, I cried as I told him the story. I asked if we could please consider moving to the States sooner than later. Over the next couple of weeks, we talked about the different cities in the U.S. where we could move, and we kept coming back to Madison. I missed my mom a lot, so even though I had promised myself I never would, we decided that moving home made the most sense. I tried not to care that in my mind, moving back implied I had failed to make it in the world. Alex hadn't even turned one yet.

LESS THAN two years later, after we were settled back in Madison, Carlos took Alex, who was three years old, to daycare one morning and stayed for breakfast because he had some extra time before he was expected to be at his job at the local bank. I was a real estate agent and showing houses to out-of-town buyers that morning. Alex was in the turtle room at Red Caboose Child Care Center (the same daycare I went to when I was little) when a man barged in with two butcher knives and held the kids hostage, badly hurting one of the teachers. Someone called 911. After fifteen or twenty minutes, the police broke in and shot him dead in front of the children who were huddled in a corner. Thankfully no children were physically injured. It was a nightmare for all the families.

Carlos was there and held Alex, covering his eyes and ears when it all happened. I was across town, showing a house on Virginia Terrace. I still remember exactly where I was standing, looking out the front window, when I took the call.

Is anyone safe anywhere? Until that point in time, the United States seemed safer to me, but after that horrific morning, and twenty years later, after way too many school shootings and deaths from gun violence, I have a very different perspective. Not being able to call 911 was one of the determining factors for us to move to the States in 2002, which today seems ignorant with my broader understanding of police brutality, police murders, and the fear that Black and brown people experience when 911 is called. Safety means so much more to me today than being able to call 911 or not.

For a month after the Red Caboose incident, I cried every day and remembered asking Carlos if we should move back to Mexico. We had only been gone for seven months. I couldn't imagine anything like that happening there. I was sure he would say yes, but he said no. I said okay. From then on, safety became a daily gratitude. Our lives can change in an instant. Gratitude kept me grounded.

I no longer resonated with the saying, "Everything happens for a reason." I believe in fate and destiny, but I also believe that horrible things happen—for no good reason—and when I find myself faced with tragedy, accidents, or illness, I trust in myself and God to help me navigate through with strength and grace. But let's be real; sometimes it gets dark, and that's okay too. It might have been a brief moment of fear when Alex was choking, but it played a part in changing the trajectory of our life. We never know when those moments will present themselves, but we can keep showing up and take notice.

Chapter 63

ALEX'S ONE-YEAR BIRTHDAY was not all happy. Not at all. I assumed it would be the most festive of times, but as the days crept up, I found myself ruminating and reliving my life a year earlier, and my birth story was not something I wanted to remember. I had not healed emotionally from the ordeal. With the one-year anniversary/birthday coming up, it was on my mind a lot, so I knew it would help to speak it out loud at an AA meeting. At the Sunday morning women's meeting, I felt safe to open up to the ten women in the circle. Tears streamed down my face the minute I started talking about it, and I had to pause to let out some sobs. Then, gathering myself, I shared the awful details. I got honest about how angry I was and how it didn't feel fair that I couldn't look back at the day with love and joy like I expected. I couldn't find a way to celebrate that painful experience.

"What would you have done differently, Sara?" a friend asked me after the meeting.

"I don't know. I haven't thought about that. It was what it was."

"But it sounded horrible."

"It was. I guess I wish I would have had a backup plan. I wish I would have called the birthing class teacher and taken her up on her offer to assist us. She would have known what to do. Maybe I wouldn't have suffered so much." The thoughts came tumbling out.

"Do you wish you would have had the baby in the United States?" she asked. She had been at the meeting when I shared the horror of

Alex choking and my fear of the medical system here.

"No." I didn't pause before answering. "No, if I would have had Alex in the U.S., Carlos wouldn't have been there, between the restaurant and immigration and who knows what else. There was no way we would be separated for our baby's birth."

"It's okay to be mad about it. It's okay to not want to celebrate. Alex won't know. You don't have to put a show on for him." She touched my arm lightly.

I hadn't realized that I felt like it was my job to put on a show for him. At that moment, I realized my definition of a good mother was to act happy and throw a big beautiful party. But he was one year old and wouldn't know the difference. So who was I performing for, anyway?

We ended up having a small party and took all the token photos with cake and smiles, but I was more relaxed and determined to be honest about how I was feeling and not put on a show for the sake of a show. It felt revolutionary.

THE WORK I was doing in AA helped me learn more about myself and how to live in integrity. I had grown up lying about so much. Getting honest—with myself and with others—was challenging and empowering.

I was learning that I could be a rebel in a healthy way, like when I ate cereal for dinner instead of making a healthy dinner and ran around in the puddles instead of staying dry.

These realizations felt liberating. I had found a way to rebel without playing in a dangerous, toxic lifestyle.

This new kind of rebellion wasn't soul-crushing; it was soul-fortifying. I could question the patriarchy, challenge the status quo, and rebel against roles and labels that put me in a box. I could object to systems of oppression and seek ways to dismantle, rebuild, and create new ways of being instead of following along when people said, "But this is how it's always been."

I was finally learning to honor my inner voice and seek her out when the contradicting messages were loud and overbearing.

CONTRARY TO THE RULES OF AA, I kept my sobriety date as February 22, 2000, even after the two glasses of wine with Carlos in the spring of 2001. Perhaps that was a rebel move, too. To me, 2/22/2000 was the date I had my last drink as a former party girl. When I drank the two glasses of wine, it showed me I needed help, support, and to make changes in my life. The decision to drink wasn't a slip; it was a wake-up call that I was living out of alignment with who I wanted to be.

I wasn't going to be penalized for that.

I wasn't going to allow a rule to erase the work I had done.

I wasn't back at square one.

Clearly, this is controversial. But it was a non-issue for me because no one knew until five years later when a toxic sponsor made a big deal out of it and insisted I change my sobriety date and seek amends. I respectfully challenged her controlling, overbearing, and rigid perspective, and we ended our relationship. That experience with the sponsor gave me pause, and I began to question the benefits of AA in my life—the rigidity of it and the guilt and shame that came with centering the disease as something I would have forever. Like something was wrong with me. And the Madison meetings lacked the spiritual connection I had appreciated in Puerto Vallarta. I quit going. And the less I went, the less burdened I felt. One day I told Carlos that I was happier not going. And that was that.

I stayed sober for another five years before I decided, with the support of my therapist, to try a glass of wine. She asked me why I wanted a drink again. I said I wanted a glass of wine at dinner; I didn't want to get drunk. She said that because I was in a solid place—my marriage was healthy, our home life was manageable, work was stable, my relationships were well cared for—she didn't feel it was a risky decision and gave me a thumbs up.

I had the glass of wine. It had been almost ten years since my last drink, and I didn't go wild. Since then, I've had a healthy relationship with alcohol. What surprises me the most, still, is how consistently I'll not finish my drink.

Addiction is complicated, and understanding more about it has helped me explore unhealed trauma. There are so many ways to not feel the feelings. AA was critical to my sobriety and offered me positive tools and support when I desperately needed it. I'm grateful. I'm also grateful that there are women like Holly Whitaker, author of *Quit Like a Woman*, for challenging the drinking and recovery cultures with a feminist lens while offering game-changing perspectives on the alcohol industry.

Choosing something different than the norm creates consequences that need to be considered. Many paths, choices, and systems of oppression impact many people. Understanding this, I could better see how my choices, and the opportunities or barriers in front of me, came with consequences—and therein lies the power of discernment.

AS ALEX GOT OLDER, some of our parenting choices conflicted with the cultural norms in Mexico. For example, our rigidity around bedtime was abnormal. No one in the family had bedtime rules like we did: seven o'clock every night, no exceptions. While that was typical in my online mom's group, it was foreign in Mexico.

Carlos and I had to be united in going against the norms, and in that regard, we were a power team. From the outside, I doubt people would have described me as a rebellious young mom, but I felt it, and for the most part, I loved it. It also had its challenging moments. The discomfort and the disdain we sometimes faced offered me moments of significant inner growth. I wasn't as scared when Carlos reminded me that we could think for ourselves and make our own decisions. I wasn't scared to make mistakes, either, because I trusted that as long as we were committed to honesty, open communication, deep respect, and love, we would be able to repair anything.

"How did you become like this?" I asked Carlos one Sunday evening.

"Like what?"

"So different from other men who seem macho and jealous."

"I don't know."

"No, seriously, Carlos."

He stopped eating and looked at me. "Someone once told me that it's always important to think. 'Piensas,'" he said. "So I thought a lot. And I thought about what I was supposed to think and what I wanted to think. I guess it helped me learn that it was okay to think for myself."

I didn't know what to say to that. I was in awe of him and so grateful that we had found each other.

Chapter 64

WE SPENT THE NEXT couple of months preparing to move our little family to Madison. Carlos graduated, and we had a big party at his mom's house and a mass in his honor. A mass to honor someone was a frequent tradition on birthdays and anniversaries of the death of loved ones. I enjoyed mass, and when I didn't understand the padre, I often prayed in my head. I liked pretending I knew the words to the songs, and I loved singing loudly when I actually did know them. When others got up for communion, I comfortably stayed back, never feeling like an outsider. I felt at home in the church even when I looked and sounded completely out of place.

By May 2002, we had booked my flight so I could be home for my sister's high school graduation. Carlos would come a couple of weeks later, giving him time to attend to the many details that remained and avoid the danger of us traveling together. Leaving his friends and family was not going to be easy. He had put the word out that he was selling the restaurant. He might have even put an ad in the weekly *Mano a Mano*, but no potential buyers showed up. I was worried he was upset about selling or closing the restaurant, but he wasn't upset at all.

"Sara, this restaurant brought us together. I got everything I could ever want out of having La Estocada. It was my baby for a while, but we have a new life together that is more important to me than the restaurant.

"And to be honest, I'm excited to do something besides working in the restaurant industry."

The possibilities were endless. I was relieved and hopeful to see him confident about what was next. "I have no idea what we are going to do. But it helps knowing we can always move back if we want to," I said. I always liked having a backup plan.

We sold our furniture, and Carlos decided to pass the restaurant on to his sisters. I had quit my job at the real estate office, knowing that real estate could be a solid option in Madison. My dreams of going back to school to become a professor of cultural studies seemed unrealistic, but now I could see that my dreams were just that—ideas to play with as I co-created something bigger than anything I could dream of on my own.

"What are you going to do?" was a popular question. It was obvious that the question referred to jobs and money. Carlos was leaving his restaurant behind, and I didn't have a job. We were trusting in our decision and knew that with our work ethic and ability to make things happen, we'd figure it out. Together.

We didn't know. And that's what we told people. The looks they gave us made it clear this made them uncomfortable. Which, of course, excited the rebel in me. And it scared all the other parts of me. It's one thing to take off on an adventure solo, but with a baby?

The known factors were that we'd have a place to land at my parents for a bit and that we'd be switching roles, with me becoming the financial provider while Carlos took on the care of Alex. We also knew how to work a to-do list:

- Get a car
- Sara, find a job
- Get Carlos' green card
- Find AA meetings in Madison and stay sober
- Move into an apartment

Saying goodbye to Carlos' family, my friends from AA, my teacher friends, my new mom friends, and the ocean was bittersweet. I didn't want to leave, and I was ready to leave at the same time.

With two suitcases, five boxes, and one large painting professionally wrapped and packaged, Alex and I were ready. Carlos borrowed a truck and brought us to the airport. I took an inventory of my emotions: sad, happy, nervous, and excited. I wasn't worried, though, and for that, I gave a nod to the universe. I strongly felt this was exactly what we were supposed to be doing. After one last tight hug in the crowded airport, Alex and I went through security to our gate.

MY THROAT TIGHTENED as I settled into the window seat. With Alex on my lap, we watched out the window as the plane shot up over the ocean and then circled, heading north. The boats were tiny on the water. We could see the white caps and the way the mountains rose high and the beach kissed the sea. My heart pounded, and my eyes watered. This breathtaking place had given me so much, more than I could have ever dreamed. This precious human bouncing around on my lap, with his big eyes and the softest cheeks, showed me I could be any kind of mom I wanted to be. My husband, Carlos, who was leaving this beautiful land for us and an unknown future, showed me I could be a committed partner and helped me realize we could create a relationship on love, trust, respect, and compassion. I was leaving a part of myself there and returning to my hometown two years sober, with a healthy mind, body, and spirit.

How do we start over? How do we balance fear and hope? How do we live in alignment with our values? How do we follow our dreams and make responsible decisions for our family?

Always so many questions. Yet, I didn't need the answers. Sometimes I just liked asking them. I trusted all would be revealed. I trusted that it would be okay. I trusted that I would constantly need to ask myself, what is working? What isn't working? Where will change benefit me? What am I scared of and why? My questions started important conversations that helped me find the next step forward.

I knew that if I stayed honest with myself about these questions, I could live the life I wanted, whatever that looked like. And if I continued to show up and find the courage for the next right step, I could keep playing in co-creation with the universe, and things would work out okay, even when they didn't. And as my mom always said, "Have faith that the universe is constantly conspiring for you, not against you."

I trust. I believe. I pivot when I need to pivot. If I fail, I can start anew or learn from the mistake and gain experience. It can be a messy experiment that just might open a door I would have never dreamed of.

I certainly didn't dream of getting pregnant, married, and having a baby in Mexico at the age of twenty-five. I had embarked on an adventure to free myself from an unhealthy lifestyle, and I trusted that wanting a different life was enough. And then I followed my intuition.

Alex slept for a good portion of the flight and was groggy as we landed. We didn't rush off the airplane or through customs to get our bags. There was no need to rush. We stopped in the bathroom so I could change his diaper and as I gently cleaned his bum, a young girl, maybe around six years old, exited a stall and boldly came right over to say hi to Alex. Her sweetness and independence made me wonder what Alex would be like at her age. Where would we be, and what would our life be like? What would I be doing? What would I be like as a mom, wife, woman, and spiritual being living a human experience?

I let my questions linger and appreciated the unknowing. It helped me zoom out of my current life and think back to five years ago. This moment would have been incomprehensible to that Sara. It was okay not to know. In fact, not knowing made my life exactly the way it was meant to be.

EPILOGUE

AFTER WORKING ON THIS BOOK for so long, it's hard to believe I'm at the point of writing the epilogue. I've procrastinated for months, and then today, as I sat outside on my back deck with my laptop, admiring the lilacs in full bloom, I realized the synchronicity of the timing. Today is May 15, 2022. It's been exactly twenty years since that airplane trip back to Madison.

It's a Sunday afternoon, and our French Bulldog, Pumba, is lying by my feet. My hair hangs past my shoulders, still dark brown but now streaked with chunks of silver.

Alex, who just turned twenty-one a couple of months ago, is in the basement with Carlos, watching a Chivas soccer game. Or maybe it's a Bucks game. Our younger son, Leo, who will turn eighteen in November, is making banana bread with chocolate chips. He's a striking, strong-willed kid who can't wait to move out and be independent. One more year, and he is counting the days.

Spring in Madison is full of everything hopeful. It's been twenty years of navigating the harsh winters, with only two weeks for our annual family visits in Puerto Vallarta. Some years we would sneak in extra trips, like this year. We splurged, and the four of us went down to celebrate Marcelina's eighty-second birthday. Pulling up at the resort where we have a timeshare, Joel, the bellboy, greeted us with hugs, and within an hour of arriving, we were in a taxi to Marcelina's house, where most of the family was already gathered around the tubs of ceviche and guacamole, taking turns flipping carne asada on the grill.

"¡Aqui estamos!" I yelled as we climbed the stairs. Our kids, taller than us now, naturally shift into speaking Spanish. The hugs and love that surround us make the trip worth it instantly.

As soon as we returned to Madison, I went to visit my mom. She's in an adult home, just ten minutes from our near west side house, being cared for by the most wonderful nursing staff. She has had Alzheimer's for eight years now. In February 2016, she was sixty-seven years old when I left my last voicemail message for her. A couple of days afterward, I found out my dad had been checking her messages because she couldn't remember her password anymore. I never left her another message again.

It's been a long, treacherous journey, but with so much grace, love, and laughter, too. Today we rolled her wheelchair outside in the sun, and I read to her and Carlos from the fourth draft of this book. I wonder if she understands any of it. I think she does. I stopped reading when Alex arrived, and she lit up as he started talking to her.

"Hi, Nana! Isn't it a beautiful day?" Alex held her hand. She locked eyes with him and beamed but couldn't get any words out.

We saw a big shift in her Alzheimer's during his high school soccer years. When he was a freshman, my mom was still driving and would pick Leo up to meet us at the games, but by the time he was a senior, she would forget which team we were cheering for, yet somehow always knew where Alex was. I get emotional watching her engage with Alex, Leo, and Carlos as best as she can. Knowing we had so many wonderful years with her brings me back to gratitude. She still smiles at me like I'm the most beautiful and wonderful daughter in the world. She makes me feel special, and I make her laugh by dancing and singing for her with abandon.

Our spirits know each other, and our souls will always be together.

I miss her so much. And our family has crumbled a bit as the disease has taken her away from us. My sister returned from Seattle last month, leaving her husband and their sweet two-year-old daughter for a quick visit. We took videos and kissed her face, telling her over and over again how much we love her, promising her we'd mother our children in all the wonderful ways she mothered us. Our dad joined us for a couple of hours on one of the afternoons. He has been her constant caretaker since she started showing signs of memory loss in 2014. It's been hard on him. Alzheimer's is hard on the whole family.

Racism is also hard on the whole family—on the whole world. Writing this book was a challenge because I had already started my own racial justice work after the murder of Mike Brown in 2014. Trayvon Martin had been killed two years earlier. I had had my head down, raising Alex and Leo and running our family-owned real estate brokerage with Carlos, when I started to read and learn more about the racial disparities in our city and the continued racism in our country, in our backyard, and our own home.

As I learned more, I examined my whiteness at a deeper level and began to change. But in writing this story, I had to tell it like it was, including the moments of my ignorance.

I wanted to leave out the part where I asked Carlos if I could call him Carlos instead of Juan Carlos for my own ease.

I wanted to leave out some of the wedding details, but I didn't. Writing them out also helped me see where my whiteness and privilege showed up in ugly ways.

I didn't want you to know that I had wanted brown babies because I know how problematic that is now. But back then, I didn't.

I WAS RAISED to be colorblind and to not talk about race, and my unlearning and relearning is a book in itself, and this one is already long enough. My mom also raised me with rose-colored glasses, and learning to take them off would make her proud.

Twenty years ago, I couldn't have imagined my life as it is today. Shitty things happen still, leading Carlos and me back to the basics of handling what comes up with love, integrity, and faith. Sometimes we bring in humor. Other times we go straight to prayer. We always keep dancing.

GRATITUDE AND ACKNOWLEDGMENTS

IN HONOR OF MY MOTHER and her beautiful gratitude practice, I have many to thank. I start by thanking her for always believing in me, supporting me, and being my ruthless editor back in the day. We write together—mother and daughter, forever. To my dad, thank you for teaching me many life lessons and for loving me. To Kat, my sister, and our extended family from Philly, to Santa Cruz, from Puerto Vallarta to Alaska ... I love you all. Thank you for your support and encouragement.

To my writer sister friends, there would be no book without you. For reals. We created a magical container, and I'm forever grateful to Casey Erin Wood, Jenn Sutkowski, Tanya Geisler, and Jessie Lerner.

Thank you to my enthusiastic community of supporters, readers, and cheerleaders. Specifically a big thanks to: Andrea Thompson, Jan O'Neill, Uncle Rob, Marisol Gonzalez, Kate Woodford, Ananda Mirilli, Amber Swenor, Tiffany Malone, Jill Cornejo, Kelly Monico, Sue Robinson, Oscar Mireles, Kristin Davis, Sandi Reinardy, Araceli Esparza, Gregg Potter, Christine Ameigh, Dina Nina, Ali Muldrow, Joanne Berg, and many more!

Thank you to my mentors, editors, and teachers for sharing your gifts and the love of your craft with me. Susanna Daniel—thank you, so many versions, edits, conversations, and support. Beth Binhammer, my wise, brilliant therapist—bless you. Allison Crow, you helped me find the courage to whisper my dream of this book in 2013, thank you. Thank you to Linda Sivertsen, Heather Doyle Fraser, Jen Loudin, Michelle Wilgden, Heidi Rose Robbins, and Madi Murphy for your teachings and inspiration. Thank you to Kristin Mitchell at Little Creek Press and Valerie Biel.

Shout out to my spirit team beyond this realm. Thanks for showing up at all the right moments and keeping it fun. 44. To my ancestors, I am grateful we can heal together. Grandma Harriet, I love you.

To my family of four—I know, I know, you listened to me talk about this book for so many years. Thank you for letting me tell this story. Alex, I am incredibly grateful for your desire to be born and that you picked us to be your parents. I wouldn't be living the life I am if it weren't for you. Period. My greatest joy is witnessing you and your brother living your lives so boldly in your unique ways. To Leo and other family members who prefer a more private life, I want to acknowledge the hard stuff. In writing this book, and many other pieces since 2013, I've learned (and made mistakes) in discerning where my story begins and someone else's ends or intersects or is clearly theirs and not mine. I share what many would consider unshareable, making it hard for some of the people I love most. Thank you for teaching me about discernment, discretion, and consent, and thank you for having the hard conversations.

Carlos, Juan Carlos, amor de mi vida, thank you for being you. Thank you for being certain I could do this, for keeping me grounded, and loving me siempre. I love our love story. Te amo un chingo.

ABOUT THE AUTHOR

SARA ALVARADO is a writer, speaker, teacher, and co-conspirator who believes that the way to handle challenges in life and business is to show up authentic, bold, vulnerable, and always ready for fun.

As a fierce advocate for social justice, Sara has published the Racial Justice Toolkit for Real Estate Professionals, a Guide for Change Agents, and is the creator of the Conversation Challenge: helping white people talk about race. Through her speaking and workshops, Sara creates awareness and inspires change with her straight talk and loving ways.

Sara built her real estate business into a successful brokerage with her husband, Carlos, who now leads the Alvarado Real Estate Group. Working in real estate and for racial equity led her to co-creating OWN IT: Building Black Wealth, a groundbreaking initiative working toward eliminating substantial barriers to wealth and homeownership for Black and brown families. She is named founder of Step Up: Equity Matters in the Workplace, Badger Rock Middle School, and Nuestro Mundo Community School.

Sara is a lover of love, spirit, dance, and adventure (with the music turned up) and enjoys family fun, traveling, challenging the status quo, and writing. To connect, please visit SaraAlvarado.com.

Learn more about this memoir, and view photos at SaraAlvarado.com/dreaminginspanish.

www.ingramcontent.com/pod-product-compliance
Lightning Source LLC
Chambersburg PA
CBHW051634160425
25059CB00002B/70

* 9 7 8 1 9 5 5 6 5 6 4 8 1 *